BOWERBIRD

The art of making theatre drawn from life

Alana Valentine

CURRENCY PRESS
SYDNEY

First published in 2018
by Currency Press Pty Ltd,
PO Box 2287, Strawberry Hills, NSW, 2012, Australia
enquiries@currency.com.au
www.currency.com.au

Copyright © Alana Valentine, 2018.

Image section copyright: 1A © Kate Geraghty / Fairfax 2004; 1B © Katrina Tepper / Newspix 2007; 2A © Alana Valentine 2009; 2B © Alana Valentine 2013; 2C © Nicolas Bonhomme 2009; 3A © Carly Earl / Newspix 2013; 3B © Bob Barker / Newspix 2009; 4A family photo; 4B © Vicki Gordon 2016; 5A © Rebecca Selleck / Museum of Australian Democracy 2017; 5B © Glenn Ratcliffe 2012; 6A © Vicki Gordon 2017; 6B © Tiffany Parker / Bangarra Dance Theatre 2017; 7A © Hannah Robins 2013; 7B © Vicki Gordon 2009; 8A © Vicki Gordon 1996.

Copying for Educational Purposes: The Australian Copyright Act 1968 allows a maximum of one chapter or 10% of this book, whichever is the greater, to be copied by any educational institution for its educational purposes provided that the educational institution (or the body that administers it) has given a remuneration notice to Copyright Agency (CA) under the Act. For details of the CA licence for educational institutions, please contact CA: 11/66 Goulburn Street, Sydney, NSW, 2000; tel: within Australia 1800 066 844 toll free; outside Australia +61 2 9394 7600; fax: +61 2 9394 7601; email: info@copyright.com.au

Copying for Other Purposes: Except as permitted under the Act, for example a fair dealing for the purposes of study, research, criticism or review, no part of this book may be reproduced, stored in a retrieval system, or transmitted in any form or by any means without prior written permission. All enquiries should be made to the publisher at the above address.

Cataloguing-in-Publication data for this title is available from the National Library of Australia website: www.nla.gov.au.

Cover design Emma Bennetts for Currency Press.
Cover image shows Alana Valentine.
Cover photography by Jez Smith.

Aboriginal and Torres Strait Islander readers should be advised that *Bowerbird* contains images and references to Aboriginal people who have now passed.

Currency Press acknowledges the Traditional Owners of the Country on which we live and work. We pay our respects to all Aboriginal and Torres Strait Islander Elders, past and present.

Contents

Prologue	1
1. Flushing out the ears	4
2. Captivated by reality	7
3. The flat above the fruit shop	14
4. Satiating hunger	18
5. Like understands like	23
6. Don't write the subject	28
7. Architect of your own emotions	31
8. My first play	36
9. Mentored by poofters	40
10. The cruellest loss	43
11. Ambition aplenty	48
12. Audience awareness	51
13. Don't squib the tough stuff	56
14. Linked into community	59
15. Establishing trust	66
16. Metaphors for experience	69
17. The value of a premise	72
18. The person in front of you	77
19. Attractions of the archive	80
20. The art of sacrifice	84
21. Selective hearing	90
22. Getting off the grid	95
23. Junee juggernaut	99
24. The talking brain	105
25. Pausing for effect	111
26. Extreme playwriting	114

27. Beyond the fourth wall	117
28. Your truest self	124
29. Doing dawn	127
30. All the beautiful students	131
31. The wounded public	135
32. Like learning a new language	139
33. Savage reality	144
34. Fear of Kong	149
35. Bodies in space	153
36. The ecstasy of Italy	158
37. Shudder in the city	163
38. Bullied with words	166
39. Humble pie	170
40. The delights of discipline	172
41. Eyes full of grit	175
42. Courage in every fibre	181
43. Wait to be asked	185
44. Best process for best practice	190
45. Inconvenient behaviour	196
46. More than words can say	198
47. No shoes, no divas	201
48. The king's man	204
49. Scientist as sentinel	207
50. Balls in the air	210
51. Now versus posterity	214
Acknowledgements	220
Index of plays for stage and radio	223

Prologue

Mostly it feels like you don't know – like you're reaching for something that you can't quite grab. Some writers talk about their fear of the blank page, but the playwright who draws work from life can have the opposite problem. Spoilt for choice. Presented with myriad possibilities and competing ideas of how to condense the source material or arrange it in a theatrically dynamic, original and compelling way. Lost in a sea of options, yet perversely obsessed with the interview not done, the perspective not transcribed, the final piece of the jigsaw forever elusive. And it's not about a lack of confidence, although that can hum away in the background for longer than you might expect. It's about not *trying* to have clarity. It's about waiting until you do.

That's how you know you're working. Rewriting your script with a perpetual feeling that you are sinking into chaos – that is what creating feels like. It can take a long time, trying things out, until you begin to hear the voice that knows why it is speaking and what it has to say. And while writing fiction can feel like drawing something out of yourself, verbatim playwriting can feel more like structuring the transcript of the party that brings all your disparate interviewees together. The story as told by the people you have met, if they were in a room together; the way they would compete and interrupt each other, and cut off anyone who went on too long or encourage someone else who was really fascinating. If they begin to brawl or riot – so be it.

While there is an elegance to the artifice of a fictional play, the craft of verbatim playwrights needs to be even more seamless, even more invisible. Like the greatest actor, the verbatim writer needs to appear to disappear, so that the 'reality' of the story seems natural and authentic, as if there were no other way to present it. Erasing the individual to privilege the collective – except when it serves the story to make it self-consciously theatrical, Brechtian, meta. And carefully, so carefully, oscillating between the suspension of disbelief and a playful rejection of it.

If you suspect that expressing the beauty of human dignity and the callousness of human cruelty begins with the tongue, you may be a writer for the theatre: 'Death and life are in the power of the tongue, and those who love it will eat its fruits' (Proverbs 18:21). It's an adage to build a writing practice on, a fascination with language as an armour, as a blanket, as a balm.

I have written *Bowerbird* for theatre students and writers, especially those interested in the many variations of verbatim or what I personally call 'close work' writing, by which I mean work drawn closely from a source – either in a community or an archive or elsewhere – and informed by the cultural and social dynamics of the world in which we contemporaneously live. It entangles my personal experience, reflections on writing and some best practice ideas. I hope it will inspire others to bring to the stage the stories under their own feet or in their own backyards.

Even if you don't want to be a writer, I hope that some of the artistic values I espouse here – of working with community to disrupt entrenched privilege, thinking creatively and taking risks, working outside siloed organisations and conventional paths, constantly reinventing both yourself and your practice, investing in lifelong learning and curiosity, and diversifying your sources of income – will be useful in a century where all of us will work in multiple settings over a lifetime.

Finally I need to mention how the global, online context has changed the consumption, critique and creation of the performing arts. Clearly the internet is a remarkable tool for both community connection and research for theatre makers. Not only archives and libraries but a veritable flood of information and resources can be found online. As a writer you can check facts with a click. But the essential premise of this book is to urge you to suit up for what might be described as 'old school' research – actually getting out into the world and talking to real people, attending lectures, looking things up in libraries. Close work writers will want to find, collect and commit to the page original, copyrightable work which presents insights, perspectives and voices not otherwise heard, or at least not in the way you sieve them through your original voice.

1
Flushing out the ears

As a child I regularly had my ears flushed out. The doctor would fill a large metal syringe with warm water and gently squirt it into my ear canal while I held a small metal kidney-shaped dish at the side of my head to catch the discoloured wax lumps that obscured my hearing. Now I say warm water because that's how he described it, but to my sensitive childish skin it may just as well have been boiling oil. The first time he did this procedure, the doctor told me it would be 'uncomfortable'. He was wrong. It was painful. The ear is not an orifice you ever want anyone to put anything into. Ever. Think of being in rough surf with a fistful of ear buds being simultaneously rammed into your brain.

The cause, he said, was my 'irregularly shaped' ear canal which caught the wax and allowed it to build up instead of flowing onto the pillow as it did from the more regularly-formed ear canals of the children in our neighbourhood. My aural disability meant that I could look forward to a lifetime of inner ear washouts, the liquid rattling around inside my skull, surging against my brain and sometimes trickling down my throat.

The upside of these aquatic canaloscopies was emerging from the doctor's surgery with the most glistening, shiny new, clean-as-a-whistle hearing. The auditory world would rush in and suddenly I could hear everything – and I mean *everything* – in the most exquisite detail. The orchestra of summer cicadas, deafening to your common or garden variety ear canal, sounded to me as if they were physically inside my head, their legs and noisy thoraxes dangling out of my ear hole. The traffic roared, speech was a shout, the shower was a thunderous waterfall. I could hear the sound of a fly's legs rubbing as it scuttled across the kitchen table, I could hear the neighbour's washing machine in its spin cycle two houses away, I could hear the thwack of the leather ball on the wood of a cricket bat in a front yard two suburbs over.

I attribute my early love of audio art to this experience of a world going quieter and quieter and then, post-procedure, ringing with presence. I did not grow up listening to the radio. My grandmother had a transistor but it was always tuned to the races, so I had no nostalgic relationship to what she called the wireless. But I first expressed myself as a dramatist in the then old-fashioned medium of radio, not in the more generationally appropriate medium of film. And from radio I learned an early love of superb diction in that most beautiful and lyrical medium for artistry, the actor's voice.

I have used this story, this revelation about my warped inner ear, as the starting point of my ruminations about my life as a playwright to illustrate the necessity of becoming a good listener. It is the foundation of all that I am and all that I still might be. Listening. *Carefully. Attentively. Hyper-sensitively.* And also to tell you that being a good listener is not about being silent. I mean, some of it is about being silent, having the self-discipline to shut up and let someone else talk. But good listening is an active process – a cat-and-mouse game where you draw out your subject by convincing them that in some ways you have become an extension of their own brain. So that when you speak you say something with which they either agree so entirely that it is a surprise to them, or something that articulates, in a distilled way, everything they have been trying to say.

Isn't that kind of conversation just the most inspiring, most world-shaking thing to do? To talk, *really talk* with someone and in that hour, in that forty minutes, be able to externalise all that has previously been residing only in their own consciousness. *That* is your aim in every interview. You have to listen closely, carefully, because this has to be the most interesting, most revealing, most self-revealing conversation that your interviewee has ever had. You are tuned to the tiniest clues about who they are, you are armed with the most sophisticated insights into how human nature works, and you are listening – with your ears, with your spirit, with your mind, with your gut. And when they pause for breath, when they stumble in their monologue, you will make the one salient point that will set them off again into new territory, saying things they didn't know they knew, had not consciously thought before. You will spin a spell over them so they are fully alive in the present moment – not recalling things they thought before, or relating stories they have already digested – but jumping synapses in their brains to new thoughts, new insights, new revelations. And when you type that up and put it on stage, an audience will hear a person on the horns of a dilemma, on the brink of understanding, in the dramatic moment of self-knowledge. And that's what will make it good theatre: transformative storytelling, instead of dry, pre-digested, factual analysis.

So flush out your ears. Concentrate on what people around you say. You'll realise that people are more elliptical, incorrect, inaccurate and obfuscating than you knew. We are seduced by faces and tones – if someone looks friendly and speaks gently we think they are being honest with us. You need to ignore the persuasions of a person's external appearance or voice. If you listen to what they generalise about it will tell you their value system; listen to who they bitch about and you will know their fears.

Agatha Christie is perhaps the last person you might expect me to invoke as a literary role model, a worthy writing instructor. All those uber-polite, abominably-genteel BBC crime shows; all that appalling expositional dialogue and creaky plotting. And yet Agatha Christie, while not esteemed as such, is one of the world's most successful writers for theatre. Her play, *The Mouse Trap*, in continuous performance since 1952, is the longest running work of theatre in London's West End. Personally I don't much like her writing or the excruciating television adaptations of it. I don't wish to be Anglo-centric or genre-validating either, or to suggest that commercial success is the ultimate arbiter in valorising her. But I do want to choose an unlikely, unnoticed female playwright (she wrote more than twenty plays) and boil down Christie's main premise, her overarching message – which is 'pay attention'. Observe the signs. Watch carefully, listen carefully. Look at things in new ways, believe what you see and hear yourself, not what other people tell you. Don't judge by façades. See through people and their smokescreen defences. Pay attention.

2
Captivated by reality

In the preface to *Aftershocks*, Paul Brown's play about the aftermath of the Newcastle earthquake, the author quotes one of the early proponents of verbatim theatre, Derek Paget. Verbatim theatre, says Paget, is 'the form of documentary drama which employs (largely or exclusively) tape recorded material from the "real life" originals of the characters and events to which it gives dramatic shape'. Paget further characterises verbatim theatre as theatre in which 'the firmest of commitments is made by the company to the use of vernacular speech'; as work based on 'painstaking, protracted and scrupulous use of historical evidence'.

By this definition I have only written one verbatim play – *Run Rabbit Run*, produced by Company B at Belvoir St Theatre in January 2004. The play is about the struggle of the South Sydney Rugby League Football Club to be reinstated to the National Rugby League (NRL) competition. It depicts the struggle of a determined inner-city working-class team and their supporters through the courts, against the considerable corporate resources of News Corporation and the NRL. The club lost an injunction and a federal court case, but won the case on appeal. Researching and writing *Run Rabbit Run* was one of the most ambitious, draining and exhilarating works of my career as a dramatist. The work extended and fulfilled me as a creative artist in many ways that I struggle to articulate but at the heart of it, I suppose, is the intense impossible faith of the people I met and interviewed.

I simply did not think it was possible for me to be persuaded of the revolutionary efficacy of what might pejoratively be called 'people power'. But it became my task as a dramatist to honour the fierce courage of this small, impoverished football team and their struggle to stand up to the combined juggernauts of change and corporate greed. In attempting to dramatise, not the goodies versus the baddies, nor the Evil Empire against the battlers, but rather the sincere sense of right with which even the most onerous of participants acted, I was stretched as a writer and artist in ways that I had not been before. The stakes for me were high in my need to 'get it right' – not only because of the confidence that Neil Armfield and Company B had invested in me in 2003, but because the South Sydney community also trusted me to honour their story. There was also my own personal history growing up in Sydney as a fierce Souths supporter and then leaving it behind to live in a middle-class theatre world which sometimes sneers at the significance of football in Australian culture and resents the attention it gets. To make known the nature of this struggle – to explain why it is about much more than sport and goes to some deeper sense of Australian community values – caused me to 'pull out all the stops' as a dramatist. When in 2005 I won the Queensland Premier's Literary Award for Best Drama script for *Run Rabbit Run*, I described to one of the other winners that the work was verbatim. 'Oh, so you didn't really write it', he said. I resisted the temptation to launch into a long tirade, and instead laughed, with a small tight smile, and begged off to get another drink. But the perception persists. If I am using the words of participants then it's documentary not drama isn't it? If I'm using the words of real people then it's not literature. Or is it?

In any work of drama the writer must decide what story they are going to tell and why. What problem do they wish to interrogate, what conundrum do they wish to articulate, what impossible truth do they wish to examine in all its complexity and contradiction and mystery? There is an assumption with verbatim theatre that the writer, armed with a tape recorder, computer and printer, merely reaps the truth that is already out there. But how do you, as the writer, decide where to point your interest and your microphone? I could have focused on the internal politics of the football club, or told a more biographical story of legendary Souths' player and chairman George Piggins; it could have been from the perspective of Lachlan Murdoch, then a News Corp executive. Instead I chose to tell the story from the point of view of the fans, a story not about football but about the spiritual and philosophical motivation for the fight. The play explores the moral courage it takes to continue to act even when your own security and self are threatened and the contradictions, imponderables and unsolvables of these questions. That is why the play is 'by Alana Valentine'. I use the South Sydney story to investigate their drama from my entirely personal perspective.

Such a proposition flies directly in the face of many people's notion that verbatim is a more 'authentic' form of theatre. Indeed, when I presented this idea to a group of students at Macquarie University in Sydney I took real pleasure in the outraged cry it provoked. One student said, 'But you're manipulating the real story to your own ends'. It was an entirely satisfying wake-up call to those who think of verbatim writers as oral historians rather than playwrights. The mantle of 'truth' is no guarantee of dramatic credibility. Perversely it is quite the opposite. The dramatist's work, as that of all writers, is to make credible, believable and feasible the entirely unfeasible, incredible and unbelievable machinations of the real world. In real life people may be unrepentant, sadistic and entirely selfish. In drama such characters are inert and uninteresting and, worst of all, 'unbelievable'.

Dramatist Jimmy McGovern at a Sydney Theatre Company forum in March 2003 put it like this: 'I usually let participants take all the time in the world to come to my conclusions'. He was talking about his community-based television dramas *Hillsborough* and *Dockers*, both feature-length verbatim works. As this remark affirms, however 'verbatim' the project, the playwright shapes the material to their dramatic needs.

After *Run Rabbit Run*, my next play for Belvoir was *Parramatta Girls*, which I described as 'massaged verbatim'. This fully dramatised eight-character stage play tells what happened to Australian children between the ages of 13 and 17 at the Girls Training School, Parramatta, between 1947 and 1974. It is a shaming story. The play is based on interviews I conducted with more than thirty former inmates and also what I learned from going to the hearings of the Senate Inquiry into Children in Institutional Care. The report of those hearings, *Forgotten Australians*, found that upwards of half a million Australian children experienced care in an orphanage, home or industrial school during the last century. That made it probable that a majority of Australians today either experienced childhood in an institution, or know someone who has. In writing the play I invited an audience to bear witness to the experience of these mothers and grandmothers. Certainly they suffered, but they are also some of the funniest, toughest, most loving women I have ever met.

One of my intentions with *Run Rabbit Run* was to surprise audiences with the lucidity, philosophy and courage of people too often stereotyped as 'uncultured' footy fans. And a pure verbatim play enabled me to assert this lucidity and philosophical sophistication because I was quoting their actual words. In effect, I had a dramatic rationale for using the direct quotes. But in *Parramatta Girls* my aim was to tell the bigger story about Australia's history of incarcerating children. Because the importance of individual experiences was their part in this bigger whole, I collapsed multiple stories into eight characters whose journeys transcended being victims to a punitive system. Instead, they had the control and volition that all characters must have in any truly complex work of dramatic fiction.

I mentioned in the Prologue my conception of 'close work' writing, by which I mean writing which may be drawn from interviews or archives, from the imagination or the zeitgeist of being alive in a particular time and place. In the deepest place of my creative inspiration, the term 'close work' more accurately describes the value system of my body of work than 'verbatim' does, though I often use verbatim material. In my terms one may be a 'close work' actor, a 'close work' novelist, a 'close work' designer, a 'close work' choreographer. All of these would be creative artists who commit a large part of their time and creative energy into engaging a community, through detailed, meticulous work that goes beyond standard research and not only gets close to the source but keeps that source close in the process. It embraces a broad awareness for the philosophical theories informing present lives, which today includes intersectionality, environmental awareness, cultural sensitivity, pluralism, democracy and post-modernism. 'Close work' playwriting in fifty years will have different philosophical and cultural contexts as living artists writing close to their times reflect the context in which they live, and dredge 'found' material from oral, written, visual, physical and other sources. I am not positing that 'close work' is superior or more valid than any other form of dramatic writing. I only hope it will make public sense of my private struggle to articulate what motivates my writing. Most of my work cannot be accurately defined as 'verbatim', although it shares with verbatim an impulse to reach into a community and reflect its voice.

For instance, in my play *Ladies Day*, the character Lorena is a writer collecting stories of gay men living in Broome, just as I did in reality. But Lorena is both me and not me. As a character Lorena allowed me to disclose an aspect of my own story that these real men forced me to see, as well as to examine ideas about my process of making theatre. The play is like 'subverted' verbatim; it begins with a consciousness of the form but then interrogates and ultimately inverts it. While based on research and including some transcript material, *Ladies Day* travels further towards fiction, not only to protect some sensitive stories but also because the junction where truth and artifice meet is of increasing interest to me. So the audience's context for the play has determined its form. This context includes other drama in early 21st-century Australia and the value of my subjective experience, the public discussions about sexual assault, along with assumptions about verbatim theatre, the unreliable narrator and questions about post-truth. The American cartoonist Alison Bechdel conjectures that for Virginia Woolf 'what fiction achieves … [is] a deeper truth than facts'. In *Ladies Day* I allowed the truth to push me out of my comfort zone and give me the backbone to become vulnerable as an artist so I could offer that vulnerability to audiences.

When I visited Broome for *Ladies Day* I got to know the smell of diesel fuel, the hum of air conditioning units, the flip-flap slap of thongs and the late night laying awake can't-get-to-sleep sweetness of the dark. I conducted my interviews in the grounds of my Broome Hotel, where the pool was a hot bath, even with four flimsy triangles of bleached shade cloth over it. It did boast a beautiful old boab tree though, with fruiting fat pods that my first interviewee picked off, broke open and urged me to eat. The flavour was of sour mango, like the dry tart jolt of reality this town handed to me on a platter of welcome.

'So you're here to write about gay men who live in Broome?' my first interviewee asked me, squinting.

'That's right', I smiled, hopefully.

'Why don't you just watch *Brokeback Mountain?*', he offered.

'Well, *Brokeback Mountain* is about American men', I said.

'Yeah, but there was an Australian in the lead, so what difference does it make?

'You mean why do I need to come over here and actually talk to people?'

'No, I can see that you need to do your background research, that you might get some good stories over here.'

'I want it to be authentic', I said.

'What difference does that make to a good story?' he said. '*Brokeback Mountain* was written by a Canadian woman and directed by a Taiwanese man and it's the most beautiful gay love story I've ever seen in my life. If I want authentic I can watch one of those documentaries on television.'

'So maybe the theatre should just do an adaptation of the short story', I huffed, defeated by the heat and the flies and the cruel logic of his insights.

'Maybe they should, I'd come and see that. Not sure about your play though.' And then he laughed in that typically Australian way of someone who abuses you in the most genial way possible, then slaps you on the back and offers to buy you a cold beer. Which, in Broome, is *always* welcome.

The validity (or not) of my investigations hung in the air between us as we headed out to the biggest event on the Broome social calendar, the opening of the Broome races. There, in the VIP bar, I met an elder of the Broome community and, as we pushed past the Broome girls tottering on their unfamiliar high heels he warned me, 'Don't move too fast or you'll topple them, darling'. We stood to watch horses run around a chocolate brown track as the punters around us got utterly smashed, 'Just like race tracks everywhere, darling'. We talked about his sissy boy past and how early the alienation and discrimination started.

In the car back to my accommodation, I wound down the windows to let in the smell of soil, freshly churned by four-wheel drives. I was giddy already with the daring red of the Jigal trees in bloom, dazzled by the cobalt of the coast, and there at reception, queer as a baroque pearl, was my next interview subject. He introduced me to *all* his gay friends and we visited Cable Beach together, where tourists ride on a procession of camels that wends its way across the sand as the sun sets spectacularly in the west. What I loved about meeting these men was the easy way in which we picked up a common conversation, the generous way they disclosed themselves, the familiarity of their issues, the similarity of their concerns. And yet under the surface was a wariness, an awareness of vulnerability perhaps, or a consciousness about not censoring or limiting themselves here. And on the breeze, sometimes, the slow odour of violence.

These men demanded that I go well and truly beyond the role of chronicler and put myself, quite literally, into the story. *Ladies Day* is a play about the nature of truth and its relationship to storytelling, a play which reflects on all my work as a verbatim-inspired, authenticity-loving artist but concedes power to the magical, fictional, self-delusional nature of the stories we tell ourselves and others. By putting it on the Griffin stage, Lee Lewis allowed the play to speak to a new generation about our lives in 21st-century Australia. Lee is a real visionary, the genuine article, and she is attracting to Griffin a theatre audience that is informed, dynamic and theatrically curious. *Ladies Day* delivered me an audience dominated by the theatrically rebellious, generationally young and young at heart. I especially remember the woman who confided to me in the foyer that she'd seen the play with her sister and afterwards they had told each other of incidents in their childhood, assaults that neither had ever mentioned before for fear of thinking they were too trivial. Not only the dramatic, or the melodramatic, is true, *Ladies Day* conjectures; truth can be much smaller than that.

In every book about writing you will be urged to find your own voice, find the persona through which you can speak, explore your motivations and interrogate your situation to reach your story. But how do you do that? How do you mine what is surging around in your own nervous system and connect it to a work for the stage? How do you abandon irony and even decency and discern what is vital and what is superfluous to the magic you want to weave?

How can you learn to know who you are in the act of becoming an artist?

3

The flat above the fruit shop

I opened the washing machine lid and spat my spinach-stuffed cheeks into the drum. I must have been about nine years old because we had not yet moved from the flat above the fruit and vegetable shop on Railway Parade, Kogarah. I had excused myself from the table and, rather than swallow the foul bitterness of this evil dark green vegetable, I had padded out my small mouth and then disgorged it into the new appliance in the laundry.

I wonder at this image of myself as a young girl – as a writer I'd like to see its metaphorical possibilities as early contempt for domesticity, whitegoods and the proper role of femininity, something very much in play when I was growing up; or a precocious refusal to swallow secondary source material, even a lack of respect for all that money and compliance could buy. But really, I was just being a wilful little brat refusing to eat my dinner. I'll give myself credit for early deviousness – it must have taken some skill to secrete the spinach in just the right way that it didn't show. And I do puzzle at my choice of the washing machine – perhaps I thought it too obvious to flush it down the toilet.

I don't remember the beating that would have come later when my mother discovered her cleanly washed clothes covered in semi-digested spinach. The threat of violence explains why I didn't just throw a tantrum at the table and refuse to eat the spinach there. I knew that would mean a hiding. The washing machine would have been precious to my mother too – after all, with my brother and stepfather, we sat on crimson plastic 'Property of Dairy Farmers' milk crates to eat our dinner. The spinach itself would have been retrieved from the skip in the back of the nearby supermarket, where unsold produce was dumped on a Saturday afternoon, back in the days when supermarkets closed for the weekend at lunchtime on Saturday. The washing machine must have had pride of place among all this poverty.

So as much as I want to refuse the delicious symbolism and laugh it off as typical spinach-hating behaviour, there is a cunning in this child, and a thoughtful, calculated cunning too. What delights me more than anything is the way in which this memory takes me back into my way of thinking as a nine year old – peering over the top of that washing machine and calculating that my mother would never see the hated little secret that I was spitting into the dark, wet depths of the machine. She makes me laugh, this perverse little girl, thinking she can outsmart the powers that be by sheer inventiveness.

My mother had remarried about a year before and our family had moved from my grandmother's house, within walking distance of the St George Rugby League oval, to a rented flat in Kogarah. My stepfather was a linesman for the postmaster-general and my mother worked at the Pacific Film Laboratories in Carlton. They soon purchased their first home, on top of a hill in Wolseley Street, Bexley. Next door was an enormous 60-metre pine tree, cut down now, which I am told was originally a marker pine used in the early colony. I can't find any evidence to support this but it is far too good a story to ignore. Roy, my stepfather, moved our small number of belongings to our new house in an old-fashioned pram with the top cut off. To get a battered, recycled wardrobe up the hill in this contraption he dragooned the balancing skills and strength of a nine-year-old girl and her seven-year-old brother.

On the day we moved into our new house my new kitten went missing. We searched everywhere but all the tears and hoping and desperate calling out proved futile. So it was almost a miracle when my mother, at the end of a long, obsessive day, pulled on a small tail and yanked the kitten out from inside the old gas water heater where she was wedged, unable to escape. We called her Sooty. Today, after a lifetime marked by repeated losses – the early death of my grandmother and my mother and three lost pregnancies – I suffer the loss of any misplaced item from a hair clip to a photo or a handbag as an all-consuming, debilitating, trembling, palpitating episode of misery. I recognise the pattern now, and try to breathe and remain calm, telling myself that the thing is misplaced, not lost. But it frequently takes some time before I can control my frantic searching and begin to look calmly and methodically. Again, I gaze back into the past and see the woman I have become in the fanatical little girl.

My birth certificate notes that my mother had me when she was eighteen. Later, long after her early death from breast cancer at the age of 49, my uncle would tell me of the day my breathtakingly beautiful mother had met my father, 'out on the end of the Manly pier'. I have photos of her in her wedding dress, her waist as small as the brim of a tight fitting hat, or as small and tight as the smiles of her parents looking on. Two years later my brother was born and two years after that my biological father, whom I have never since met, left us. We moved in with my maternal grandparents, whose foreboding at the wedding now seemed prescient.

I mention my mother's history mainly because her choices profoundly affected my grandmother, who became my primary carer as a child. I inherited from my grandmother an almost obsessive regard for education and an ambition for a life that might go beyond the fate of a pregnant teenager. Later my mother would openly tell me that I shouldn't take it personally but there was no doubt that I ruined her life. Actually she didn't say 'I shouldn't take it personally' that's just me softening the blow in retrospect. What she actually said was 'You ruined my life'. That's what she said but what she did was keep me with her, work every day to sustain me, and dress me beautifully in clothes that she designed and sewed for me herself. Little wonder that I took up the profession of playwriting, where we believe not what people say, but what they do.

When I would ask my grandmother what she wanted me to be when I grew up she would blithely tell me that as long as I didn't end up in jail she didn't mind. When I hit university (the first in my family to do so), I remember meeting many middle-class young adults burdened with the expectations of their parents to become doctors or lawyers. Smugly I told myself about the advantage of my grandmother's low expectations, ignoring the fact that I was already at university at her urging. I was convinced that I could pursue a life of writing and creative endeavour because my working-class background freed me from bourgeois concerns. Yet straight out of university, I took a job in advertising on the North Shore – jumping into the grubby capitalism that my university companions rejected – and boasting to myself about the entrepreneurial freedom of my heritage.

How wrong I was to underestimate the growing seed of a greater ambition that my grandmother's fanatical passion for education had planted in me. How naïve I was to think that merely going to university or making money would be enough for her ravenous spirit that I still carry so preciously inside me. How lucky I was that my mother's tough love fitted me for a profession in which rejection and public judgement come with the territory. The Australian novelist Christina Stead said that in order to make an artist one must take a sensitive spirit and crush it under the wheels of the world. So when you, the emerging writer, find yourself feeling and actually being crushed, remember that one day those wheels will move on and your unique vision will emerge.

4
Satiating hunger

When I was growing up food was often in short supply. Some night's dinners were a lucky dip as Nanna saved money by buying tinned food that had no label. She had a cupboard full of the stuff. They must have improved the label glue in more recent times because I have no idea how the labels came off. Perhaps my wily, cash-strapped grandmother removed them herself and then asked for a discount.

There is no more persistent memory of my early years than the rare occasions when I ate more than my fill. The time my grandmother got my brother and I a job putting Kelly's Liquor Store pamphlets in letterboxes for three days and there was enough money to buy two whole lamb chops *each* for dinner. The time when Mr Kinney from church gave us a piecework job screwing nuts onto bolts as part of some industrial scheme and we had the money to buy three Flake chocolate bars for me, my brother and my grandmother to eat. In an advertisement at the time, a young woman carefully unwrapped an upright Flake bar and ate it with unbridled erotic passion. Viewed now it would look like she was giving the bar a slow blow job. But for my brother and myself, this ad represented the visual embodiment of our deepest longings and fantasies. Flakes in hand, we waited for the ad to come on television that night so that we could eat with the girl and share in her ecstasy of oral gratification. I can still remember the three of us, moaning and munching those Flake bars, as if we had never tasted anything so wonderful.

If I learnt anything about mathematics or supply-and-demand economics in my childhood it was from analysing the contents of Easter show bags and calculating minutely which bags were the best value for money – chocolate wise. Once bought, the bag's contents were forensically checked to make sure it contained everything promised. At home, the bounty was calibrated, inventoried and apportioned to make it last for as long as was possible, taking perishability into account.

My grandmother used to walk us down to the Rockdale Plaza, 2 kilometres from home, to save a few cents on the purchase of something, and then ask my brother and me whether we would rather have an ice-cream or get the bus home. We always chose the ice-cream and endured the agony of the long walk. When I was twelve years old, a man sitting next to me on a train exposed his penis to me while balancing an unopened bag of Twisties on his lap. I was more concerned that it would forever cruel my love of those wriggly little orange snacks, than about the sight of his wriggly little pink willy.

The question of hunger has become compelling for me since the Charles Perkins Centre, assisted by philanthropist Judy Harris, commissioned my proposal for a verbatim play called *Made to Measure* in 2016. The Charles Perkins Centre is a world-class science facility focusing on metabolic syndrome, especially obesity, diabetes and kidney disease. My idea is to interview couturiers who make wedding clothes in order to write a play that dramatises people's relationship with their wedding day appearance and how this expresses hopes, dreams and truths about their lives.

Designers and tailors can provide a perceptive route into the *stakes* involved in getting married. The wedding day is a critical dramatic moment when individuals want to look like their ideal version of themselves; to personify their own (and their intended spouse's) image of a desirable partner. The public pressure of the wedding day is unique and excruciating, even for someone with a secure and mature body image: an affirmation of love and possibility in front of one's entire family and social network; and a moment frozen in time by the wedding photos. Rarely is the body and how it looks so undeniably fundamental to the narrative of the day.

My professional intuition that dressmakers and tailors would have hilarious stories about disastrous dieting, impossible clients, spectacular failures, incredible transformations and scandalous liaisons has proven accurate. Already, my interviews have thrown up an entertaining diversity of insights into the Australian psyche as it relates to body shape, nutritional discipline and cultural expectations.

There are so many fertile dramatic ways in which the relationship between a designer, seamstress or tailor and a potential bride or groom will license me as a writer to confront audiences with some harsh truths about health issues. I'm hoping it will be a clever way to interrogate the conflict between healthy body image and fat-shaming. I'm planning to include science and research under the guise of a bullying seamstress or a tolerant tailor. A writer, particularly a playwright, needs metaphor to carry the subject so they can intrigue an audience through character. You can't write a play about obesity, nutrition, body consciousness or science. You *can* write a play about an intimate relationship of trust, though, and how that trust is tested, betrayed or strained as the wedding day approaches – a touching, funny and ultimately revealing insight into the Australian body on its wedding day, and beyond. The premise in *Made to Measure* is that individuals can do anything they want to do, if the reason is sufficiently compelling. I want to articulate deep aspects of these reasons, rather than define them, so that the imponderable aspects of human nature play a mysterious part in the drama.

I didn't grow up with the obesity epidemic, surely one of the biggest global health challenges of the 21st century. As I said, lack of food was a constant issue when I was young. In fact, I first went into a church because I was hungry. If you think that sounds unlikely, perhaps you have never been hungry. If you have been hungry you'll understand the motivation. My local Methodist church provided food with after-service suppers, morning teas and other community events. It provided books as presents for anniversary celebrations, too, and entertained us at Sunday School with terrific, attractively preposterous stories. The local church developed my public speaking skills by asking me to read at services, and told me I was special and beloved and destined for great things when no one else at the time was saying anything of the sort.

Still, I managed to get to my teens without having, well, converted. I had thought about it a lot. I wrestled with the whys and why nots but late into my teens I was essentially there for the cream cakes and illustrated storybooks. I had friends who were people of faith, I even went away to you-beaut Christian camps. Well, they got me out of the city, fed me and there were fun 'activities'. I also got to meet nice, long-haired, guitar-playing boys who didn't put too much pressure on me for sex. No more than was welcome anyway.

But at an Easter camp when I was seventeen, the question of faith developed an urgency. I was beginning to feel genuinely uncomfortable about not believing, not taking a leap of faith, not being able to buy the 'saved for your sins' angle of the story. On the first day of camp we were asked to write a poem about Christ's death on the Cross. I wrote a piece about how it was not really that incredible that Christ died on a cross. After all, I mused, plenty of people die, lots die unfairly. Some even die willingly, as he did, for a cause or a belief. What distinguished Christ, the budding little theologian in me argued, was that he died to save us from our doubts. He was so faithfully convinced that he could triumph over death that he was prepared to die, horribly, brokenly, to vanquish all our doubts. Doubt was the antithesis of faith and faith, I wrote, was the most precious thing in the world. When I read it out there was a long silence, then the woman who was leading the exercise came over and took my page, read it again and embraced me. 'That is the most wonderful poem', she said. 'Can I keep it?' And I didn't say 'Yes, but I retain copyright'. I said, 'Sure, it's all yours'.

That was Good Friday. I spent the next two days crying. Confused, really badly confused. Longing to believe but not able to. Danced up Saturday night, but slept badly. Got up to the dawn service on Easter morning and believed. It wasn't quite an act of will but it was at first, somehow, close to an act of surrender. I straddled a divide that was nowhere near definite. I could almost feel my arms and legs back in the disbelieving category, while my heart and my head had gone over to the other side. I could look back and still know all the doubts and fears but now I was looking at them through the lens of grace. And I was still crying. Crying with relief, crying with doubts. I mean, how did I know that this was real? How did I know I wasn't just buying into the absolutely perfect narrative of being converted on Easter Sunday? The stone rolled away from the tomb.

After many years, these three remain – faith, hope and love. What you choose to have faith in is up to you – art, love, community, divinity, anarchy, justice, freedom – what you choose to test out through your life will shape your work and define your oeuvre. In a world where there is so much information, so much science and so much fear, I believe the 21st century will be defined by what we choose to value, what we ethically and morally prioritise, what we do with what we *already* know. A grotesque intergenerational theft has been perpetrated on the coming generations, not only of resources but also of hope, and so the work you may choose to do as a writer for the theatre must reflect the things in which *you* have faith, hope and love.

I believe that a profound hunger to have your voice heard is the number one ingredient for an artist to succeed. Talent is essential, discipline is indispensable, opportunity from your community is all. But every great writer, actor and director I have worked with uses their art to satiate and understand the hungers in their own life. Hunger is a finger that prods at you until you satisfy it, it rages the next day as ferociously as it did the last, hunger is undiminished by age. And *really* being hungry is not the same as what you feel when you are dieting. Hunger is seeing the food right there on the shelf and not being able to eat it, standing in the foyer with an artistic director who knows your name but has never given you access to their audience. Hunger is like a brand that sears your soul, and spits and sizzles as it marks you. You have to have experienced real hunger to know it.

5

Like understands like

When you start thinking about working with a community that interests you, your first port of call should be someone who has an idea of what a playwright might be. It's a hard but salient truth to realise that some of the most interesting people in the world have never been to a theatre, or have even the vaguest idea what a playwright does. After you tell them that you write for the stage they will persist in referring to your 'novel'. Long after you have been working with them they will ask how long you take to learn your lines. And, hey, there's no reason to get snooty about this ignorance – I wouldn't know what electrical engineers do or the language they use to describe their work even though they designed the computer I am writing with as well as the system that delivers the electricity to power it.

Once you realise that not everyone knows what a dramaturg is, let alone the difference between prompt and OP (opposite prompt), you will seek out someone who at least understands the slippery nature of truth. It might be someone who deals with journalists or publicists. When Belvoir commissioned me to write *Run Rabbit Run*, about the struggle of the South Sydney Rabbitohs to get back into the National Rugby League, the first person I rang was Norm Lipson, the club's marketing manager. As a former journalist, he had a strong idea of how to tell a story – indeed, I attribute a large part of Souths' successful fightback to Lipson's talent to spin a story that captured the public's imagination. He knew that a story did not simply 'exist in the ether' but was 'constructed' by the person writing it. When he directed me to people, he knew that who I spoke to, and even the order in which I spoke to them, would influence what I wrote.

In 2008 the Alex Buzo Company commissioned me to write a companion 'response' to Buzo's landmark play, *Norm and Ahmed*. When I began to investigate the play that would become *Shafana and Aunt Sarrinah*, I contacted an interfaith organisation called Affinity. I drove out to Auburn on a rainy night and climbed the stairs to their offices, directly above a gorgeous pink and white Turkish delight shop, where I met Makiz Ansari. During the interview she revealed her struggle in deciding to don the hijab, when her own aunts had vigorously resisted doing so. I later spoke to one of her aunts as well as other Muslim women and organisations, and even gained access to a housing centre for Muslim women. An interfaith organisation does not necessarily know what a playwright does but they are familiar with dealing with the unfamiliar. Since their *raison d'être* is to forge links with people or groups who don't understand Muslim culture, they are inured to the idea of broaching understanding. It turned out that Makiz Ansari was *the* find of the research process, but it is hardly unexpected that such an incredible, intelligent, insightful person would be working in an interfaith, cross-cultural forum.

When I visited Hobart in 2010 as a guest of the Tasmanian Writer's Centre I didn't have a car so I took to walking everywhere around this small jewel of a city. My meanderings from Battery Point and the purportedly haunted Writer's Cottage led me to the Queen's Domain where I found an avenue of trees planted in 1919 by the families of Tasmania's World War I casualties. Contemporary relatives of the soldiers had recently restored and replanted this unique and beautiful avenue. The walk among its 520 trees was tremendously moving for me and it connected to my long association with veterans' stories and experiences, beginning with free athletics classes in my childhood provided by the local RSL that finished with the 'Ode of Remembrance'. I had marched as a child in the Anzac cenotaph commemorations in Kogarah, and in more recent years the Australian War Memorial commissioned me to write *Radio Silence*, a short play set during World War II in which a member of the Women's Auxiliary Australian Air Force (or WAAAF) is listening and waiting for the return of her fiancé, a Lancaster bomber pilot. Through this work I realised that while soldiers' stories are told with considerable detail and a great number of artefacts, memorabilia and context, few stories feature women and the different ways they have suffered, contributed and survived during wartime.

I mentioned my response to Hobart's Memorial Avenue to Jo Duffy, the incoming artistic director of the Ten Days on the Island Festival, which led to a number of enthusiastic meetings with Hobart Council. I conceived *The Tree Widows* as an interactive, outdoor performance in the Queen's Domain through which audiences and performers would explore the unique connection of this living monument to Tasmania's past as four actors delivered a series of character-driven monologues. The monologues would be based on stories drawn from real-life relatives and friends of the soldiers memorialised by the trees. My idea was to create a living link to Hobart's past for an audience of local residents and visitors to the Ten Days on the Island Festival as they moved from tree to tree, exposed to the elements and aware of other random park users. The trees would be a potent metaphor, a living set, a harrowing reminder and a poignant memorial, immersing the audience in the immediacy of their urban environment, and reaching past complacency and other defences to bring them into the present moment of this outdoor space in a powerful way.

When I learned that the man who was responsible for the recent 'resuscitation' of the avenue was an ex-teacher I virtually did a jig up the walls of my apartment lounge room. Before I spoke to him, before he had the vaguest notion of what I might propose, before I had even checked the website for a contact number or email I *knew* he would get it. Teachers are intellectuals, teachers are storytellers, teachers traffic daily in the contract between entertaining and informing their audience and, I might add, they work some of the most difficult audiences in the world (teenage young adults) and live to tell the tale. And so it was. When I spoke to Adrian Howe he could see the possibilities of making an outdoor work of theatre, he put me in contact with the families who had the 'best' stories, he even knew what verbatim theatre was. I was spoilt rotten with Adrian and the production of *The Tree Widows* was, I hope, a tribute to his vision, creativity and industry.

In addition to Adrian, I discovered among the Friends of the Soldier's Memorial group a close-knit community compelled to resurrect the overgrown avenue where name plates had been stolen by looters, and which had been chopped up by the mowing operations of a once-neglectful council and even, at one stage, made into a rubbish tip. The group had publicised their outrage at this mistreatment, cleared away the strangling wattle and other small trees and installed plaques in their effort to revive the avenue's fortunes.

In *The Tree Widows* audiences were invited to walk with performers at assigned times of the day. They learnt some information about the soldiers through the monologues, but the object was to create an emotional empathy both with the soldiers who died and the lives and hearts of women who were left without them. Relatives can have conflicting or confronting feelings in these circumstances – some become virulently anti-war, others rage against the indifference of citizens to the sacrifice made on their behalf.

The Tree Widows won the 2017 Errol Award for best writing as well as the Judges' Award for 'creative integration of community, culture and heritage'. Jane Johnson was nominated for best female actor and I was nominated for best direction. Best of all a Tasmanian critic wrote, 'Her gift to Tasmanian audiences is this sublime meditation on the way we make sense of our own lives through private and shared memorials to the dead. Spanning generations, this is one of the very rare plays in which you feel yourself rubbing up against the cultural DNA of an entire city'.

So find your metaphorical thinker, your media liaison officer or, worst comes to worst, the most brilliant community gossip. The person who likes to know everyone else's business. The person who 'can tell you a story or two that would make your hair stand on end'. Find the community-appointed or even self-appointed town crier. Find the maverick. When I was undertaking the internship for my postgraduate degree in Museum Studies at the National Maritime Museum, I met Paul Hundley, curator of the museum's USA Gallery. He unabashedly told me, 'If I'm not in trouble then I'm not doing my job', and I thought, 'Now *that* I can work with'. Find someone who is not afraid to stir the pot a little, who has worked with so many people in so many incarnations that they can tell immediately that you are not a time waster or a wannabe. Find the person who can take you to their own personal lookout to give you your first overview of the community you have chosen. Their perspective will not be yours, but it will give you a very good starting point.

6

Don't write the subject

No play is about a subject. Well, I guess bad plays are, and perhaps they give verbatim theatre its reputation for worthiness. An industry professional once told me that, 'verbatim is the cod liver oil of contemporary theatre: good for you but not very nice to swallow'. This followed a public reading of my play *Tricky Girl*, a reworking of *The Taming of the Shrew* commissioned by Bell Shakespeare, developed after I visited high schools and canvassed young adults about their opinions of the gender politics in *Shrew*. The comment betrayed a tedious and general misunderstanding of the verbatim form that can culminate in the label of 'documentary' theatre.

As I say, no play is about a subject. All plays are about the same thing – human nature under pressure, in crisis, in conflict. The subject is the cladding that contextualises the crisis of this particular set of human beings, if you like; the lens through which you observe the effects of the pressure. But the interest of a dramatist is always the same, at least mine is: it's in the perversions, complications, details, surprises and disappointments of human nature. A close work playwright is interested in the specific way individuals articulate their perceptions and insights today, contingent on all the ideas and politics and identity issues which inform the way they think and speak. Like all dramatists we believe in what people *do*, not what they *say*, but this style of theatre has a particular interest in how language obfuscates and reveals character.

In June 2013, when I was enjoying the research delights of a Harold White Fellowship at the National Library of Australia, I spent a dizzying three months in Canberra. I became so unreservedly besotted by the city, its residents and its impeccable archives that the fellowship assistant, Beth Mansfield, quickly dubbed me a boomerang: 'One of those returning fellows who seem to come back year after year'. And I did – dredging the archives and renewing my respect for the data management skills and meticulous persistence of researchers and academics.

Towards the end of my residency, Margy Burn, the assistant director of the library, invited me to accompany her to meet the serving governor-general, Her Excellency Quentin Bryce. I was suited up in a Wadeye screen-printed fabric by artist Alenga Nganbe, with fluorescent orange and purple dilly bags, which I had sewed on my trusty HR Princess sewing machine. We drove down Dunrossil Drive to the Yarralumla residence. Quentin wore a tailored blue suit with an Yves Saint Laurent scarf artfully folded at her neck but her bright blue crocodile-skin shoes betrayed a more playful nature (I never addressed her with any appellation so I can't say we were on first name terms but, in an Australian way, it was implicit). We were invited to sit on the couch in her office, and Her Excellency urged us to eat a pretty tier of petit fours in front of us, which, she told us, 'had just been especially made by my pastry chef'. It wasn't the moment to mention that I followed a gluten-free diet, so I dutifully popped one in my mouth, hoping that the typical irritability and bloating wheat causes me wouldn't manifest itself until after our audience had concluded.

I understood that Margy often helped the governor-general with her speeches, using the remarkable resources of the National Library's research collection to give historical accuracy and piquancy to her public addresses. They talked about that for a time before, politely, she turned and asked me about my playwriting. 'What have you written about that might interest me?' she said. I mentioned *Parramatta Girls*, and talked about the national apology to the forgotten Australians, to which she nodded gravely and then I brought up my play *Run Rabbit Run*, about the Souths fightback. 'Oh, yes', she said, using the full panoply of her diplomatic skills to urge me on. I didn't think I was nervous but I certainly wasn't in control of the conversation. 'So it depends if you are interested in football', I ventured. 'Well, I'm not really', she confided, 'though I am the patron of a number of important sporting groups that I support'.

And then there was that terrible thing, a pause. For my part I was nearly choking on my semi-digested petit four as the hideous thought ran through my brain, 'Oh God, I'm meeting the most interesting woman in Australia today, the most visionary, most fascinating, probably the most socially high status person I've met since I fumblingly shook the hand of the Duchess of Cornwall at NSW Government House, and I'm making conversation about football'. And now she was turning her head slightly, retreating to the conversational certainty of the National Library, when I threw out, like a javelin, a sentence that might spear her to my spot. 'Well, in truth, my play was not really about football at all. It's about the conflict between tradition and change, about how to balance the heritage of the past with the demands of the present and indeed, preparation for the future.'

As low as I'd gone was as high as I now flew. 'I think about that all the time, of course', she said, brightly. 'As merely the most recent inductee in this role I don't think I have the right to change everything about the office that I may not favour or like, but I am very mindful of the need to keep the role contemporary and relevant, so that it continues to genuinely be able to influence change.' Wow. She flowed, she chatted, she bubbled brightly in contemplation of the conundrum. Brave enough now to raise the GG-issue teacup to my lips, I congratulated myself on having turned the disaster around, but of course it was her skill, not mine. She had the ability to engage sincerely with even the tiniest life raft of conversation that floated her way.

Not about football is why women from the audience at Belvoir St used to come up to me after the performance of *Run Rabbit Run* in tears, wringing my arm and between sobs confess 'I hate football but I loved your play'. Not about the subject is why people watching or even just reading that play laugh and cry and scrunch up their fists in anger. And not about the subject, phew, is what saved me from a humiliating disaster and turned it into a triumph of personal revelation with a woman I admire without reservation, Quentin Bryce. At least, that's the way I'm telling it, and, without a transcript, that is my creative prerogative.

7

Architect of your own emotions

The means to fulfil my grandmother's ambitious dreams for my teenage self was as an English teacher. The person I admired most in the world was my English teacher, Miss O'Sullivan. Also a teaching career came with a scholarship. So I applied for this marvel, this scheme where the state paid for your further education, and I worked like an unnaturally socially isolated teenager to score big on my HSC. I barely slept for longing as I waited for confirmation of my educational and financial liberation to arrive in the post. It was due on the Friday. On the Wednesday I got a letter saying that I had been accepted into a BA in Communications at the NSW Institute of Technology, now the University of Technology Sydney (UTS). I barely remembered applying for it. (The school had urged us to apply for lots of placements, in case we didn't get our first preference.)

I looked the course up in the handbook. It was a degree in media and writing. Well, I had never wanted to be a writer, I wanted to be a teacher. But there were all these really cool media facilities there and you got to make radio programs and films and hey, this actually looked pretty interesting. The more I read about it the more it intrigued me. But a lot of it was about writing. Hmmm. My Geography teacher, Mrs Cappalletto, always used to tell me that the reason I got such good marks in Geography was because I was such a clear writer. Writing was also intrinsic to my status as fourth speaker of the school debating team, although I hadn't thought about it like that before now. Still, it struck me as an interesting proposition. Maybe I wanted to do a BA in Communications, I would have to work several jobs to pay my way through whatever I did. Maybe I could change my mind about teaching.

And so, like a bride who flees the chapel unwed, and uncannily close to the altar of a brilliant pedagogical future, I decided not to become a teacher. At which I would have been very bad and by which I would have been made utterly miserable. When the offer of a teaching scholarship and a BA in Education placement came on the Friday I did look at it. But now I wanted to go to UTS and be a journalist, a writer, a professional communicator. There was no scholarship so I would have to find the money, somehow. But suddenly, wanting to be a writer made sense of years of observing the world, participating in theatre and dance classes, and filling journals with poems, plays and overheard conversations.

During my degree I met Jenna Price and John Kavanagh, who were editors of *Newswit*, the student newspaper, and they trained me up to become an editor in my own right, with Amanda Collinge and Kerry Brown. Everyone thought I might become a journalist but instead I secured a mentorship, an apprenticeship really, with the Advertising Federation of Australia to work at the Monahan Dayman Adams (MDA) agency in North Sydney for nine months. So while all my feminist student buddies went off to work with the Australian Broadcasting Corporation (ABC) and women's health organisations, or a host of alternative media outlets, I trotted off to dress myself from the conservative ladies' dress shop and put my hand up for a life in the filthy lucre of the advertising business. I passed through a somewhat gruelling selection process, including written and verbal interviews, that culled a couple of hundred applicants down to seven trainees who each received nine months' employment on full pay. We were to be immersed in every area of the advertising business including management, media and creative (in my case, copywriting).

A month later, there was a ceremony to confer our Traineeship certificates, and after the ceremony, another trainee had invited us back to her place for what she called a 'small celebration'. Her address was Point Piper Road. The number was low so I think ... no water view. To put it in context this was the 1980s and the sides of my head were shaved with a comb-teased mullet on top. I co-fronted a late Wednesday night program on 2SER FM of punk and new wave music, and my girlfriend was a motorbike-riding bass player in an all-girl rock band. Point Piper was not my usual haunt.

I should have suspected. I had turned into Point Piper Road what felt like several days ago and I was still only in single figures on the house numbers. Man did these houses cover a lot of territory. Finally I came to the house and, yep, it was full waterfront, white gates, high tech security system, the lot. There was, I kid you not, a double banister staircase with a crystal chandelier in the entrance hall. I was certainly not keeping my head above water on this one, no way. But I laughed and nodded when my hostess told me that she was going to Paris for the summer break. 'I've worked my butt off to get this traineeship', she said proudly. I pasted a small, glazed, appropriate, convivial smile on my face, ate the mingy little snacks provided (I later learnt to call them *hors d'oeuvres*), drank the champagne and contemplated the fact that my time as co-editor of the student newspaper *Newswit* had in no way prepared me for this.

But I'm caught in a delicious nostalgia about my first look at seriously rich people, people who might actually vote conservatively (such creatures were the stuff of legend in my childhood) which has diverted me from the point of this chapter, namely, that there are some things that you shouldn't try and butt your head against in this country, in this culture of Australia – theatre or otherwise. I served my mentorship with MDA for nine months after which Paul Wilson, the creative director, offered me a copywriting job. I was still a definite oddity in the department but I was doing good work on the Qantas, Estée Lauder and News Limited accounts which required regular, junior copywriting. Come Christmas, MDA threw a party and asked us to come in fancy dress.

My Aunty Jess from Forster had recently died and I had inherited a fully pinned felt wad of all her lawn bowls badges. So I bought a white bowling uniform, cut the hem to the length of a dangerously short mini-skirt, bought black fishnet stockings and suspenders, and a child's beach ball which I painted with black acrylic paint. I hunched over like a crazed granny on speed, clutching my bowling ball between my hands and twisting my mouth into a shape that might have resembled false teeth. I looked absolutely brilliant ... weird, accurate, subversively sexy and fun. When I broke onto the dance floor the contrast between my Afro-Jazz dance moves and the pensioner I was channelling must have been a hoot par excellence.

I can't say I had much competition so I felt I was a shoo-in for the Sony Walkman which was the top prize for the best costume. A Walkman, for anyone born in this century, was the digital music gadget of choice in the late 1990s. There was a young man from Accounts got up in his mother's clothes but, being the veteran of several Mardi Gras parades by then, I didn't even notice him. I mean, it wasn't even bad suburban gothic drag. This was just outright, unadulterated bad drag. You could see the streaks in his foundation. And advertising agencies, if not a hotbed of political dissent, were still arbiters of style and excellence. Here was a roomful of some of the most aesthetically inventive and gifted fashionistas in Sydney and this guy was not even in the amateur league. But you know what comes next. Mr Junior Account Executive carries off the Sony Walkman and Miss Strange Little Random Bowling Lady from Creative wins the basket full of Estée Lauder cosmetics. Second prize.

Was I pissed off? Hell, I'm still talking about it. I was so infuriated, so outraged, so utterly gobsmacked by the injustice that I have never forgotten it. But it taught me a deeply memorable, indelible truth about life as an artist in this country. For me it was 'You can't beat a man in a dress'. For you it will be something else – but the lesson will be the same – you can't compete with whatever is 'cute' or 'trick' or 'fashionable' at the time you begin. That is not the way to your original voice. Don't avert your gaze. Look hard at what is fashionable, the flavour of the month, or the year, or the prejudice that is embedded deep right now in Australian culture and expressed in the theatre. You may have to spend a lifetime working against it. But first you need to examine what it is. Understand everything about what perspectives are privileged. Because it's only by being objectively, forensically aware of the cultural limitations around you that you can find and articulate your individual power and confidence.

Look at the theatre of your time and how you either align with it or push against it to formulate your own aesthetic, your own original ideas. What you don't like, what beats you, what pisses you off is as valuable, maybe even more valuable, than what inspires you. It will keep you awake at night, distract you, make you daydream, confuse you and compel you. Learn how to articulate what you think about the theatre of your time, precisely and analytically, not just emotionally, and definitely not just as a patron. Closely observe what works with audiences moment by moment – spend as much time looking at the house as you do the stage. Look at the way a playwright constructs a scene with more than two people in it – as in count the number of lines before a character fades out of the scene. Playwriting is the architecture of emotion, it is a magnificent machine built to deliver meaning over time. The way you beat the pretender in the dress, I've learnt, might be by donning one of your own (as my characters do in *Ladies Day*), or it might be by inventing something entirely new. In any case your strategy must be to wait until tired, clichéd, predictable ideas have *had their day*. Your day will come if you stay close to your deepest source of originality and truth.

8

My first play

I stayed for another nine months at MDA as a junior copywriter and learnt a lot about lateral thinking, commercial realities and alcohol poisoning. I discovered that you could put an idea into this system, this machine for making meaning, and a shiny piece of persuasion would come out the other end. I never objected to the moral vagaries of advertising – it serviced a business with money wanting to buy slick communication. MDA refused to take on tobacco companies as clients and I would have pulled myself off alcohol and oil companies if they ever signed them, which they didn't. So it was tabloid newspapers, beauty products and airline tickets – not a list to cover yourself in glory but not exactly evil incarnate either. And I met some seriously clever creative people. Problem solvers and lateral thinkers par excellence. I decided to leave because I wanted to do other things. I had gone into advertising, as I said, because my working-class engines were revving to make money so I could be independent (knowing there's no-one to bail you out if you fall on your face is a strong motivating factor). But once inside the money-go-round of advertising I think I saw that the real trick, the real measure of being clever, was to make a living doing exactly what you wanted to do.

I found cheap share accommodation in Lavender Bay. The owner had been committed to a mental institution so the real estate agents couldn't fix up the property or sell it. Instead they had to rent it out in all its dishevelled disrepair to the kind of dishevelled, shaved-headed punks that I was now running with. I applied to work with JNP Productions on *A Country Practice*. I wrote a sample script and they offered to put me on as a production assistant, 'to let me get to know the series' with the possibility of moving into the writing area. I declined their offer. 'Why?' asked script editor Forrest Redlich. 'Because I'm writing a play', I told him. 'Ha', he laughed, 'Aren't we all?'

So I'm in this room in the dilapidated mansion where I'm living and I see in the paper that the Sydney Theatre Company are running a competition for Young Playwrights. I decide to enter it and write a play about a teenage alcoholic called *Multiple Choice*. Why theatre? The waking of my fate, the rousing of my vision, the stirring of my purpose. And the appeal of the prize money.

I entered the award but I didn't win. In fact there was no award that year. But by the time the outcome was announced I had moved into the inner city and got a job on the Belvoir St bar. I showed my play to the theatre's general manager Chris Westwood, known more ubiquitously as West, and she urged me to take it down to the Australian Theatre for Young People (ATYP) and show it to the artistic director Colette Rayment. I did. She liked it, she programmed it and soon I was at the opening night in the foyer of the Old Sailors Home. In the lead roles were Lisa Hensley, Emily Nevin-Crook (now Emily Russell), Adam Cook and Imogen Banks (my future agent). Also on stage was my girlfriend's band Fun'n'Only, punk girls from the Blue Mountains playing havoc with the somewhat sheltered North Shore cast.

Alex Buzo was offered to me as a mentor during the production in a scheme called the Master and the Apprentice Mentorship. I refused to participate unless it was called the Experienced and Emerging Mentorship. Our first meeting was at the Red Rose Cafe in Macquarie Street where I ordered a pie and chips and he a packet of Peppermint Blizzards. He told me that if I would like an actor to emphasise a certain word in a line I should simply underline it. I told him that the ATYP director Colette Rayment had told me that acting was a subtle art form and I should not try to predicate the way a line should be said. 'Nah, underline it where you think the emphasis is', he told me. He also advised me not to use direct address to the audience in my first stage play. But I did so despite his warnings. He came up to me on the opening night and told me that he was 'quite wrong' and that the direct address had worked a treat. To me that has always stood as a measure of great courage – this incredibly gifted and experienced writer willing to be surprised and revise his judgement of a young writer who was really no more than an opinionated upstart. I still see it as a genuine brush with his greatness as an artist.

Playwright Louis Nowra has noted that Buzo's plays are about language and how people 'use language as a deliberate tactic to put other people off guard'. *Norm and Ahmed* was the first play in which I deeply identified with the way Australians were presented – along with the fumbling inarticulate attempts at lucidity chronicled in Patrick White and the charming warmth of Peter Kenna, with its brutal undertow of aggression veiled in genial, irreverent humour. But Buzo's influence persisted long past this first encounter with him. 'The most common road sign in Australia is "form one lane"', he wrote in the *Adelaide Review* in November 1998 in an article titled 'The Narrowing of Theatre in the 1990s': 'During the thirty years I have earned a living as a professional writer I have learned one thing. The theatre will recover and become an art form again. I am sure of it. No longer will everything come from one lane'. I still have the copy of Terence Rattigan's *The Browning Version* which he gave me. 'Study how he structures the exposition', he told me.

The production of *Multiple Choice* was terrific, and garnered great reviews – I was accused of being 'promising' and 'precocious'. Suddenly I thought, 'Hey, maybe this would be a good thing to do with my life'. The play was even produced again at the Sydney Festival the following year, in Wharf 2. This time I invited my family. My grandmother asked, 'How do you know so much about teenage alcoholism', to which I answered, smiling, 'I did a lot of research'.

I wrote a radio play called *The Story of Anger Lee Bredenza*, about a mother and daughter, a kind of parable in which the spirit of a dead child is returned to the land in Central Australia. I entered it into the Ian Reed Foundation award for a new radio play. Ron Blair, the Commissioning Editor for ABC Radio Drama and an esteemed playwright, wrote me the most wonderful opening line of a letter I have ever received, 'We like your play and want to buy it'. He did. I was so enthusiastic during the production that he said, 'I think you'd quite like to direct one of these yourself'. This led to three years of full-time employment at ABC Radio Drama as a producer and director.

Audio arts are the most wonderful apprenticeship for a young playwright. At the ABC I had access to the best actors in Australia, for the three days it took them to record the play. Usually as a playwright you have to work through youth theatre productions and independent productions and small theatre productions to experience rigour and a bruising apprenticeship before you reach the main stage. I'm not saying that you don't get access to the best actors in those productions … but in radio drama in those days you could call in the most experienced actors of their generation – the people who were playing the Opera House and Belvoir at night and they'd come in to do a radio play with little, barely-experienced you. My first radio directing gig was the production of a Jennifer Paynter play called *Balancing Act* with Melissa Jaffer in the lead. I will never forget her patience, brilliance and consummate professionalism in dealing with my hesitant, self-conscious and, I'm sure, barely-useful direction.

I went from being a contract employee to a full-time, fully fledged staff employee of the ABC. I could have stayed there for the rest of my career. But in 1994 my mother died and, frankly, I just couldn't handle the stress of office politics, illogical management and full-time work. So I resigned. People thought I was mad. People walk across hot coals to become a permanent ABC employee and I was resigning. No redundancy, no nothing. At my farewell I remember a fellow from the radio station Triple J saying to me 'What will you do on Monday?' And I said, 'I'll get up and write'. He laughed.

But I did.

9
Mentored by poofters

It is hard to imagine now, she says with an ironic flourish, but in 1991 it felt like there was no-one interested in what I might be writing for the Australian stage.

But then there was Arthur Frederick Dicks. A stern, scathing, tough-love theatre maker, Arthur was an Englishman who had come to Australia in the 1970s as head of design at NIDA. With Gae Anderson and Paul Hastings Booth he put his own money into the formation of theatre company In the Pink. They showcased my play *Southern Belle*, loosely based on the life of American author Carson McCullers, in the downstairs theatre space at Belvoir as part of the 1991 Sydney Gay and Lesbian Mardi Gras Festival. I learned more from watching it on stage than all of the feedback I had ever had.

I have read books by novelists and poets about their passionate, dependant, almost erotic love of words. Annie Dillard describes the line of words as 'a miner's pick, a woodcarver's gouge, a surgeon's probe. You wield it, and it digs a path you follow'. And yes, of course, playwrights love words too. But beyond words we have a covetous, disturbed, irrational admiration and longing for theatre spaces and the language of bodies in space. Playwrights do not write text; they incarnate ideas, they interrogate what happens despite words and underneath words, enraptured with the possibility of an authentic emotional exchange between the stage and the audience. Inside a theatre, the boards of the stage whisper their echoes, the walls rumble with memories, the lighting rig illuminates the dust and glitter and spittle of the past. We breathe in the possibility of imagination transforming the world into truth and sense.

Even today when I go to the theatre I always go in early because I like to watch as the audience come in and fill up the seats. It's an intense and transformative experience, an irrefutable acknowledgement of the power of architecture, heritage and history in this most ephemeral of art forms. As a playwright, the anticipation of seizing the forum, the public space, to address and entertain one's community, the careful rehearsal and preparation for 'the two hours traffic of our stage' drives you back again and again. This space makes you become shrill and insistent about the importance of gender parity and cultural diversity; strengthens you to rebuff opposition and ignorance and outright hostility to pipe up again and again; and makes you dedicate your life to getting it right.

I wouldn't be making my living as a writer today if it wasn't for the patronage of Arthur Dicks and the encouragement of Gae Anderson. When Arthur told me his theatre anecdotes about touring in the UK and gossiped about NIDA and insisted that I explain every single choice I made – from where scenes were set, to why characters spoke, to how the drama might unfold – I listened. When Gae did auditions and met actors for coffee and discussed casting with me and Arthur, I listened. I had been to NIDA myself, for the playwrights' course in 1989, but when I reflect on where I got my first confidence from, NIDA didn't come close to the real world, real blowtorch-wielding mentorship of these two gifted professionals, prepared to publicly come out about their sexuality at a time when it was courageous to do so.

Three years later, in December 1994, Arthur Dicks died and I attended his funeral at the Walter Carter Funeral Home in Bondi Junction. That was a year of too many funerals for me, including my own mother who died three days out from her fiftieth birthday in March, and actor Tim Conigrave who died in October. Tim's funeral was at St Canice's Catholic Church in Darlinghurst. His fellow actors gave tribute: Victoria Longley spoke with love thumping from every word while Jennifer Vuletic sang like a seraph. Nick Enright invited everyone back to his house in Newtown for the wake.

I was a fledgling playwright living on hope and Nick Enright was the real deal, living the life. When I was employed at the ABC, in 1989, Nick had written a play produced by Jane Ulman called *Watching Over Israel*. To me it is one his most moving, most astonishing dramatic works. It concerns a banking executive who is walking to choir practice in Darlinghurst when she stops to help a young sex worker. Like all works of great beauty it is built on a powerfully simple premise: 'What would happen if we stopped to help someone who asked us instead of walking past?'

In one scene the choirmaster invites a young sex worker to his home. Uncomfortable and nervous, he leaves the young man in his lounge room while he goes to the kitchen to get them both a drink. The radio audience then hears a high-pitched scratching and wonders what it is. When the choirmaster walks back into the room we understand we have heard the sound of the young man removing vinyl records from their covers and scraping a knife across their surface. Without ever saying the word 'knife' it looms larger in our imaginations than it could ever physically appear on screen or stage. For years I used it as one of the finest examples of how to 'show, not tell' in radio. The play won the 1990 Australian Writers' Guild Industry Excellence (AWGIE) Award for Radio.

When I got to Nick's house for the wake there were people in every room drinking, laughing, crying and sharing their memories of Tim. In Nick's study, there was a pin board covered in index cards and I remember standing, peering at it. It outlined the structure of one of his plays, *Good Works* I think. So this was how a real dramatist worked. I remember being surprised that he hadn't tried to cover it up, instead leaving the skeleton of the work pinned up there to be observed, all exposed, with no flesh or muscle to disguise it, so I could look straight into the mind of the writer. Nick came in while I was shamelessly staring. I thanked him for having me in his house, I commented fondly on Timothy's acerbic wit and then I left. With my next waitressing pay I went and bought a pin board and index cards.

10

The cruellest loss

The cruellest month, according to TS Eliot, is April. He was talking about weather in the Northern Hemisphere but for an Australian playwright it feels dead on the money. In April you begin to get an idea if any theatre companies will program your work for the following year. By June–July you know. In September they announce their seasons. So, no, maybe every month is brutally, savagely cruel if you are a playwright, relying on selling your work to be able to eat in the year ahead.

Mostly you spend your time wishing you were cleverer. A finer writer so you could solve what needs to be done to make your work a good play or, better still, a great play. Mostly when you watch the work of other great writers you do not envy their skill in some petty, egotistical way, you covet their talent, you long for their inventiveness. You have a sly admiration for the genius of other writers, profoundly wonderful because it is so bittersweet. You love it but you wish it was yours. You wish you had thought of that first. Despite all your ideas and ambitions, all this aching to be programmed inside you, you have to face the fact that you have no control over what happens, no influence whatsoever. And then it gets worse. Because as a playwright, a person whose gift it is to imagine *all* sides of the problem, you can actually understand and imagine what artistic directors are going through. You know it is not simply about writing a great play.

Michael Gurr put it brilliantly when he wrote in his beautiful memoir, *Days Like These*: 'Having begun the conversation in hope, you find yourself boxed into sympathy for the Literary Manager. He's having a very hard time. How can I help him? Oh, I know. By going away'. Michael and I were both at the 2005 Byron Bay Writers' Festival. We were on several panels together, public readings of our work, and we got on, as they say, like a house on fire. I was utterly besotted. I wanted to have known him all my life and I felt like I had known him all my life. He noted in his memoir that I corrected his assumption that this was the first time we met and reminded him about the 1997 NSW Premier's Literary Awards dinner when we were both nominated for the Play Award and he won for *Jerusalem*. Then he paid me the ultimate compliment, 'Alana says something that I make a note to steal. She says that at the heart of every play there should be an unsolvable question'. *That he makes a note to steal!* Somehow I managed to impress a man who had bested me at the State Literary Awards all those years before.

Is that the real measure of deep, deep infatuation? That you give yourself over to the kind of clichés you might, under usual circumstances, resist. I've been thinking about Michael all day because on Monday, 2 May 2017, he died. And I am unreasonably, irrationally affected by his death. Because I loved him, of course. Because I admired him, undoubtedly. Because he was younger than me by three months and his death acquaints me hideously with my own mortality. I'm sure this is by far the most powerful reason. But it is also more than that. Here was a man who lived, who struggled here in Australia, to be a playwright; to express his politics and his passions and his artistry. He was me. Not exactly, but sort of. His society valorised him young as the boy genius, but it punished him later for being so hard-line, so serious. Having been feted younger, he told me, he didn't know how to hide his true feelings later, how to hide his opinions, as women so routinely learn to do. So he moved into politics where the expression of real opinions, the courage of your convictions, is the job. And now I stand at the sink, washing the vegetables for dinner, my hands muddy with the mix of potato dirt and water, my eyes clouded with the pain of his passing.

I don't want him to be dead because I cherish the fact that he was ever alive. I love that a man like him, a spirit like him, a soul brother, a vivid, living, writing, thinking, feeling man in a relationship with another man like him was alive in the world when I was. But I will do what I often do with my grief. I will fold my memories of him up inside me and think of him and speak to him when I need to conjure him back into being.

To the young writer, the aspiring writer, the emerging writer, the established writer I say this – do not be afraid to love others, especially other writers. They are more than refractions of yourself but you will not know until they pass how profoundly liberating it was to have that person in the world, someone who knew about reaching for perfection in an art form that is so cruelly elusive. And beyond the sentiment and idealism, think of this pragmatically. Writers record history; they set down in words a version of their times. There are writers today enjoying great success, there are directors who are hailed in their times. But the artists who will be remembered are the ones who take time to encourage, groom, mentor and inspire younger writers. You can be as hot as you like in your lifetime but unless someone who outlives you wants to immortalise you, you will disappear into the vapour of the past. Michael Gurr will never suffer that fate because so many people loved him, including me.

Tony Ayres is another one to whom I owe a great debt of psychic and actual thanks. And director Aubrey Mellor who gave me my first production on an Australian main stage and wrote me long, perceptive, instructive responses to my work, praising its theatricality and believing in me when I hardly knew, as my grandmother would say, 'my arse from my elbow'. Dramaturg May-Brit Akerholt has been a lifelong inspiration and that rarest and most precious of colleagues, a person who is utterly experienced, brilliantly informed, rigorously thorough and who uses all of her considerable intelligence to tell you honestly what she thinks and explain why. It is not about agreeing, but about having a terrifically knowledgeable response to push back against. These people, and so many more, reached out their arms and put their hands in mine and pulled me up and into my fate.

Of course, Mr Ayres is now an internationally recognised filmmaker, producer, writer and show runner but when I met him and his partner Michael McMahon, he was wearing red sequin shorts and dancing in a room surrounded by thousands of bare-chested men. We were at a Sydney Gay and Lesbian Mardi Gras party and I was wearing sequins too, big blue disc sequins on a super-tight tube dress. Alex Harding, the writer of *Only Heaven Knows*, had given me the dress when I made my first trip to London, his home town. He told me he would only give it to me if I wore it on the plane and walked through Heathrow wearing it. *That*, he said, should be my entrance into London. I took the dress to London but 24 hours on a plane in sequins was more than even I could do, so London got to meet me in skinny black jeans and a pink leather jacket instead.

But now my sequins were searching for every light in the laser-filled dome and Tony and I were laughing and dancing and drinking and talking. He was a serious artist already, he'd made a couple of utterly beautiful short films and he later showed me some stunning screen-printed artworks from when he studied in Canberra. He introduced me to Penny Chapman from the ABC and later drove me down to meet the tattoo artist eX de Medici in her studio in Canberra. I knew of eX's work because she had done a full body tattoo on Geoff Ostling, another friend at the time. Through Tony I met actor/writer Tim Conigrave, author Sophie Cunningham, playwright Andrew Bovell, photographer William Yang and … oh just *everyone*. But the most important person he ever introduced me to was Nellie Flannery at Robyn Gardiner Management (later RGM Associates) who took me on as a client and became my first agent.

Tony is a profoundly gifted artist and visionary, and a deeply generous person. He told me that you could see other writers as the competition, or you could accept that you were only going to get some of the jobs some of the time and reap the rewards of being part of a community. It was among the best advice I was ever given. Because of this insight I worked on the boards of the Australian Writers' Guild and the Sydney Gay and Lesbian Mardi Gras where I was also Festival Liaison Director; and at numerous volunteer organisations in the interests of other artists. I have had the privilege of meeting and working for common goals together with some of the best writers of my generation.

Nellie Flannery invited me to come into her office to talk about my work and I was so incredibly nervous and proud and excited by her responses to my ideas and plans. I stayed with RGM for thirty years – after Nellie left to go to Shanahans, my agents were Nicholas Papademetriou, Imogen Banks and Dayne Kelly. When Sharne

McGee, another of my agents at RGM, set up a branch of Creative Representation in Sydney I joined her. Your agent will be your confidant and your confessor. They will stand beside you in raw disappointment and sweet victory. Choose wisely. I could not have wished for a more perceptive, more loyal, more dedicated group of agents, and Sharne is the hardest, most brilliant diamond of them all. Wendy Howell has now taken up the task and she earns my thanks in advance.

Before I left ABC Radio in 1994, I received a Churchill Fellowship to go as an observer to Raidió Teilifís Éireann (RTÉ), the Irish broadcaster, and to the BBC in Wales, Northern Ireland and London. I also went to the Royal Court summer school. The dramaturg on my Carson McCullers play, *Southern Belle*, was Phyllis Nagy, the American writer of *Weldon Rising* and, in 2015, the screenplay adaptation of Patricia Highsmith's *Carol*. About my play she was harsh, ruthless and incredible. During the summer school people kept checking in on me to see if I was 'okay' because Phyllis had a reputation for being really tough, and she was, but I appreciated tough and learnt a lot from her. I remember going to her house where she lived with her partner, the literary agent Mel Kenyon. They had this incredible scratching post for their cats – an elaborate, high-rise, carpeted thing that I'd never seen before but which the cats seemed to really enjoy. We went out for lunch at a local cafe which served a huge plate of steak, egg and chips that Phyllis thought was much better value than all the trendy places near the Royal Court. When I returned to Australia, Phyllis and I corresponded for a while, terrifically witty letters which took me more time to write than my plays. During that trip I also made a big connection with Lucinda Coxon, the author of numerous plays and, in 2015, the screenplay of *The Danish Girl*. So blue sequin dress or no, I developed a love of the London theatre scene and made some precious, lifetime friendships with writers. So, dear emerging writer, I recommend that you join the guild. There are reasons to be part a community of writers that go beyond calculations of how you can be immediately advantaged.

11

Ambition aplenty

It's four in the morning and I am walking down a Melbourne street, towards a hotel reception. I'm not staying there. Playbox have put me in a suburban apartment they own and the hotel is the only place open to get a newspaper. My first play in a mainstage production at the Playbox Theatre Centre, *The Conjurers*, had opened two nights before and the *Age* was publishing a review. I was so excited and nervous, so full of hope, that I couldn't sleep. So I put on my clothes and walked down the street to the hotel, declaring I was willing to pay whatever they would like to charge me for a newspaper. When I opened the paper and found the review the headline was, 'Ambition Aplenty: but play fails to capture the magic'.

It's hard to remember now, after years working as a playwright, exactly how I felt. It was a bit like having one of the keg-laden beer trucks I had seen going back and forth to the nearby brewery come and park on my chest. The pain was distracting enough, let alone the inability to breathe. But the worst of it was that at the time I really thought that reviews *meant* something. That they had an effect not just on the box-office, which they absolutely do, but on your career, which they absolutely don't.

The Conjurers is a play about two female magicians travelling along the Great Ocean Road. Gala, the younger of the magicians, conjures out of the sea the ghost of a Sea Captain. It's a meditation on grief in the style of magic realism. Aubrey Mellor, the artistic director of Playbox, had commissioned and produced the work. Because in one scene Gala, played by Maya Stange, propositioned the older magician Beth, played by Margaret Mills, it was considered a lesbian play. I remember someone in theatre management conveying to me her personal disgust at seeing a number of female patrons 'use the opportunity to make a public display of their affection'.

The play actually did quite well and was remounted a year later in Brisbane at La Boite with Deborah Mailman in the lead role of Beth. It's never been done in my home town but it will be, one day. The premiere season gave me my first experience of the strange, out-of-body discombobulation that happens to a writer when the play is first read aloud. Suddenly you hear and see what it looks like in space and time instead of as words on a white page; that is, in three dimensions instead of two. Playwrights talk about craft, and endless books discuss three-act structures, inciting incidents, climax and resolution, and one scene flowing into the next. I have the greatest respect that it somehow all makes sense to them. For me, craft is simply the ability to have what you imagine on the page correlate with what works as drama on a stage.

I had developed *The Conjurers* at New Dramatists, a playwright development organisation in New York City, and they presented a public reading of the play with Allison Janney (later famous in the *West Wing*), in the role of Beth. Peregrine Whittlesey, a New York agent, was in the audience and afterwards she signed me up as her client and I have been with her ever since. In 2015 she sent me to a meeting at the National Theatre in London with Sebastian Born, the remarkable Associate Director (Literary), and I pitched him the play that would become *Crossing the King*, a co-commission between the Sydney Theatre Company and the National Theatre. Only months after I had signed the contract that she engineered, she emailed me to say that she had sold my play *Soft Revolution* (known in Australia as *Shafana and Aunt Sarrinah*) and the stage adaptation of my BBC radio play *The Ravens* to a women's theatre company called Venus, just outside of Washington in Maryland.

So I can look back at that scared, crushed young woman, standing in a hotel foyer in suburban Melbourne and say to you, who may be standing in a foyer of your own, excoriated by a tough review: really, don't give it any more power than an uncomfortable day or two. If you're like me, you might notice a pattern. On day one, the day the review comes out, you go down into hell. You hate everyone and everything and swear you are never going to write again and detest all humanity and all divinity and especially everyone associated with the production who failed to tell you what a crock of shit you were putting on stage. On day two you wake up, still damaged beyond belief and still furious but affecting a 'don't give a rat's about anything' swagger. By day three you will be writing again because, well, what else are you going to do? The hardest thing is that *every* time you go into hell on the first day you will think, 'This time is really the one. This time I won't get back up. This time they have destroyed me'. Inside the first day no reminder of previous resilience matters. It's not till day three that you will remember that this is usual, this is the process, this is the gig and you will survive it.

When you are deep in the throes of your bottomless disappointment, this won't help but you might like to consider it anyway: *just because it's not in the comments section online, doesn't mean no-one is disputing it*. I have had people come up to me in foyers, or write emails years later to say, 'I've admired your work for a long time'. And it's humbling and staggering and incredibly surprising. You want to grab them by the shoulders and say 'Who knew?' In Australia, people watch and wait for a long time before they speak. People might be discussing your efforts in small rehearsal rooms, and bars and elsewhere even if you aren't there to hear it. Everyone knows it's *hard* but no one is going to give you the armour you need. You have to draw the scar tissue out of your own body and suit up for valid criticism and also for what can seem to be harsh, irrational prejudice. Remember that most critics also need courage to put their opinion in words and stand by it publicly. Done well that can, in its own way, be an incredible act of generosity. But no writer, no theatre artist, escapes the prejudices of their time. *No-one escapes unscathed*. Think of yourself as one of those punching bags with the heavy base – you know the ones, no matter how much you whap, whap, whap it, it just keeps popping back up.

12

Audience awareness

In the production of my play *Swimming the Globe* at the Civic Theatre in Newcastle, a journalist character 'filmed' the two aspiring Olympic swimmers, in the style of media interviews. The interviews were shown on stage using a live action camera. But on opening night, the camera refused to work for the first four scenes. Then, in the middle of scene five, it suddenly began transmitting images to the screen on the back wall. Up in the dress circle, alone, I was having kittens. The live action was illogical and bizarre. How could I face the opening night audience? With resigned fatalism, I thought, and trudged down the stairs, all my dreams and ambitions for the work in a shattered pile at the bottom.

After *Multiple Choice* at the Australian Theatre for Young People, *Swimming the Globe* was my next produced play. I had borrowed Nick Enright's play *A Property of the Clan* from the City of Sydney Library, and seen in the front of the book that Brian Joyce, the artistic director of Newcastle's Freewheels Theatre-in-Education Company, had commissioned the work. So I wrote to him and asked if he would commission a new play about two young swimmers aiming for the Olympic Games. I got the gig. This says much more about Joyce's incredible openness and spirit of adventure than it does about my initiative in writing to him, but take note of that audacity too if you like. Who knows if an email to an artistic director will yield a gig today? It certainly can't if you don't write it.

Humiliation and rejection will be the most frequent, reliable and consistent emotional experiences of your life as a playwright. I'm not just being negative. It will start early on and continue through all the spectacular rabbit-out-of-a-hat moments when you expect only applause, long into the years when you think your persistence should count for something. Abandon your pride and learn to eat humble pie. There's nothing I can say to make it any easier. Rejection will always hurt, always. Anyone who tells you it doesn't is just being a brave little darling. Rejection will come with your morning cereal, your lunchtime sandwich and your evening cheese platter. It will come from people who were once your staunchest supporters; and from irrational people who have never met you or even seen your work. I'm trying to resist a pious adage about 'making rejection your friend' because, well, it sounds like so much sanctimonious rubbish. But the ugly truth is that you do have to look rejection in the face and say 'Come on then, over you come. Sit here by me. I know you're going to anyway'. And it's not just the bloggers or other critics. When students were studying my play *Watermark* I received an email:

> I had to do your stupid drama script Watermark for my play and I hate it so much and its so bad, that I want to roll in mud and die. Good for you for writing a play, but the next time I have to do one of your plays I am going to scream. Xoxoxo a mad drama student Love you just kidding

and

> … what a crap play. i hate this play, i have to learn all the stupid lines of this pointless play WATERMARK IS THE WORST PLAY IVE HEARD OF AND HAD TO REHEARSE FOR!!!!!'

but then later,

> Hey, I just sent you a bad hate mail and I'm sorry, I'm just really emotional that I have to do this play for my VCE. X.

Yeah, sticks and stones, suckers, sticks and stones.

But back to the opening night of *Swimming the Globe*. When I got into the foyer no-one said anything about the missing video projections. Instead, lots of people congratulated me on the play, and, of course, praised the actors. There wasn't a single comment about the malfunctioning camera. It struck me like a train – they didn't know what was supposed to happen! They weren't commenting on the video projections suddenly coming to life in the middle of Scene 5 because, guess what, they didn't know it wasn't planned. They would only know there was a disaster if I told them. And why would I do that? To assert my 'version' of the show they should have seen? Would that not make them feel robbed, even humiliated, if they thought it had been great? It would be like saying 'Silly you, you couldn't even pick that it was all going wrong'. And so I said nothing. I smiled and nodded and thanked them for their response. And in that moment the work became about so much more than me, and my controlling desire for the play to reflect exactly my idea of what it should be. In that moment I became a collaborator and to this day I thank Brian Joyce, and even the technical little gremlin, for giving me the gift of insight that helped me to know it. Even when another playwright tried a tentative, 'Inventive use of video', I just smiled and said, 'Wasn't it?' I never let the cat out of the bag.

In theatre things can go wrong. But as I discovered that night, when they do, whatever happens, never tell your audience.

On the first preview of my play *Run Rabbit Run* at Belvoir St I told Neil Armfield that I was dismayed at the cheering and booing of the Souths-supporter-stacked house. 'As if they're at a pantomime', I said, contemptuously. 'Or a football match', replied Neil. I laughed. 'It's just that I've gone to so much trouble to give a balanced, complex view of the problem. Like, John Hartigan from News Limited makes some valid points and all they do is boo when he comes onto the stage'. Neil shrugged, 'You can't control the audience', he said, sagely. He was so right. I could build in jokes I knew they would laugh at, I could build in conflict that would make them gasp, but I couldn't, ultimately, control their response. One Souths supporter grumbled that George Piggins had no *long* speeches in the play. I tried to explain that, rather than have George speak at length, instead he spoke inspiringly at every major turning point. He was the visionary leader, just as he had been in the real life story. I tried to tell this fellow that dramatic power is not about number of words but the weight of the character in the dramatic action. I'm not sure he bought it. To him, the most important person had the most lines.

Implicit in Neil's casual acceptance of the power of the audience to take its own course was a lesson in trust. I had to trust that the Belvoir subscribers and general audience would see the complexity in the play, while the cheering and booing Souths-supporters could give them something that neither Neil nor I could ever control. They provided a glimpse into the stakes and lived reality of this actual community, alive and vibrantly 'going off' in the Belvoir space. And to conjure *that* into the theatre, *that* was really something.

A similar thing happened, again at Belvoir, at the second preview of *Parramatta Girls*. The Department of Community Services (DOCS, now Family and Community Services [FACS]) had been persuaded by Bonney Djuric, of the Parragirls support and lobby group, to pay for preview tickets for some forty or fifty ex-inmates of the Parramatta Girls home. Before the show went up it was chaos. Many of these women had never been to live theatre before and they couldn't find the box office. Maybe thought they were at the movies because they talked all the way through the play. Fuelled by being together as a pack and seated together, they made their presence well and truly felt. At the end of the first act the character Marlene, played by Leah Purcell, finds that the gate to the home has been left open by the garbage men. She tells another girl who immediately makes a bolt to escape. She tries to drag Marlene along too but Marlene can't escape. She is rooted to the spot. It's a scene about how when you're institutionalised it's not just the walls that keep you locked up, a scene about how you carry the institution walls within you. But the ex-Parramatta inmates in the preview audience were having none of that. Suddenly Leah is standing on stage and fifty boisterous ex-inmates are shouting at her, 'You go girl!', 'Get out of there, girl', 'Get out of there now!' I'll never forget the look on Leah Purcell's face as she stood on stage, knowing the script required her not to go, but wanting to go with every fibre of her being, to fulfil the long-held desires of every ex-inmate in that room. I have to say that this preview transformed all eight members of the cast. It was as if they *became* the Parramatta girls – their disrespect and attitude and toughness now inherent, not acted, vivid in all its dysfunction and wildness and fury. During the interval Ralph Myers, who was the production designer, came up to me and told me how a

Belvoir subscriber had stopped him and said, 'Can you ask those women to be quiet? They're spoiling the show'. To which Ralph replied, 'Well, they really *are* the show'.

You can't control the audience. And, really, you wouldn't want to.

13

Don't squib the tough stuff

I first heard about the Parramatta girls from the ABC television show *Stateline*. Sharon O'Neill reported on the return of three Indigenous women to the dungeons in the home, the site of their childhood incarceration, in anticipation of a much bigger reunion later in the month. I contacted O'Neill and after a lot of convincing she agreed to pass my phone number onto one of the women, Coral, who lived in Wollongong. Days passed before Coral called me, but eventually we made contact and I arranged to meet her at a cafe in the Gong. We sat for two and a half hours as she sometimes cried, we often laughed and she generously opened her heart and her life to me. She told me how she was supposed to speak at an Indigenous Health Conference as a local elder, about the local stories associated with Mount Keira but, as soon as she got up to the microphone, she found herself blurting out the story of her abuse and mistreatment at the Parramatta Girls Home. A journalist in the audience followed up her disclosure with a story in the *Koori Mail* the following week and after it appeared, she received many, many responses from others who had been in the institution. So they got together and organised a full weekend reunion for a large group of Indigenous women. They planned a visit to the home, a Captain Cook cruise as well as several other activities (including a hilarious bus ride through Kings Cross which is chronicled in the play).

Coral invited me to a large group dinner at a restaurant in the Rocks that concluded the weekend. 'Come to the dinner', Coral said, 'meet the women and tell them what you want to do with the play. They'll soon tell you if they want to help you or not'.

And so I went along, more than a little nervous since this introduction would make or break my ability to write the play I was planning. If the Indigenous elders didn't want me to tell the story, that would be the end of it. The incarceration of 'uncontrollable' girls and 'delinquent' boys was an Australia-wide phenomenon (as evidenced in the Senate Report *Forgotten Australians*) involving up to half a million Australians, black and white. From my perspective, though, I needed the permission of the twenty or more Indigenous women I was about to meet.

It was a proper slap-up feed – steaks, salads, prawns, fish, vegetables aplenty. The party was upstairs at a local hotel, it took up a large balcony area with bench tables arranged on three sides, topped by large white umbrellas. I let them have their meals in peace and then, as the desserts emerged I began to move from table to table. Coral introduced me. She told the women that I was planning to record their stories, gather their lived experience and historical evidence and put it all on stage using actors. It was only because Coral clearly trusted and endorsed me that the other women were prepared to listen. But once they did, many of them enthusiastically embraced the idea. They had been silent for thirty years, they told me, because they genuinely thought no-one would believe them. They had been convinced that, as 'bad girls', their testimony would be discredited and now they urged me, some even began to insist, that this story must be told.

At the last table Coral introduced me to Marlene Riley-Wilson. Even in a space full of astonishing, strong, powerful, impressive women, Marlene had special power and authority. She wore one of her signature picture hats – an enormous purple confection that would not be out of place at the Melbourne Cup. When Coral briefly told Marlene what I was planning she stared hard at me for a long time. I met her gaze and, unflinching, said nothing. I had paid attention to the instruction of enough Indigenous elders by then to know that this should be my first response – to say nothing, ask no questions, listen, and *wait*, for however long she took, for however long she wanted, wait for her to take control of the situation and the exchange. Display my respect for her authority, display my respect for her pace. It is uncomfortable to be silent with someone you don't know. It is compulsive for some whitefellas to speak, to take control of the situation, to fill the void with chatter. She was testing me, testing to see what I knew and, if I can put it this way, maybe looking to see where my spirit was sitting – how big it was, what courage I had to listen, what knowledge I could hear.

After a moment a smile broke out on her face. She leaned closer to me, so close that the brim of the enormous hat she wore was almost touching my forehead, and she said, in a hushed tone, 'Alright, I'll tell you my story, Alana', her gaze never leaving my face, 'but only if you promise not to leave out the really tough bits'. I nodded, and also smiled. 'Marlene, I promise you, the tough bits are what I want to hear more than anything.' She continued looking at me and said, 'Yep, I'll tell you everything. I'll put it all out there. But only if you don't squib the tough stuff'. I gave her one of my prepared pages, detailing the project and my contacts. She took my pen and wrote her number on the top of the page and handed it back to me. 'You call me', she said, 'and come visit me in Glebe. I'll tell you everything'.

Marlene's story became the backbone of my play, her courage and defiance in climbing the roof, throwing tiles at the superintendent, instigating (with others) the first riot at the home and continuing to live her life on *her* terms inspired me in the most profound and sustaining way. I met many deeply courageous women as part of the research for that play. I heard heartbreaking stories that sometimes defied belief and which, to be honest, rubbed away my defences so that my heart ached with horror.

And therein lies the rub. You can't squib the tough stuff but there *will* be a cost. You will sacrifice a small part of your own innocence. When you listen to thirty or forty people telling you their pain in all its brutal detail, it transmits some of their trauma into your own being. You need to find the artistry to transform that pain into understanding, perception and even hope.

14

Linked into community

One of my most important discoveries about gathering community-sourced material is the need to create a chain of connection between my interviewees. This has two advantages to you as an interviewer and is mandatory when you are working with sensitive or traumatised people.

The first advantage is that you will have an immediate point of connection with your interviewee if they know someone you have already interviewed. And if they trust that person they may be more disposed to trust you, than if you have rung up out of the blue. It can help to relax the interviewee if you open your interview by chatting about your 'shared' acquaintance – how they take their tea or what bright colours they like to wear, or some small shared perception. Obviously you should not betray a confidence, or give away any private information. But a small observation will create an intimacy of sorts.

The second advantage is more of an ethical consideration. If the interviewee might experience flashbacks or bad memories because of your discussion, it is both ethical and responsible to know that they have someone they can call if they need to debrief. We are not trained counsellors. We are not trained to deal with the people whose memories and pains we are rifling through. It may be at their invitation and you may think, well they're adults and they can make that decision for themselves. But we have to be strategically responsible even to people who think they will be fine.

And probably will be fine. Indeed, most people benefit from telling you their story. Sometimes you are the first person they have spoken to about their past pain and they find it liberating; the telling can help them to heal. I have seen that happen to a large number of interviewees and it helps me to keep going. A highlight of my working life as a writer was on the opening night of *Parramatta Girls* when one of the interviewees, a Wadi Wadi elder, grabbed my arm with tears in her eyes and said, 'Thank you, Alana, you've given back to me the twelve-year-old girl who was taken from me all those years ago'. That moment was precious beyond all expectations.

My responsibility, and yours, is always to the play you are writing, not to your subjects. But nothing is more important than their physical and psychological safety. Nothing – not even your play – can ever be held to be more important than the well-being of another person. To assuage any concern I have about the psychological well-being of the people I interview, I always make sure there is someone they can reach out to for help, if nasty, greebly-faced nightmare images and memories pursue them beyond the interview.

Of course, having said that, I know some people might argue that your art needs to come first, that you're not a social worker and you don't have to protect anyone. And yes, of course, you can be that selfish, naïve and destructive. But if you go into a community and make them out to be fools, or sluts or criminals, ask yourself what you are trying to achieve. I would question why that work should be privileged to the public stage. And while you are not there to proselytise on behalf of the community, my advice is to take every precaution not to trigger a psychotic episode, an addiction relapse or something worse. Of course if it does happen you can't blame yourself. I'm not suggesting you can control the real world, but you can take every responsible step in advance, according to your own moral and ethical framework.

For instance, in my research for *Parramatta Girls*, I favoured interviewing women who were already connected to the Parragirls support and lobby network, or who had some discernible support structure with other inmate survivors in place. I got a lot of calls out of the blue from individuals who had never spoken to anyone about their time in that institution (and others). I listened to them and put them in contact with people I knew. I also gathered background from their stories but I almost never went to record an interview with them or featured their particular recollections in my play. I was conscious that I was asking these women to talk about memories that some of them hadn't considered for thirty years or more, and it could trigger an unexpected fallout.

Care was even more necessary when I was working with adult survivors of child abuse. First, I worked with a reputable organisation, ASCA (Adults Surviving Child Abuse, now the Blue Knot Foundation) and some interviewees found out about my project though their website. I also went to ASCA workshops for health professionals, where I met therapists and doctors and asked them to recommend any patients they thought might be 'ready' to speak about their ordeal. I received interest from interviewees through local church groups, local community organisations and elsewhere. But there was always someone who knew both me and the interviewee. I texted interviewees the day after to 'check in on them' and invited them to the public showing of the work. I maintained my contact with the Blue Knot Foundation long after the public event took place, in fact I am still working with them. I make a professional commitment when I work in a community to develop a trust relationship, and invest time and self and work.

Make no mistake – it *is* life and death and exceptionally serious to peer into someone's life, to ask them to disclose their story. Your ethical considerations are very different to those of a journalist, though journalists, too, are conscious of their responsibilities (well, the good ones at least). You are not looking for the scoop but the revelation that they haven't made before, the original thought, 'the emotional news' if you will. And you need to wait for them to come to it in some gentle, helpful way, not rip it from them and sprint away.

In 2013 Merrigong Theatre Company produced a play called *Dead Man Brake*, on the tenth anniversary of an horrific train crash that had occurred at nearby Waterfall. A decade earlier as part of a new writers' attachment to the Sydney Theatre Company (STC) called Blueprints, I was asked (along with others) to write a 30-minute play 'ripped from the newspaper headlines' of a particular week. For me it was the week of the Waterfall train disaster. A State Rail train travelling from Sydney to Port Kembla had derailed just south of Waterfall station, killing seven people injuring dozens of others. A Special Commission of Inquiry concluded that the accident could have been avoided if earlier safety warnings about the 'deadman's emergency brake' had not been ignored. At the time I wrote my Blueprints play the Special Commission had not been convened. But I conducted a verbatim interview with a Salvation Army chaplain who had overseen the chaplaincy response to the disaster. His name was Lieutenant-Colonel Don Woodland and it turned out that he had attended as Chaplain almost every Australian disaster of the last thirty years, man-made and natural. The man was astonishing: he led the team that went into Port Arthur after the massacre in 1996; the following year, he was at the Thredbo landslide by 4 am (less than 5 hours after it happened), he attended the 1989 Kempsey bus crash and the 1977 Granville train disaster. His insights into the healing and human response of people after such events were unique and original. I wrote a 30-minute play that was given a reading at the STC and I heard that a lecturer had used it at Wollongong University a couple of times but it was never produced.

But I noticed Merrigong Theatre's success with locally produced stories, especially Version 1.0's *The Table of Knowledge*, so I sent the short play off to its artistic director Simon Hinton pointing out that 2013 was the tenth anniversary of the disaster. He decided to commission a full-length version of the play and we had a public reading in September of 2012. It received warm and congratulatory responses from the audience and then a small, stooped older woman with a plastic bag full of cuttings made her way towards the actors who were sitting on the stage. This was Ljudmila Božič, the mother of train driver Herman Zaides who was killed in the crash. When she took the microphone and told the assembled audience who she was, there was a profound silence in the theatre – a deep, breath-held listening that goes far beyond the absence of noise. A silence in which time seems to slow and an awareness of being alive in the present becomes vividly real. I arranged to meet and interview Ljudmila and her sister Olga Kocyan, who both made remarkable contributions to the play. I also interviewed ambulance and police officers who attended the scene. They all came to the opening night. As well as undertaking interviews, I read the 6000-page report from the Special Commission of Inquiry into the Waterfall Rail Accident and used other material on the public record.

A feature of the play was the poems I wrote that Daryl Wallis turned into songs to make a kind of verbatim musical, or, as we started to call it, a requiem drama. The songs attempted to capture not the individual speaker, but a sense of the community – to shape broad phrases, ideas and feelings that I perceived from the interviews. For instance, many people I spoke to shared a survivors' guilt but did not express it in a way, dare I say it, that was succinct enough to make it into the play. So I shaped their response into poems and the sentiment became part of the song lyrics instead. When I was asked at a forum where the lyrics came from, I described them as 'generic verbatim'.

Another feature of this work was that I created pairs to tell of the story. Elsewhere in my verbatim work I have used relationships between people, sometimes interviewing them together but never before had I used such a large number of duelling monologues. The first pairing in the work happened in one of those fortuitous ways for an artist that you might call 'coincidence' at the beginning of your career but over time you begin to perceive that such coincidences occur again and again if you are open and responsive to what's around you. A kind of metaphysical liaison with your subject. In this instance, I went to interview journalist Nonee Walsh at the ABC, who was on the train, and she mentioned Johnny, a friend who had been on the train with her. It just so happened that, without knowing their connection, I had scheduled an interview with Johnny, who had contacted me via my website that same afternoon. So Nonee told me that she and Johnny knew each other and, coincidentally, I am scheduled to speak to them on the same day. In the play I have them telling their story of the crash from alternating perspectives, including the moment when they meet on the train.

> JOHNNY: So, the train's on its side and I get up and go into the vestibule area and stand on the doors. And I'm sort of standing there and then I saw this woman totally ashen, dust all over her face and everything, like a 9/11 survivor and then out of this white powdered mouth are the words, 'Johnny, Johnny it's me'. I didn't recognise her. I thought who the hell is this? Because I was just so out of it and then to have this person come through and call me by name. And she said, 'It's Nonee'.

NONEE: I said 'Johnny, it is you' and he's going 'Nonee, what are you doing here?' It was bizarre.

JOHNNY: It was a hell of a shock to have someone know my name after that incident. It was disorientating and almost depressing because it brought you with a slap into reality more somehow because there's this person you know and you have to like be you. It's like I wanted to be in my own head space. I wanted to be like totally spaced out, which I was.

So by having them know each other I created stakes and a relationship on stage, just as any playwright does. The other pairs were Mark Rees and Steve 'Smokey' Dawson, two paramedics who were both at the scene; Olga Kocyan and Ljudmila Božič, so they could both talk about their grief; and Father Patrick Vaugh (a priest at the scene) and Don Woodland (the Salvation Army chaplain who attended the families). This technique allowed me to give the play a sense of connectedness that is not always apparent if you just have one individual speaking after another.

There is an instructive example in *Dead Man Brake* of listening to what people do, not what they say. At one point paramedic Smokey Dawson is talking about body parts on the track after the accident and he says that 'out of respect he wouldn't say anymore'. He also told me that, 'out of respect', he would only share the details and graphic, ugly descriptions of grotesque and horrific injuries with nursing colleagues and paramedic professionals. But I noticed that several people who talked about not saying things 'out of respect' then went on to describe the horror they saw. The paramedic said he was *not* telling us the story, but, when I listened carefully, I realised that, in fact, this *was his way of doing so*. The phrase 'out of respect' seemed to reassure a number of people that they weren't going to offend the relatives. But a compulsive and psychological need prompted them to describe the scene anyway. When you are using verbatim material you cannot forget first rule of dramatic characterisation on stage – don't believe what a character says, look at their actions. In theatre, just like in life, what people say isn't always what they do (or don't do).

The bold acumen of Simon Hinton in commissioning *Dead Man Brake* is part of a wider paradigm-busting movement in regional

Australia. In the contemporary performing arts, the regions are creating some of the most urgent, revelatory, community-connected work in the country with a diversity of writers and theatre makers, debunking the tired, old notion that city companies are bolder and more diverse. In her 2017 Currency House paper, *Restless Giant: Changing Cultural Values in Regional Australia*, Lindy Hume argues that this counter-urban movement, as she labels it, should be embraced as an equal forum for creative excellence and innovation. This is certainly my experience. Aside from Simon, for the past several years I have worked with passionate creative directors such as Caroline Stacey at the Street Theatre, Raina Savage at Griffith Regional Theatre, Charles Parkinson at the Tasmanian Theatre Company, Jo Duffy (at both the Darwin Festival and Ten Days on the Island), Jane Cush from Goulburn Regional Art Gallery and Canberra Glassworks, Chrisjohn Hancock at the Leider Theatre in Goulburn, Narelle Lewis and many valued others from Performing Lines, Toni Tapp Coutts and others at Katherine Regional Arts Centre, and Amy Hardingham when she was at Outback Theatre in Hay. Just as technology and mobility is rendering geography less immediately relevant in business, so too is it opening up life-changing and status quo disrupting activities in the arts.

15

Establishing trust

Impolite, ruthless interrogation does not equal great art, nor does strategic, careful encouragement mean you lack rigour. The question I get asked most at verbatim theatre workshops, lectures or panels is, 'How do you get people to trust you?' My answer can seem disarmingly simple: 'Be trustworthy'. Keep the promises you make, act honourably, be honest about your intentions. It's not rocket science, though it can sometimes be hard to do.

When you record an interview, ask your interviewee to sign a standard release form that allows you to use the material you record. It should say that you can use the information you record, but there's no obligation to do so and make clear there is no remuneration. The form is a legal document that, like all other contracts, formalises an understanding between two parties.

Andrew Denton, the genius comedian and television presenter, once asked me to change a word he'd said in an interview for *Run Rabbit Run*. At the time he'd been in trouble over using scatological language at the Logie awards and he didn't want to appear obsessed with the posterior of a certain media mogul. It didn't change the meaning of his sentence so I obliged. In truth, Andrew was still delivering some of the hardest tough talk of the play, an insider questioning the capacity of Souths for gratitude and change, and so a single word was of little consequence to me. If he had wanted to remove the essence of what he had said, it would have been more difficult. But he didn't – just one loaded word. And it was one of the only times I have been asked to do this.

Any reaction to a work of theatre, especially where deaths have occurred in the real world and people are still grieving is, of course coloured by an understanding of our personal relationship to the 'sacred'. How should the playwright handle sensitivity around an 18-metre flood in Katherine where three people died, or a train crash which killed seven people when there are living relatives to consider? Some community members and relatives might consider it disrespectful to stage a play about the event. What exactly is the balance between respect and artistic daring, integrity and risk?

Let me make clear that an urge to be trustworthy does not, under any circumstances, mean that you can resile from your first obligation as an artist to present the truth in all its complexity and ugliness and confronting diversity. You are not there *just* to make this community feel good about themselves. But if you are authentic, strategic and genuine, you may become a broker between the wider public and the specific community as they sit together in the audience. If you are really inventive and creative about it, you can confront the community with the uncomfortable truths they already know but are at pains to avoid. And when they look those truths in the face, as you reveal that community to itself, you will help it to heal in the way that only an artist can.

This is why I argue so passionately for more community-sourced close work on our main stages. The act of seeing oneself on stage, in all its unpleasant truth, is a human right and not simply a middle-class one. Close work theatre does for unfamiliar, marginalised voices and communities what the mainstream theatre does for the middle class. Our theatre should not be another way to strip the poor, both financially and culturally.

I struggle to find both the tools and the language to argue why it is so important to write about and consider the voices of 'the other' in this century. In fact, I usually argue that I don't want to be bored to death sitting through endless stories about adulterous middle-class marriages or worse, on-again, off-again romances between rich twenty-somethings. Be intimate with who you like, I say to all those guilt-ridden writers, just don't write any more plays justifying it. The truth is that stories about teenage girls incarcerated and abused by the state, gay men trying to survive in Broome, people who got married at the Wayside Chapel and scientists trying to convince people to stop killing themselves with food are more interesting to me because they can vividly articulate the realities of the world around us and surprise us with its diversity, complexity and beauty. I love to be reminded not to spend my time in tiny enclaves that agree with me or suffocating cliques that reassure me, I long to be astonished by startling originality, by the alternative perspectives and dynamism of insightful voices. You, the writers of today and tomorrow, have things to tell me that will shock and confront me and I say: bring it on you writers, bring it on.

I earnestly believe that tyranny needs to be named and resisted, that corruption needs to be punished. I vote on the basis that public policy should address the needs of the group, not the individual. I think that democracy must protect the marginalised and help the poor. I am grateful for the law reform that has brought human rights to people previously marginalised by their gender, sexuality or race. I believe all these things and I am sure about them. But what I write about are more often things I am not sure about, conflicts that have no answer, or complex solutions, or morally slippery circumstances. While your political certainties will colour your voice, your human doubts will inform your art.

When it comes to trust, the formula is basically to treat others how you would like to be treated. Push the envelope but don't tear it into a million pieces. Behave with integrity. You *know* what that is, but you need to practise it when it would be tempting not to have to bother. Just like in life.

16
Metaphors for experience

Previously I wrote about first meeting the Parramatta girls at their get-together in the Rocks, following an Indigenous ex-inmates' reunion weekend. During that weekend the women had planned to go on a Captain Cook boat cruise for the day. One of the attendees later told me about what happened and I included it in the play. The way she told it, the cruise assistant, seeing the large party of Aboriginal women at the front of the crowd, asked them to go to the back of the line so she could board the individual passengers first and board them as a group second. Now I don't know about cruise safety and crowd control protocols but I do know what it is like to wait in a queue. And I'm not an elderly, Indigenous, ex-Parramatta inmate who had just spent a weekend renewing my fighting spirit of rebellion. Innocent, ignorant or just plain officious it was a major miscalculation to tell them to go to the back of the line. These women spat the dummy back at Miss Captain Cook Cruise and refused to board. The organiser, Coral, demanded a refund for the entire party and she got it.

As a dramatist, the sub-textual implications of this event were too delicious to resist. Yes, it was funny and conflicted dramatic action but metaphorically it was so much more. I had been listening to women tell me that they carried the feelings of worthlessness and social humiliation long into their adult lives. But how to dramatise that? You can't have a character stand on stage and *tell* you about their feelings in any form of drama. As human beings we just don't care enough about people who *tell* us how they feel. We care more when characters (or the writer) *show* us how their lives have been affected. If you find an event, an anecdote or a story that *shows* the effect, *that* will rouse our understanding and our empathy.

In their refusal to get on the boat I believe I found the best way of dramatising how these women had carried feelings of worthlessness with them into the present day. Even if the cruise assistant had been polite and explained there were safety reasons behind her request, I wonder if these women would have heard it. They've been told to go to the back of the line, the end of the queue, the bottom of the heap for their entire lives. All they will hear is 'go to the back of the queue'. And there it was – the pain, the hurt, the anger – bubbling to the surface again. Perhaps, in that moment, the play became about more than the ex-inmates of a dreadful childhood institution because it gives an insight into something we all do – we hear the thing that has been said to us again and again, the negative thing that we secretly believe about ourselves. We go looking for the rod to beat our own back. I wanted to show the scar left from the Parramatta Girls Home that could never be massaged away. The legacy that can't be explained which is evident in every decision. Well, that's what I was aiming for. In the play they don't re-enact the moment. It may have been an even funnier scene with one of them playing the cruise assistant. But I chose to service the audience's perceptions of that moment as one of collective, rebellious solidarity. The fact that Indigenous women were boarding a Captain Cook cruise ship was also painfully ironic. I knew it would tickle the Aboriginal elders.

During the run of the play, the director Wesley Enoch had a frank discussion with the people from Captain Cook Cruises who did, all credit to them, understand the dramatic purpose of the scene. As I've said, from my point of view the scene wasn't about whether the cruise people were in the wrong but what the women could *hear*. I was surprised when I received a couple of letters saying that 'poor old Captain Cook got a rough ride in the play' but since one was from a person who also said that 'there were no Aboriginal girls even in Parramatta' I wasn't too concerned. When I asked the Aboriginal women elders about that comment they actually laughed. Marjorie said, 'Think about it. If they didn't see you as Aboriginal were you going to put your hand up? We'd been taken away and put in Cootamundra because we were half-caste and so had lots of other kids. They could see we was Aboriginal. But like it shows in the play, lots of Aboriginal people were teaching their kids not to say they were Aboriginal so they wouldn't be taken away. Don't judge them for that. And anyway, it didn't make no difference. They still locked you up whether they thought you was or not'.

At the beginning of the script of *Parramatta Girls* it says the play takes place in the present and 'the remembered past'. Whose version of history gets told is profoundly and threateningly political. I knew it, the Aboriginal women knew it and so did every single ex-inmate. If you don't know that in every fibre of your being, if you aren't ready to suffer misunderstanding, abuse, disdain, patronising disrespect, and open hostility to fight to get a version of history on the public record that tells an uncomfortable truth, then maybe life as a writer is not for you.

I was fortunate to have Eamon Flack as my dramaturg on *Parramatta Girls*, in his first job for Belvoir. Eamon is meticulous about narrative clarity, passionate about originality and daring and specificity in the writing, and sincerely political in his vision for what to privilege to the Australian main stage. My future work was indelibly marked by my encounter with his quiet but relentless curiosity for how to solve the creative challenges of this work, the way in which he persists, even after one solution has been found, to keep digging down into the possibilities of a moment, to draw lessons from classic structures and writers. When you encounter a remarkable creative mind you will be struck by this intense focus on the creative question at hand – a laser-like concentration that transgresses politeness or propriety or self-consciousness. And in the glare of that cleverness you will benefit if you can forget to be deferential, or appropriate or compliant. An encounter with a gifted theatre maker can be an intimidating experience and you need to learn not to respond with a defensive crouch. Don't retreat back to a fragile certainty, or sulk or sneer about the interrogation. Instead take the opportunity to grow and learn and step out into the arena of the play-maker to find your own way to defend your vision.

17

The value of a premise

I remember one night at a youth hostel in Florence, when I was travelling alone across Europe. The Italians are so civilised that you could buy a glass of wine to have with your dinner while every other youth hostel in the world was dry. So sophisticated, I thought, settling down for my spaghetti and vino at a shared table. Three other Australian girls were seated a little up from me and soon asked me to join them. I noticed that they weren't having any wine and they did look a little, well, sour, but I was feeling gregarious and in the mood for a dose of home. The source of their problem soon emerged. 'We have this schedule that we worked out before we left Australia', they said and showed me a neat, handwritten diary. 'We have "see David at the Accademia" in the morning and then "visit the Uffizi" in the afternoon. Every day is planned'. There was a silence and then a sort of sob, 'But there are things we weren't expecting that we can't fit into the schedule'.

I tipped back my spiky black hair, rattled my silver bracelets and peered at them through my heavily kohled eyes. 'So why don't you just change the schedule?' I suggested. They looked at me as shocked as Queen Victoria apparently was when she first clapped eyes on Michelangelo's masterpiece, sans fig leaf. 'Can we do that?' tried one girl. 'But then we won't see everything', said the other. 'That's right', chimed the third. I leered with my best gothic stare, 'But what you do see you'll really enjoy. At the moment you're seeing everything but not enjoying any of it'. I have no idea what this little trio resolved, they retreated to their dormitory while I stayed for another glass of wine and got talking to an American woman who repaired helicopters for the army.

Creating a stage play about a community is a little like being confronted by all the splendours of Italy – you aren't going to be able to put everything in and it's going to make you miserable if you try. You need to come up with a question, a notion to interrogate, a dramatic premise that will guide you as you move through your interviews. You may not have it on the first interview or even the second. In fact, it could be really useful to see what emerges as a common concern in the community. But you're going to want to have it more or less in place by your fourth or fifth interview. A common concern of the community, or a source of conflict there, is not necessarily a good premise for a stage play. I could have written the *Mahabharata* about the South Sydney Rugby League Football Club and I was told a lot about the club's internal politics. But who's really interested in that outside of the club itself? Of course David Williamson wrote a play about the politics of a fictional football club that serves as a fascinating forum for human nature in extremis. But if you're writing specifically about a particular community you're going to want a dramatic premise, an unanswerable dramatic engine, that will make their machinations interesting beyond the narrow confines of the community. The dramatic premise at the heart of *Run Rabbit Run* is the conflict between tradition and change, between the loyalties of your childhood and the realities of your adulthood, about the commercial demands of professional sport in the 21st century and the community values of kindness, tribalism and loyalty. About three interviews into my research, when I sat across the table from a well-to-do man who spoke with passion about the injustice of the big end of town riding roughshod over 'the little people' in the club who had little else but their football team to inspire them, I began to see the drama at the heart of this story. I began to wonder how this team, which hadn't made a semi-final since the early 1970s, inspired people to sacrifice so much time and energy and, yes, even their own self-interest, to fight. And I began to be scared by the possibility that I had come across people of genuine moral courage.

Why scared? Because it is much harder to tell a story about the best in human beings. It's easier to be cynical and damning of human nature. But here were people of sincere faith, genuine commitment and sacrifice, of utter communal goodness. I had to put that on stage without making them faultless saints. I had to find their Achilles heel, their fatal flaw and lay it out in front of them. By the fifth or sixth interview I knew what I was looking for – I was looking for that spark, that drive, that belief that they could change the world. I was digging for the lucid, working-class philosopher, the revolutionary, the men and women of vision. Every question narrowed my focus. It's like starting a jigsaw puzzle when you spread out all the pieces. Maybe you group them into particular colours to divide it into sections. But as soon as you find your first piece the next thing you're looking for is a specific piece that will fit with the previous one. And so on.

So, I like to be random enough to respond to what is there, rather than approaching the story with preconceived ideas, but avoid drifting on the surface of the community like a cork bobbing in a sea of possibilities. Your premise also has to connect with what intrigues, obsesses or terrifies you personally. The motor of your muse as a writer is specific to your experience in life and your own mangled, neurotic wad of fears and pleasures. When I wrote *Parramatta Girls* I was shamed by their story and fascinated by their survival but, four years into the project and with my own mother and grandmother dead, I had to acknowledge that I also wanted to be around a whole lot of tough older women. That said, I think a playwright's instinct for a great story as opposed to simply a good one is probably more consistent than we might think, just as, when in Florence, we're both going to want to see David's cute little arse.

So be led by both your politics and your perversions, by your sense of justice and your sense of humour. And have a plan, but be prepared to change it if a better one swims into view. Whether you are working with oral interviews or material from the archive or writing a play with entirely fictional scenes, you always need to bring a unique perspective. Constructing a full-length work of theatre basically means making thousands of decisions – which bit, what words, set where, said by whom, and then what and then what – a thousand times over and over again. You need an idea to steer those decisions in order to create something with glorious insights and entertainment for your audience.

How do you develop ideas, theories, premises? Well, clearly you need to be able to think, to consider, to understand yourself and the world and, most particularly, your characters. You need to see a lot of theatre and understand its language. But beyond all that, you must have something to say. Something you believe. There are millions of ways for artists to interrogate and understand what they believe. You might keep a diary, you might be part of an artistic collective, you might read extensively and shape your own ideas by testing them against the ideas of others. Each time I write a play I find that I need a different process to 'crack' the premise of the work, which is kind of annoying. You might think that experience would teach you how to 'do it'. But for each play you need to perceive the material in a way that no-one else has done. This perception is what you are selling or presenting to your audience, a 'take' that they will find intriguing.

So sometimes it takes weeks of feeling unproductive, misdirected, lost, stalled, confused, frustrated, irritated and bored before the penny drops. Partners who live with writers know this – the writer pleads that this time, this time, they really don't know what they are doing, as they enact a version of themselves that the partner has never seen before. They may be uncharacteristically ebullient until the partner remembers that they are writing a kids' show. They are anxious about disaster lurking around every corner and the partner remembers they are writing about a tragedy.

When I was writing my archive-based play about letters written to Lindy Chamberlain-Creighton, I found myself going through my untouched-for-some-time cupboards, drawers, files, storage boxes and cabinets. And not just in my office. Western consumerism means that all of us, even the poorest and youngest, store things that we don't look at for years, forget we have and fail to sort through, catalogue, file or process into functionality. There is a delight and amazement, unparalleled by fresh purchases, of rooting through a cupboard to find something you have put away for 'special' but now want to bring out for daily use. Nostalgia and a flood of memories can be unleashed by a set of drawings that you haven't looked at for a long time, you can chronicle the shock of change as you look at some despised piece of clothing that you now think might just be the right thing. There's joy in finding old things transformed by time into something new. The small shock of that transformation builds new synapses for translating old ideas about what you are working on into fresh perceptions. It's as though finding something new in the familiar affirms your faith that you can also do this in your work.

I'm out on a bit of a limb here because I'm trying to wrangle to the page the mysterious processes of creativity and, let's be honest, it's not like I'm spending all my writing time sorting through old trunks and obscure kitchen shelves. Especially in the case of my play *Letters to Lindy*, a huge amount of the work was administrative. That is a challenge in itself – visiting the library, copying the letters, typing them up, getting Lindy's permission to use them, writing to the correspondents themselves seeking permission, scouring the electoral roles when the letters come back 'Not at this address' and so on. The last thing I needed, frankly, especially in this play, was even more sorting. At first I found myself thinking that I was procrastinating – tidying up rather than writing. But then one morning I woke up knowing why I thought Lindy had put so much energy and love into her own archives, understanding what I thought it was about. Drawing breath I realised that, right or wrong, I finally had my personal take on the material. I knew how to spin it on stage. I had been unconsciously mimicking Lindy, though I promise you, this never occurred to me until I came to the page and it suddenly became clear.

One of the things about an artist is the ability to see new ideas in hoary old truisms about human nature – romantic love, the lust for power and the conflicts inherent in being alive. The most original way to do this is to strain those ideas through the filter of yourself. You do that by being relentlessly (some would say selfishly) absorbed with your own experience. It's a perverse truth that close work theatre, which looks to all the world like stories about other people, is really you parading your own concerns, perceptions, values and interests up on the stage. So give yourself over to the unconscious process. It may lead you to make a mess or tidy up – either way, you'll be getting inside your characters from your own unique perspective.

18

The person in front of you

When I was doing a postgraduate degree in Museum Studies at the University of Sydney, we were given a group assignment to write a report about a particular exhibition at a museum of our choice. I had recently seen a brilliant exhibition at the NSW Justice and Police Museum called 'City of Shadows' so I suggested it to our group of three. I also proposed that we interview the curator for some background on the curatorial philosophy behind the exhibition. Before we headed down to the Rocks we put together a number of questions and delegated who would ask what. It wasn't until we were in the interview that I realised that my confidence and experience as an interviewer was seriously freaking out Ming, one of our group. She asked her questions exactly as we had planned, as did the third group member. When I got to my assigned questions I asked the first one as planned and then sort of began to 'feel my way' around both the areas about which the curator had spoken with passion and the areas where I thought he was either consciously or unconsciously obfuscating.

Interviewing can be like poking at a sore till it bleeds. An ugly metaphor but I hope a useful one. If you can get someone speaking about the things that really move and inspire them they will begin to lose that self-conscious, careful word choice that can sound stilted and pre-digested when performed on stage. Everyone has something that really rings their bell, everyone, but you have to share their interest to find it. Similarly all of us are in denial about something, and an interviewer should also listen carefully, almost ruthlessly, to identify the things your interviewee doesn't want to talk about. In short, you really need to be *listening* to them, not just for what you want to hear, but for what they want to say – or not say.

As we spilled onto the streets of Circular Quay after our museum encounter, Ming strode off in a passive aggressive huff. We caught up with her at the station where she was waiting for the train. I asked her what was wrong.

'What were you thinking?' she spat, exasperated. 'You didn't stick to the questions we agreed to.'

'But don't you think I got some interesting responses out of him?' I tried.

'You didn't get him to answer the questions we agreed to.'

'But I got more interesting answers.'

'More interesting to you', she said, crossing her arms.

In fact, she was right. I didn't get him to give us generic answers to generalised questions. I didn't get him to hide behind rhetorical patter instead of revealing something of himself. I didn't get him to talk to me as if I was a high school student. I got him to speak to me as if I was a colleague able to negotiate the genuine contradictions of his choices. I guess that's what makes me a playwright, if not a good group member. I was seduced by the possibilities of getting under the skin of the person in front of me. Maybe what I elucidated from him was more relevant to a stage play than an academic group assignment. In the end we got a distinction for the assignment and Ming is still sending me Christmas cards from Singapore so my little breakout moment didn't cause any irreparable damage.

You have to interview the living human being in the room with you, not the idea of the person you conceive before you meet. I write down questions beforehand to make sure I cover the things I want to speak about. Yet sometimes an interviewee may speak about things more interesting than you imagined. At other times an experienced interviewee might actively change the topic to avoid answering your question and you might doggedly pursue it. Just remember that you are searching for the thing that reveals their character to us, and perhaps even to themselves. If you become the aggressor, pursuing one single admission or revelation, you stand to lose much else.

An interview usually has what I admiringly call the Jana Wendt moment, after the journalist and broadcaster. It's the moment when, after being their friend for, say, thirty or forty minutes, you gently shock your interviewee by more robust questioning. This kind of forensic examination of their assessment or their assertions, testing it for its veracity at every turn is what journalists do – quickly, brutally and highly effectively. As a playwright you'll need to play a slightly longer game; you're going to want to use whole swathes of what your interviewer says, not just pick the juiciest, most provocative bits. So let them feel comfortable for a while, let them tell stories that show themselves in a good or even self-deprecating light, let them persuade you they know their topic and then quietly, velvety, slip in a moment of scepticism, a turn of favour against them and see how effectively they rise to justify their perspective. It just might be interesting enough to type up and put on stage.

19

Attractions of the archive

I pulled a small blue Christmas card from the archive box with a picture of Santa on his sleigh on the front. Inside was a small concealed speaker with the words, 'push for music'. You've got to wonder what compelled me to comply so easily in the hushed confines of the Special Collections Reading Room in the National Library. It was such a small card that perhaps I presumed it would have a pretty flimsy range, not capable of much volume. No. Really, I was seduced by the promise of making something *happen* as I pressed softly on the speaker.

Ding ding da ding ding ding ding. The tinny but all-too insistent tune of 'Rudolph the Red-Nosed Reindeer' blared from the card. Other researchers in the room – stern-faced academics – looked up at me with scowling faces. I pushed the card again, harder this time, trying to stop it, but the tune continued enthusiastically. Now others studying in the room turned around to express their displeasure, like irritated commuters in the quiet carriage of a southbound train. But the little try-hard speaker in the gremlin-possessed card was taking this chance for all it was worth. So long repressed in the archive and who knew when it would ever get another opportunity?

The librarian was craning her neck over the desk and twitching her face in strong disdain. In another moment she would have to get up and then I would be in real trouble. Spoken about in the staff room. Forever referred to as that playwright with the reindeer card routine. The butt of ho, ho, ho and Christmas choir jokes when I signed in each morning. All this flashed before me but prod as I might I could not gag the ebullient little tune coming from this deceptively frail card.

And since the card was part of Mrs Lindy Chamberlain-Creighton's restricted access, special permission material, I couldn't run out of the room with it either. I tried to muffle it under my Canberra-issue scarf, so that the music sounded like it was deep in a well. Now the librarian *was* getting up and coming towards me. Just as she neared my desk the tune came to a sudden end. Smiling, I quietly opened the card to show her the 'push for music' command. 'Oops', I said, and hurriedly dropped it back into its blue manila folder. She went back to her desk, only the slightest shake of her head betraying how truly pathetic she thought I was for pushing it in the first place.

In 2013 I was awarded a Harold White Fellowship at the National Library of Australia to explore, with her permission, the letters, cards and other material sent to Mrs Lindy Chamberlain-Creighton. They ranged over the thirty-three years since her daughter Azaria was taken by a dingo at Ayres Rock, or Uluru as the local Anangu call it, on 17 August 1980. More than 20,000 items in paper and card, thousands more emails and text messages still flowing in, two out of three of them now apologies.

Lindy had placed 199 boxes of material in the NLA and I had three months to look at them with a view to creating a stage play. One of the NLA curators told me that creative artists such as novelists and playwrights rarely scored the fellowship, not because the library doesn't value such writers but because in the competitive environment of the fellowship, the *research credentials* of fiction writers look woefully meagre against the many academic applicants, most with PhDs, some of them professors. In other words, they don't doubt that creative writers would find the fellowship interesting, but screeds of research-heavy applications win out in the end. She told me that it was clear from my 'documentary-based' plays that I was well used to handling large amounts of research material without becoming overwhelmed or defeated by it. Good call.

It is like walking into infinity, walking through the doors of the NLA. I found out later that they have some 21 kilometres of manuscript material in their holdings. 21 kilometres! And that's not counting the books. Legislation requires that a copy of every book published in this country is deposited in their vaults. So it is more than a little sick-making to think of all the myriad of obscure, weird and wonderful material that you are *not* accessing during your stay. You have three months so you *should* have time to get to know the place. Then again, there are 199 boxes on the topic of your choice, and you're pretty sure you're not going to get through more than about two-thirds of them.

It's genuinely giddying and sometimes overwhelming. The value of having a premise to guide my investigations really kicked into its own right then. Of course I did many random searches, ordered copies of oral history recordings that were tangential to my Lindy work, sidelined on some other research concerning a dance project, and generally acted like a pig in information-studded mud. But I also stuck to the main game. I knew how to do that from my previous research forays.

I've used the archive to create theatre work throughout my career. My play *Singing the Lonely Heart*, which started life as *Southern Belle*, came out of a three-month pilgrimage to the United States, travelling on a Greyhound bus, researching the early life of writer Carson McCullers. I stopped in Texas, where the oil-rich, philanthropy-blessed libraries hold archives of many of America's greatest writers. Walking back from my research one day I passed a Southern Baptist church with its doors open and ducked in the back just in time to see ten congregants being baptised in a font the size of a swimming pool. She was an 'odd woman', the librarian in Columbus, where Carson grew up, told me, 'no wonder the Georgians found her hard to understand'. And I went on to New York City where McCullers lost her savings on the subway, befriended Tennessee Williams, made her name as the playwright of *Member of the Wedding* and wrote, on and off, many brilliant novels and short stories.

When I was researching a play called *The Sex Act* about the passing of the *Australian Sex Discrimination Act 1984* by Senator Susan Ryan, I discovered the Parliamentary Library in Parliament House. After writing a pleading letter to the Head Librarian, I gained photocopying access to their unimaginably wonderful files. I was delighted and astounded to learn that every MP has a file which contains every newspaper article written about them and also transcripts, yes transcripts, of every media appearance they make. An utter boon.

In 2003 I travelled to the Getty Museum in Los Angeles to research the collecting history of a woman named Jean Brown, who had bequeathed to the museum the most incredible archive of Dada and Surrealist material. I used to travel to the Getty every day via three buses, caught after standing on empty, drive-by-shooting-likely streets for what seemed like hours. Once there I caught the little on-site train up to the museum and used my special pass to gain access to the library – pencil only, no bags. It had a treasure trove of crazy stuff. I never managed to secure a commission for the work but I've been unearthing that research again. In the life of a writer, ten years is a sneeze.

My postgraduate diploma in Museum Studies inaugurated a passion for interpretive theatre in museums and other cultural institutions that led to a large number of commissions from, among others, the Australian National Maritime Museum, Hyde Park Barracks, the Australian War Memorial, the Museum of Sydney, the Sydney Jewish Museum and Sydney Observatory. Consequently, through the curators of these institutions, I got my hot little hands on primary sources and revelled in making my own judgements, unimpeded by academic writings.

The primary attraction of the archive is that it gives you access to material that is no longer available in the real world. Historical records especially, but archives also gather papers from a particular group of people in a distilled form. It would take me years and be impossible to interview the 20,000 people who wrote to Lindy Chamberlain and, even if I did, hindsight would radically obscure their recall – particularly given that Lindy has now finally been exonerated after one of the grossest miscarriages of justice in Australian history. I want to see what people said when they didn't know the outcome, when they were in the thick of the drama. For that, the archive is unmatchable.

The other attraction of the archive is to service those misanthropic, low oxytocin, just-want-to-be-left-alone periods in a playwright's life. No pesky actual human beings to interview, charm and wrangle, none of those irritating spanners that bureaucracy or avoidance or denial can throw into your works. It's a lonelier journey but your detective skills and political value system, along with your individual personality will determine the story you draw from the records. A community not in the flesh, but in archive boxes – their voices, like my little 'push for music' gremlin, struggling to get out.

20

The art of sacrifice

My process with close work is, where possible, to take the work back to its community before it is produced on the public stage. This services the community's continued input and ownership of the work, alerts you to any developing issues related to the profile of the community and also creates excitement and anticipation. The first time people see and hear themselves on stage is a magical and precious thing. You will want to witness this in a 'community-heavy' environment. In this context, their 'family' can reassure, support and bolster confidence and self-esteem.

When I developed *Parramatta Girls* with Company B at Belvoir St we had two public readings before the play went into production in 2007. The first consisted of pure verbatim transcripts from some of the thirty-plus interviews I had done, with the actors playing multiple parts. It was important to use their exact words at this early stage, because the women had consistently said to me that they didn't speak for thirty years for *fear that they would not be believed*. They grew up being told no-one would believe them because they were 'bad' girls. The evidence of their own lives had persuaded them that this was indeed the case. Even now, in the interviews, this legacy of self-doubt lingered. Putting their exact words on the public stage, in front of an audience of invited guests and industry professionals, including inmates of other orphaned and incarcerated children's institutions, was profoundly important. It allowed me to gain their trust so I could move the project forward.

In that first reading, as thirty or so different voices echoed and repeated themes, some similarities emerged. While in real life each person was unique, in a theatrical context the brain groups stories together, to find 'collections' of behaviour and recognise patterns and 'archetypes'. I realised it might be possible to 'collapse' the stories into eight characters and dramatise the reunion at the home. With their permission I retained the names of some of the women I had interviewed, telling them that I would create 'characters' – versions – based on their story but also using bits of other people's stories. Because they had seen the first public reading and noted how 'confusing' it was trying to follow 'who was who when', they understood the logic of my decision.

This choice also served another purpose. Some stories were too personal, too confronting, too difficult for someone to 'own' on the public stage. For instance, admissions about how the legacy of their childhood had affected their treatment, and in some cases led to the assault of their own children; or disclosures about friends who had taken their own lives because of their unresolved pain. It was a big ask to stage stories, revelations and confessions in a particular individual's voice that could potentially be re-traumatising. Collapsing verbatim interviews into a massaged form would maintain authenticity but allow a small cloak of fictional 'anonymity'. This meant I could include scenes about self-harm, illiteracy, domestic abuse and sexual exploration without relegating this behaviour or legacy to specific 'real' individuals. As I say, this was to protect them. But since these factors ran through the life stories of all the women, it was also disingenuous to choose which women should 'wear' them publicly.

So for the second public reading I collapsed the stories into some five or six characters and created fictional characters to portray the guards, the offspring of the women, and others mentioned in interviews. I felt it was important to dramatise the ongoing legacy of the home on the women's lives, since so many had spoken about this in the interviews. Many of the interviewees brought their children and other family members to the second reading. Afterwards Neil Armfield had a word with me. 'I can see why you would want to include the offspring and the guards and the others in their story', he said to me, 'But truthfully, we're really not interested in anyone but the women. You need to find a structural way for us to see the entire story through their eyes because it's only really them that we want to follow'.

It was a remarkably succinct piece of dramaturgical feedback and proved the key to my rewrite. Of course we only wanted to see the women! But perhaps we could see them both in the past and the present. I was going to be working with skilled performers – couldn't they play the women at the age when they were in the home and also when they returned for the reunion? Of course they could, and provide the audience with bravura performances in the process. I could show the legacy of the home on them as adults, *not* by moving into a realistic portrait of their adult lives but by theatricalising the differences. By showing the audience how they changed, rather than telling it through extraneous characters.

Head Full of Love, my play about kidney disease in the Pitjantjatjara community, also had two public showings with community stakeholders at the Alice Springs Beanie Festival. The play was conceived after a trip to Alice Springs when I visited the Western Desert Nganampa Walytja Palyantjaku Tjutaku Aboriginal Corporation (or Purple House), an independent kidney dialysis facility and met Sarah Brown who introduced me to many of the Central Desert mob living with kidney disease. At the same time Louise Partos from Artback Theatre had created a connection for me with Jo Nixon and Adi Dunlop, matriarchs of the Alice Springs Beanie Festival. I had spent an extensive amount of time interviewing, adventuring, crocheting and conversing with Pitjantjatjara community, beanie artists, kidney dialysis nurses and Alice Springs locals. Then I took all my recordings, research and impressions as well as my fumblingly created beanies to Tasmania where, perversely, in the chilly surrounds of the Hobart Writer's Cottage, I wrote my first draft.

The Darwin Festival, who had commissioned the play the previous year, had already scheduled it for production in August 2010. So when the Beanie Festival rolled around in June, the community presentation enabled us to check back in with the story's source and iron out or tweak any aberrations. The second reading, during the day, was attended by a large group of Pitjantjatjara women who sat down the front of the theatre, laughing and responding, as did the rest of the non-Indigenous audience. The applause at the end was warm and sustained, as it had been the night before, but I already knew there was a bee in their collective beanies.

In both presentations the character of Nessa had talked to Tilly about masturbating in Scene 8, after they talk about men. Tilly talks about the death of her husband.

TILLY: Need to find 'nother one.

NESSA: Yeah, I don't know if I can be bothered.

TILLY: Nessa have some that fun.

NESSA: Oh, I like sex. I'm no prude. Not like our mothers. No, we were the generation who learned to get what we wanted weren't we?

TILLY *looks at her, blank.*

I masturbate of course.

TILLY *giggles.*

Oh, come on, we all do. [*Beat.*] People don't talk about it anymore but everyone does it. Do you know I think the young ones are more prudish about it than we were. But they're at it too. I used to babysit, Tilly, I used to babysit three or four children – friends' children as well as my son – and from the age of about two you'd go into the cots at night and there'd be this thump thump thump as they're banging away. Lord, it's the first thing we discover isn't it? And, I've got quite good at it over the years too. I don't use a dildo or anything, might buy the odd vegetable every now and then for my sins. Know what I mean? You've got to pay more attention. I'll tell you what Tilly there's always room for a little nod and smile when you see another middle-aged woman buying a single large carrot.

So, pretty harmless in the 21st-century, Sarah-Kane-eat-your-heart-out-scheme-of-things don't you think? Well. There was outrage, there was anger, there was disappointment. One elderly non-Indigenous woman, I kid you not, grabbed my arm at the end of the reading and said, 'That was wonderful dear but that bit about self-abuse, listen, older women just don't do that!' Another young woman, high up in the Beanie Festival hierarchy told me, 'I was embarrassed to sit next to my mother during that bit'. Outside an Aboriginal woman visiting the festival and sitting among the Pitjantjatjara women told me that they strongly disapproved of that section. 'The play is so wonderful', she said, 'so important and so insightful and so necessary. And then you go and spoil it with that piece of smut in the middle of it'. I received a huge amount of positive feedback from both readings. Most especially, I secured a connection with Beth Sometimes, who speaks Pitjantjatjara and who agreed to help tutor the actors' pronunciation for the production in Darwin. But again and again people told me that the masturbation moment was inappropriate. Colette Mann (who played Nessa) and Roxanne McDonald (who played Tilly) reported similar conversations in their feedback. With typical wry wit, Colette said, 'I think they might have gone with the wanking, darling, but the carrot was a bridge too far'.

So. There are three things you can do when faced with the same piece of feedback on one particular theatrical moment. You can ignore it, you can change it, or you can cut it. The sexual radical, no wait, excuse me, the *realist* in me wanted to keep it. 'Older women just don't do that!' Please. Of course they do. I don't doubt that *Portnoy's Complaint* was no bestseller in the Alice but 'just don't do that?' Well, frankly if they don't they should try! I talked about it with the director Wesley Enoch, especially the feedback from the elders via the spokeswoman (none of the traditional Indigenous women had actually said anything about the 'moment', when I had asked them how they liked the play they had smiled and nodded their approval). Wesley said he liked it and I should keep it in.

I thought about just cutting the carrot. But that took all the fun out of it. I thought about leaving it in. But having endured fifty conversations about 'what a great play, pity about the carrot moment', I imagined that conversation multiplied by ten performances in Darwin. It would be *the* thing people would talk about in the foyer as it was here. It would blitz any other moment in the work and unbalance the whole. It was a throbbing prominence in an otherwise sandy desert. It was a clump of sequins on a rustic beanie. Much as I had the shamelessness to include it, I recoiled from the certainty of this play about kidney disease and reconciliation, with all its important provocations, being reduced to the 'play with the carrot'. The Central Desert Women's Council had asked me to tell this story because of the crisis around kidney disease in Central Australia. They had given me permission to include the Pitjantjatjara perspective because this story was so important to get out to the Australian theatre-going public. Yet, above and beyond that, this was an artistic work. What was the greater compromise: to include it and unbalance the whole, or to remove it, and allow the rest of the work to move as a piece with moments of humour, pathos, understanding and confronting difference?

So I decided to cut it. The entire section. Binned the carrot to the compost bucket and saved my perceptions about older women's sexuality for another play. Often one scene, or one moment, or even one glitteringly beautiful line can overwhelm the whole piece and you get to know, as a writer, that you have to cut it. Artistic balance is not the only reason you may have to cut a script. On any project drawn from life I take legal advice to protect the company who will produce the work and myself as well as the community and other participants. Just like I don't want the 'carrot' moment to swamp the whole, I don't want a legal issue to draw all the oxygen from a project. For *Letters to Lindy*, the archive contained many orphan works, that is, works where the copyright owner could not be found. But I posted, combed the electoral rolls, the yellow pages, explored every avenue possible to get in touch with the original letter writer.

Head Full of Love is just one example of when I needed ruthless discipline to cut a special moment. In *Parramatta Girls*, I wrote a scene in which one of the Aboriginal inmates was learning to cook and another inmate forced her face into the flour. When she lifted her head up from the bowl her face was white. It was a lucid metaphorical moment, theatrically dynamic and beautiful, and it was based on a real story told to me by an Indigenous woman. But it came in the middle of the second act and it just didn't push the narrative forward in the way that every scene needed to do in the second half. Neil Armfield, again in his discreet but canny way said to me, 'I love it, it's a beautiful moment, but I don't know why it's there'. And so I cut it, at the end of the third public preview. Just before we opened. Because it wasn't serving the whole. And that is the gig.

21

Selective hearing

I used to think that knowing whose feedback to listen to was one of the most important things a writer could learn. I now know that ignoring the naysayers, the do-it-how-it's-been-done-before merchants and the enemies of your original voice, is the only thing to know. Of course you need tools, of course you need craft but, above all, you need to find a way to back yourself, rejection after rejection. An emerging Tongan-Australian writer recently asked me, 'How do I know what to listen to and how do I know when to stop listening?' As her mentor, I told her that when responding to feedback on a script in progress, she might find the phrase, 'I'd like to think about that' very useful. Wesley Enoch used to laugh with me about that phrase, when we were working on *Parramatta Girls* and *Head Full of Love*. He said he was always impressed by my prodigious ability to listen to and respond to feedback. 'But when you started to say, with a small smile, "I'd like to think about that", it was always my cue to move on. The great thing was', he told me, 'you always did think about it'.

There are two components to feedback. First it might indicate a lack of clarity or a gap in the drama or an inconsistency with character. Second it might proffer a solution. Your job is to use any rewrite to deepen the drama and clarify the character choices. Even when the feedback does not articulate exactly what the problem is, a moment in the script that causes the reader to pause or be pulled out of the drama lets you know there is an issue. Listen to what the dramaturg says. How that moment made them feel might be *exactly* what you are aiming for. Beware of conventional or unimaginative responses when people give you feedback. As for the proffered solution – you never have to follow that. Listen if you like, but it's not what you have to *do*. Bad feedback will try to suggest how to make the play more like the one the dramaturg would like you to write. Good feedback asks what you were trying to do in that moment and tells you that you need to work harder, more creatively, to achieve it. Great feedback pinpoints a problem you can see straight away. And maybe the proffered solution is an absolute gift which loans you the brain of someone smarter, more perceptive and more experienced than you. How do you tell the difference? You think about it.

Another phrase you may find useful is 'I'll put a flag on that', which means that every time you hear that section or that line, you consider whether to keep it or cut it. It's kind of like pinning something on Instagram to remind you to come back to it later. Use it when you know that there is something needed, absent or overstated in a part of the script but can't yet determine the solution. Or when people tell you the line needs to be cut, but you want to see it in rehearsal, sometimes in preview, you want to see if the line might carry the laugh you anticipated and surprise everyone. You want to see if it can earn its keep.

Finally, I find that it helps to make an audio recording of feedback and dramaturgical advice so that I can play it back and reinstall it on my brain when I come to work on rewrites for a project. No amount of notes can take me back to what I was thinking during such a session. I also find that I am less defensive, less needy and less self-conscious when I am listening to feedback on a recording rather than in person.

There are, of course, common dramaturgical problems that almost every writer can benefit from examining, a kind of checklist in your brain when you read through the work. In particular, these might include:

- *Show, don't tell*: Is there a place where you are letting the characters tell us what they think instead of showing us through an action? In the theatre you are looking for a way to theatricalise this notion, to express your ideas urgently on a stage. This principle is important in any dramatic work.
- *Personal story as a metaphor*: How are you using the story for a bigger overview of your society or culture? The end of

a work, how the drama is resolved, is not necessarily your recommendation for how this problem should be solved in the real world. The notion of using theatre as catharsis (from the Greek κάθαρσις meaning 'purification' or 'cleansing') argues for the process of releasing strong or repressed emotions in a safe context, rather than in the real world. If your character must leave her family and her culture because it is repressing her, then the story urges change in the real world so that such a drastic solution is not required.

- *Your favourite line or moment*: Have you included something which everyone tells you is an indulgence? Maybe it seemed essential when you began, a pivotal speech perhaps, but now you're encouraged to cut it. Rather than lose it, should it, perversely, be increased? Spread throughout? Or maybe it *should* be cut. Acknowledge the problem, but experiment with the solution.
- *Something to say*: Something profound, original, urgent. If you've got it, work it. And hang onto it with both hands. Don't let anyone bland it out.
- *The title*: Does it summarise your premise? Does it have an intriguing, elusive (and possibly) double meaning? People found my title *Shafana and Aunt Sarrinah* hard to pronounce, but, it was important to me to use it in Australia, since it was commissioned as a companion to *Norm and Ahmed*. In the United States, however, they used the published subtitle *Soft Revolution* instead. A title that has been used several times before, or is a common phrase may be a problem online too. But, maybe you want that. Bring it on.
- *Avoid bald exposition*: Find a clever way to reveal things to the audience. Audiences remember things that they think they have discovered for themselves better than when they are told them.
- *Less is more*: The stage offers the vitality and beauty of gesture and voice and intonation, and the active silence of the actors. Then there's the invention, imagination and

surprise of the director. Live theatre offers all the remarkable unspoken and astonishing things that presence and relationship, subtext and situation give us. The stage doesn't reduce your characters, it liberates them from a page into physical reality. Imagination is not reduced by becoming more specific – it is focused and augmented, it is dramatised and animated.

- *Ambiguity and paradox in relationships*: Work hard to retain humour that lands not on the line but between the lines. Find speeches where people contradict themselves and their stated values and beliefs, and have another character call them on it.
- *How does your text create and invoke music?* Aside from the poetry and rhythm of the words, is there space for song or original music? The director will have strong ideas about this but often writers can suggest musical ideas which will profoundly enhance the text.

When other people give you feedback, remember what you are writing. There is no reason to listen to someone who tells you to up the genre aspects of your work if you are merely using those tropes to tell another, more interesting social or cultural story. There is no point in feedback that says 'make it more of a television crime procedural' when you want a work of art that interrogates cultural tradition. There is no sense in imposing a conventional three-act structure and hero's journey on a play if it reduces your work to cliché and banality.

I met with Sally Sara, the courageous ABC foreign correspondent, at Luke Nguyen's Red Lantern restaurant in Surry Hills in 2016. She had seen my play *Ladies Day* at Griffin and emailed to ask if she could buy me lunch. *Ladies Day*, she told me, had inspired her as she was writing about her life as a foreign correspondent. She was making great progress, interviewing family members and loved ones to find out how they felt as she repeatedly threw herself into the face of danger. She was surprised and intrigued because their responses differed from what she had expected. The ambiguities of real life intruding in remarkable, complex ways was going to make for a beautiful work. But, she said, she had been told to make the work more structurally conventional, more compliant with the Robert McKee brand 'hero's journey' and she was finding it oppressive. What should she do?

'Junk the feedback', I said.

'Really?' She was immediately in assent.

'If it's suffocating your inspiration, if it's gagging your creativity – bin it', I said, with as much cavalier rebellious attitude as I could, stuffing peanut sauce and pork into my mouth. 'You know how to tell this story, you know the dimensions of it because you are living it. Get it down in as messy and contradictory a way as you can. Order can be imposed later'.

She later emailed me and said that it was 'by far the most helpful talk I've had about the whole process'.

The truth is that a dramaturg who can give you good structural advice at the right time, a mentor who can force you to tear down the structure and rebuild it, a director who can reject sloppy plotting or inert scenes – these people are your best friends. But they are not needed at every step of the process. The dramaturg's unique role is to ascertain what to say and when to say it. The person who sat across from me was a skilled journalist, a highly experienced storyteller who had been presenting professional work on air for decades. At that moment she needed someone to tell her to ignore the rules and go for it. She needed the confidence to be an artist, not the discipline to be an architect of story. The dramaturgical hard yards would come later (the only way out is through) but right then they were not useful.

As a dramaturg you have to be able to determine if the writer in front of you is lazy and intransigent, or overwhelmed and becalmed by too much or too harsh feedback. Kate Gaul once described it to me as 'like putting a marshmallow near a heater', when a director puts the dramaturgical blowtorch onto a new or emerging writer (or even an experienced one) and the effect is to turn their idea to a charred crisp. Sometimes the idea that the dramaturg or director has *is* more original, more interesting, more theatrical, more wonderful in every way. But if the idea is not coming up from *your* gut, prodding at you in *your* sleep, nagging at you in *your* dreams; if it's not *your* idea, it's not going to assuage your artistic hunger in the way that it needs to. Dare to believe that the person you need to please most of all is you.

22

Getting off the grid

'You can drive!' said the co-ordinator of Booranga, a writers' retreat at the Charles Sturt University in Wagga Wagga.

'Well, yes', I said. 'Is that unusual?'

'As a matter of fact it is extremely rare', she said. 'Especially the poets. None of them have licenses and they all need to be driven around. My job is mostly being a chauffeur to poets.'

It is 2000 and I have a residency at Booranga Writers' Retreat to spend a month overlooking the Charles Sturt vineyards and write. And while many of the visiting writers, according to this co-ordinator, liked to sit out at Booranga for a month alone – working, reading, thinking – I couldn't think of anything worse. So before I got to Wagga Wagga I secured a commission from Radio National to make a radio documentary feature called *City of Glass* about the National Art Glass Collection at the Wagga Wagga Art Gallery. That way I could spend my time having lunch, dinner and drinks with all of the most interesting people in this terrific regional city – glass artists, gallery curators, and dissenters. I also planned to drive around to Tumbarumba to visit the high school and the library and to Albury High School and, while assessing who made the best morning teas (I do not jest, morning tea is high-stakes in regional Australia), record interviews, observe, soak up stories and generally expose myself to people, opinions and perspectives that were new to me.

Of course, I also made contact with the local theatre company, the Riverina Theatre Company, whose artistic director was Mary McMenamin. I was used to allowing forty-five minutes to get to the theatre in Surry Hills from Redfern (less than 2 kilometres away), factoring in traffic and parking, so it took some getting used to the idea in Wagga Wagga of leaving at five minutes to eight to make an eight o'clock show (no traffic, no parking issues, a straight through run to the auditorium). With Mary I began to discuss the idea of making a verbatim-based play to celebrate the incredible cultural diversity of Wagga Wagga – the big Sri Lankan and Indian communities, the Russian community, the Korean and Chinese and Japanese migrants who had lived there for years. Did I have an idea, Mary asked me, that would bring these disparate groups together? A concept to get these culturally diverse women talking allowing them to compare their experience and find their commonality?

I suggested the women might share their ancestral knowledge of healing – literally compare old wives' tales about treating all kinds of ailments. I asked the women to bring to a workshop *one* story about their mother or their mother's mother's healing remedies. I needed to do little else. The women were climbing over each other, and me, to regale the wisdom of their forebears, to impress us with tales of miracles and healing, to compare, exchange and engage with the lessons of their ancestors. And to wonder at the similarities between some of this female-focused knowledge. It was an incredible workshop that generated some astonishing revelations. But how to turn it into a stage play that Wagga Wagga audiences would come to see?

That's where the Bard came in. Regional audiences at that time loved Shakespeare, and probably still do. It was a slam dunk way to get audiences into the space. I conceived a play called *Titania's Boy*, about a divorcing Indian couple whose son Pradepan began to identify with the changeling child in Shakespeare's *A Midsummer Night's Dream*. The idea came from stories that several women had shared with me about the pain and challenge of marriage breakdown after the isolating journey of moving to a region. It was a three-hander, with the performers playing the divorced wife, the son and his sympathetic teacher and doubling as Shakespearean characters from the *Dream*. When Nick Clarke replaced Mary McMenamin as artistic director he made *Titania's Boy* one of his first productions in 2003 with Georgina Naidu, Alex Papps and Zeke Castelli.

The play benefited from the time I spent at Shakespeare's Globe in London, where I was introduced to the dramaturg as uber-research assistant, a person who, instead of interrogating your structure or dramatic ideas, provided you with interesting and inspiring information about, say, the subtextual knowledge a Shakespearian audience might have of astronomy and child-rearing and gender politics. It was creative stimulation par excellence, feeding me fascinating facts that inspired my imagination.

In the 21st century, the idea of a writer getting 'off the grid' is as important as it ever was – time to be quiet and listen to the truths that hum up from your subconscious, time to challenge your routines and perceptions, time to make new observations and new realisations and see who you are without the scaffolding of your usual life. If you are a playwright, I recommend that you arm yourself with some kind of project which will allow you to access a broad cross-section of people – an investigative adventure which will yield conversations and contacts even while you are not quite sure what you are *actually* writing about. In 2014 I travelled to Central St Martin's Art School in London to attend a short course called 'Cool Hunters, London'. It's designed to teach students how to think like a fashion trend predictor, how to sharpen their powers of observation and see beyond the surface of now to the texture and shape of the future. I made a short radio feature for ABC's Radiotonic about my travels but I gathered material and insights and perspectives on an entire bevy of international young fashionistas attending the course that will brilliantly inform a play I am writing about the Professor of Fashion Madge Garland and her work on British *Vogue*. Good research, deep research is never a straight line. So if you want to be a theatre maker, especially a writer, travel as much as you can, but always have a little project of enquiry tucked up your sleeve to give your enquiries a frame and a direction. And when I say travel, think broadly – it's not about going a long way. The French writer Xavier de Maistre famously travelled around his own room. It's about finding a way to journey to the new, wherever that may be found. Lin Yutang wrote in *The Importance of Living* in 1937:

> The true motive of travel should be travel to become lost and unknown. More poetically, we may describe it as travel to forget ... A true traveller

is always a vagabond, with the joys, temptations and sense of adventure of the vagabond ... I may suggest that there is a different kind of travel, travel to see nothing and to see nobody ... There is all the difference between seeing things and seeing nothing. Many travellers who see things really see nothing, and many who see nothing see a great deal. I am always amused at hearing of an author going to a foreign country to 'get material for his new book' as if he had exhausted all there was to see in humanity in his own town or country ... We come therefore to the philosophy of travel as consisting of the capacity to see things, which abolishes the distinction between travel to a distant country and going about the fields of an afternoon.

23

Junee juggernaut

Yorta Yorta / Kurnai writer and director Andrea James phoned me in September 2011. She had been invited to do writing workshops in Junee Correctional Centre with Aboriginal and Torres Strait Islander men. She couldn't do the job, did I want it? Sure I did. The gig would involve going into the jail for five days, running workshops to get the men writing and producing a short video to show at the Wagga Wagga Ngiyaginya Aboriginal Festival. I had spent some of my childhood visiting a relative in jail, Junee was a minimum-security, privately-operated facility, and this was my first introduction to Shine for Kids, an organisation that works with children who have parents in NSW correctional facilities. As part of their liaison with inmates and their families, Shine had two Aboriginal elders working in a dedicated cultural centre in the jail.

When I arrived in Wagga Wagga, the festival organiser picked me up and took me to a share house where I was assigned a room. It was obviously someone else's room – her clothes were on the clothes rack, her cosmetics were on the dresser, her detritus was on the carpet. Oh well, I guess this is a regional arts festival operating on a minimum budget. No airs and graces necessary. I was assured that the sheets had been changed and the others staying in the house, all men, were lovely friendly chaps. Now, unlike some writers I actually like staying in people's houses, I don't always demand the privacy or the security of a motel room. The rub here was that I had not been told that I would be spending the night in a room with an unlockable door in a space with three other men I didn't know. This had nothing to do with the integrity or otherwise of the other residents, turned out they were nice fellows, all theatre workers and the like, all very fine, but it was a little unusual.

The jail visit started well. I think there was a real doubt that these 'workshops' could work, about whether the men would open up and participate in writing exercises at all. On the first day, I treated the men as I had worked with participants in verbatim writing workshops elsewhere. I had spoken to Wesley Enoch who had worked with Indigenous men in a correctional setting and he told me about getting these incarcerated men to build a cubby house. I had neither the time nor the resources to do that but I did take a leaf from his book and asked the men to tell a story about something they had been taught as a child by a relative, preferably their father. I asked them tell this to another inmate and have the second inmate relate the story back to the group.

This had several advantages. Talking about their childhood meant they could tell something real and personal while the memory of someone teaching them awakened feelings of being valued and inspired. Sharing their story with another inmate demonstrated trust and attention and initiated the men into a verbatim technique. The exercise honed their storytelling, their perceptions and their facility for detail and also made them realise that I wasn't going to try and preach to them about 'literature'. Instead they would participate in exercises enabling them to articulate their relationship to culture and reveal their personalities. Plus, it would break the boredom of prison life.

The highlight was the day I asked them to role play 'refusing the request of another'. Boy, did they have a catalogue of experience to draw from. An eerily accurate account of a social worker denying benefits; an hilarious scenario of a drug dealer refusing to supply a client; a father withholding ice-cream from his children as an act of tough love. As performance always does, these improvisations showed to me, and each of them, the complexity of their understanding, the vagaries of their life experience and the progress of their rehabilitation

There was always one or two Aboriginal female elders from Shine for Kids who participated in the sessions. This imprimatur was fundamental as I carefully won the men's trust through a series of theatre games, writing exercises and stories about my work in the theatre. I still had to have the chops to persuade the inmates to follow my lead but I wouldn't have been able to get to first base without the trust and co-operation of the elders; they held the door open for me. Here, seriously, is life-changing work done by real, unsung heroes.

One participant was popular and outgoing. Young, good-looking and exuding confidence, he was often the first one to jump in when I asked for someone to share what they had written. When we did an improvisation exercise he clowned it up with exuberance and genuine creativity. Some of the others had to be brought out of their shell, but this particular man seemed to have easy access to his feelings and appeared to be emotionally stable. 'A bit of a peacock', one elder confided, as he preened and paraded in front of me and the others, culturally proud. He had managed to retain a modicum of hope and vitality inside the prison routine.

After working with the inmates for three days, I wrote a short poem called 'The Ballad of Junee Jail' to act as a frame for their work. I used rhyme to help the men memorise the words. The task for day four was to film the men performing excerpts of the poem. They had to memorise one or two lines, look into the camera and say them, and then it would be on to the next participant. In the film, these lines would be cut in with documentary footage from the workshops that showed the men reading their own work, doing improvisations and discussing culture.

Sounds simple. Mostly it was. After a bit of procrastinating, male-on-male goading and teasing, participants said their lines into the camera in turn, often with a sly smile. They'd have a couple of attempts at it, sometimes I'd make suggestions and encourage them to relax into their own rhythm and energy. The others would egg them on as well, then slap them on the back in congratulations when it was done. I was buoyed by their community spirit and cultural strength. They were exhibiting the pride and camaraderie of an ensemble of theatre actors after their first preview.

Then we came to our peacock. He had two lines to say:

> One of the walks we do a lot
> is a walk down memory lane

The first time it was good. But he said, 'No, let's go again'. 'okay, sure, try it again a little bit slower.' Which he did. 'No, I can do it better than that.' 'okay', I said, 'but that was really good, we can use that'. 'Let me go again, I can do it better.' And he did, again and again. And then he started getting the lines wrong, 'One of the walks we go is down …' 'No, not down, One of the walks we do is into the lane of the memory.' 'No, no. Stupid. Stupid …'

He was getting rattled. The more he couldn't do the line, the more angry and agitated he became. He began to turn the anger on himself. It was like watching a video of builders dynamiting a solid multi-storey brick building. One moment it is standing and then, an explosion, and the entire thing is careering to the ground, a pile of rubble and rocks and choking dust.

'It's okay, I think we've got it', I said. But it was no longer about the line. He was humiliated, in front of the female workshop co-ordinator (me), in front of the other inmates and he thought the guards were laughing at him. In fact there was no-one nearby except myself and the camera operator, though some others were watching from the sidelines as he worked himself up into more and more of an angry state. As he began punching the top of his thighs with his fists and repeating 'stupid, stupid', the corrective services officers came closer and told us to take a break. A couple of the older inmates came over to him and squeezed his shoulder. They took him over to have a cup of tea. After a break I said nonchalantly that I thought we had it and could use some of the earlier takes. He seemed happy with that. It wasn't long before he was joking around again and laughing, gently taking the piss out of the entire project and reducing the importance of 'performing' in front of the camera. I said it was a pretty lame poem actually and he agreed. And then we moved on.

As a workshop tutor you need to work hard to protect participants from moments like this. But, in truth, any work that involves creativity and people offering themselves cannot be made entirely hazard-proof. The best you can do is to build a sense of genuine solidarity among the participants and trust that they will hold each other up, which in this case they did. In a prison situation like this I knew not to ladle out faux sympathy thus drawing more attention and making him feel like a failure. Tough love, unemotional, on with the job was the only way to go. The next day, my final day with the participants, I said nothing about it and only underlined how much I had enjoyed the work. This allowed the peacock to fade back into the group and be part of the general acclaim and positive response to the full week's workshop. We had cake. We said it needed to be a regular feature of jail life. We affirmed each other's humanity and displayed mutual respect.

But the moment of pain and shame was hard to get out of my consciousness, less because I thought it would have lasting effects on the peacock himself (I was reassured by the visiting elder that he was fine) but because of how it brought to the surface a glimpse of a pattern that can take hold, most especially in vulnerable people, but I think a little in all of us. The danger when you have low self-esteem and find something that gives you even a small amount of confidence is that you expect to be perfect always. For me the lesson was, don't judge yourself too harshly – or at all.

Others might reflect on this moment as a metaphor for what can happen to a young culturally diverse person when they try to put into their mouths the words of someone else. The poetry in this case was not in his natural voice. If he had been allowed to say the sentence in his own words he may never have floundered. Perhaps on reflection he might draw conclusions from his response and recognise that he loses his stability when he is overwhelmed by rules and unfamiliar behaviours. Or maybe he'll just learn not to beat himself up when things don't go exactly to plan.

I have told young writers that the trick to keeping on writing (which you need to do to get any good at all) is never to judge yourself. Never. Don't scrutinise whether your idea or your writing is good or bad, don't become self-conscious about what you are doing, don't decide if it is working or not. A great writer, I believe, is someone who has an infinite capacity to try again. Try to care enough about what other people think to learn and grow and improve, but not so much that it becomes a monkey on your back, ripping off your head and your arms in a violent act of self-sabotage. I say to a young writer what I would like to say to my Junee peacock, 'let up on yourself', 'give yourself a break', 'have fun with this'. I once heard Michael Gow say at the Australian

National Playwrights Conference 'The best advice I can give to a young writer about dramaturgs is to tell them to fuck off.' At the time, as a young writer, I thought, 'Yeah, well, that's alright for you Michael. You can tell them that and they'll still come back to you'. But I have never forgotten it. And now as an experienced writer I think I know what he meant and thank him for saying it. He was not talking about the arrogance that makes you impervious, but the courage that allows you to keep going. He was saying, learn how to protect yourself from unrealistic expectations, especially your own. Learn how to strive but more importantly, get out of your own way and learn how to play.

24

The talking brain

During the Q&A after the production of *Dead Man Brake* at the Merrigong Theatre Company in August 2013, one of the teachers with a school group asked me why there were less 'ums and ahs' in the play than in *Run Rabbit Run*. 'Did they just speak better than some of the other people you have interviewed?' she asked. This is a complex question that I have often addressed by differentiating between pure verbatim and other forms and now I use the umbrella term 'close work theatre'. Early on I used the term 'massaged verbatim'. Pure verbatim focuses on exact transcripts of the interview material, where the contract between you and the audience is that the actors repeat *exactly* what the interviewee said, and as a playwright the focus is on their precise words. In massaged verbatim I am still interested in how they speak, but I don't reproduce the dialogue word for word; rather I use my skills to polish or boil down the interview material and create for audiences the *essence* of their speech. This can include characteristics not discernible from pure transcripts but apparent in the moment when interviewing a number of community members.

But massaged verbatim is only the start of it. I've already discussed how I coined the term 'generic verbatim' to describe the poetry sections and song lyrics in *Dead Man Brake*. I did this to harness comments, perspectives or phrases characteristic of the community's language when they were not able to sustain a full speech on their own. With *Dead Man Brake* many people talked about how they irrationally blamed themselves for getting into the wrong carriage, how they thought that they 'should have known' not to get on that train even though rationally that didn't make sense. This became the poem, then the song, 'Wouldn't it be nice'. Johnny Franko sings it in the play and while many of the phrases in the poem are his, I augmented his words by manipulating and arranging similar expressions from other people. So it's definitely not classic verbatim. At the same time, it reflects a community voice since I am reproducing their collective phrases, patterns and perceptions.

So when I answered the teacher at the *Dead Man Brake* Q&A, I encouraged her to look beyond verbatim as dramatic speech with all the ums and ahs left in, and to guide her students to look at the other aberrations of speech which betray intent and meaning, or aspects of human nature.

It's also true that people process their grief and pain in stages, and this will affect how they respond to you. The most confronting thing for an interviewer to recognise is that the interviewee's interaction with you may be part of their healing process. Over time this may cause your subject to express their story in different ways. So they may be teary at first, and later ashamed and reluctant to speak, after that they may become cavalier or even flippant, as if it is of no consequence, it's in the past, not worth talking about. As the writer you are going to choose which manifestation best serves the story and structure of your stage play. But you will also remember that this is a human being and ethical responsibilities will colour your choices.

The originality and beauty of using verbatim material is to observe not what people say but how they say it – how they warp it, interrupt it, pervert it; how they cloak it, deny it, twist it; how they lie to themselves and to others; how they encourage, discourage and protect themselves with their own self-talk.

The Parramatta Girls often spoke with ice-cold, clinical clarity about 'Doctor Fingers' and the brutality of the medical examinations which greeted them on their admission to the Parramatta home. These descriptions were frequently unemotional, distinguished by specific, I might even say, forensic, detail about the procedure. I learnt, as a writer, to understand that it mattered exactly how many fingers were inserted into their vaginas, and for how long, the specific questions they were asked, and precisely what was written on their admission documents.

On the other hand, some interviewees who wanted to admit something painful or difficult would tell me two or three other things before they got to the hard stuff, perhaps to test my understanding and ability to 'go with them'. This was especially true in the interviews I did with the adult survivors of child abuse for my play *Swimming Upstream*. An abuse survivor cannot always admit candidly or describe explicitly what happened to them. Sometimes they just won't go there. They talk around the subject and get to a certain point in the conversation where they expect you to *work it out* or even *say it for them*. 'So that's when he assaulted you', I might say after a lot of half-finished sentences and veiled implications. And the interviewee would nod, gratefully, relieved that it has been spoken aloud but still unable to say it. *Comin' Home Soon* was another play in which interviewees often avoided direct references to the topic.

Comin' Home Soon was commissioned in 2012 by the Goulburn Regional Art Gallery, which for several years had sent Indigenous artists into Goulburn Correctional Centre to conduct visual art workshops with inmates. Jane Cush, the gallery director, contacted me because the inmates had told these artists incredible stories of their lives and experiences which she wanted to chronicle and present to the public. Jane had heard about my Junee workshops and asked if I could come up with an idea for both a visual art exhibition and a play, constructed around the inmates and their stories. I expressed interest and I asked if I could include work which I was doing with Shine for Kids, an organisation working with the children of prisoners. Jane enthusiastically agreed.

We prioritised the attachment of an Indigenous Project Associate and an Indigenous visual artist to the project. But the visual artist soon withdrew (entirely without acrimony, she just got other work) and suddenly we had to come up with an idea in consultation with the inmates themselves.

They agreed to draw black-and-white outlines of cultural totems and animals of their choice, like large children's colouring-in drawings. I then took the drawings to the Shine for Kids children (also Indigenous but not directly related by family), so they could colour them in. The creative work of drawing and colouring provided a terrific activity and conduit for discussion and a distraction that made the storytelling a fun, expressive, creative way to work towards a public exhibition, instead of a formalised interview process. By making handmade colouring-in templates for the Indigenous Shine for Kids participants, the inmate artists took the time to focus on and privilege a child's needs, which their incarceration prevented them from doing for their own families. Through their large, beautifully planned and executed outlines, they asserted their esteem for their own children, whom they missed, instilling a love of cultural knowledge and exhibiting guidance about the value of discipline and self-expression in the pictures they were making. The pictures were detailed and careful, they contained cultural symbols and a relationship with nature that the children responded to and the inmates longed for. But, most importantly, they required a child's hand to bring them to life. And in all of them, as the men and the children made art together, time continued to pass both inside and outside the jail walls, time that was being remade and readjusted into a productive future through this act of collaborative art, time that ticks and clicks and taps away from all of us every day and for them, every day inside.

The exhibition, mounted in 2013, showcased these artworks – made during and between my visits to the Aboriginal inmates in Nura Warra Umer at Goulburn Correctional Centre and then completed primarily by the children of Aboriginal inmates at the Shine for Kids complex at Silverwater Correctional Centre. During my visits to both centres I conducted workshops with inmates and children and invited them to talk, use their imaginations, tell me about their lives and reflect on their circumstances. The artworks were coloured in by the children, with creative assistance from Alison Murphy-Oates (Indigenous Project Associate), Leeann Turley (Manager of Community Programs, Shine for Kids), and me. Sometimes the children sat quietly in a circle and the only sound you could hear was of crayons scratching the surface; at other times Alison told them what her own father had taught her about the symbols in the artwork. Children came and went as relatives left to visit inmates in the adjoining complex and, when their arms got 'colouring-in fatigue', they jumped up for a little Wii tennis or foosball. One young artist was so engaged with the artworks that she was still experimenting with glue and glitter and colourful feathers as we were packing up.

Alison was an absolute boon at these the Shine for Kids workshops, regaling the children with stories that made them squeal with laughter and playing a mean game of foosball in the common area. I couldn't take a recorder into Goulburn, so the men wrote their words in exercise books and watched me scribbling copious notes as they revealed their feelings. The children played games and spoke freely about their hopes and fears and their ways of surviving. The volunteers and workers from Shine for Kids took a moment's breather to give me the benefit of their many years of experience.

For the play I compiled and reflected on everything shared with me during my visits. Much of it is verbatim transcripts of interviews and the rest is inspired by, or contains aspects of, stories told to me. During a public reading of the play in Goulburn in January 2013, a number of people commented on the lack of swearing of the inmates, the 'sophistication' of both their language and the children's, and the diversity of things they chose to talk about. Some even ventured to wonder if they really 'sounded' like Aboriginal inmates or why the children sounded so very 'grown up'.

A playwright using verbatim material lives and breathes for such comments and, frankly, does a little dance about them because they demonstrate how close work theatre has a unique power to surprise and shift audience assumptions about how individuals and communities express themselves. What an inmate might say privately to another inmate, a police officer or to their Aboriginal elder is one thing; my contract with the audience was to pass on words and stories said to me. And through the children we hear a story which so often is poignantly and destructively unsaid. I rejoice they found their voices and had the courage to be so candid and honest with me and, through me, the audience.

Ultimately the play is about the contradictions and pains of trying to be a parent from jail, about how children try to hide their parent's incarceration from their school and others, of how too often the general community believe that the children of prisoners also deserve to be punished. It was produced by the Lieder Theatre in Goulburn, Australia's oldest amateur theatre, directed by Chrisjohn Hancock, and involved a cast of seventeen, seven of whom were Indigenous. In a

Q&A after one performance, an audience member said that she failed to empathise with the men in the play because, she didn't know what crimes they had committed. I tried to explain that the play was about the problems of parenting but soon became exasperated. Alfie Walker, a cast member and the Chair of the Pejar Aboriginal Land Council, jumped in and said how this was no longer Alana's play but *our* play, and he also spoke very movingly about how the project made him realise that these incarcerated men were part of the Goulburn community.

Comin' Home Soon won the AWGIE for best Youth and Community Play in 2014 and is published by Snowy Owl Press. Here is one child's perspective on where her father has gone and why:

> He got washed down the dunny. He got flushed down the dunny for throwing my chinese african american half human bunny called honey down the dunny. it was only funny when he tried to get out of the dunny. He finally landed in asia and ran off with a runny shark chinese african american bunny that had flushed the dunny and he got flushed back to me.

25

Pausing for effect

I had just parked the car at the local supermarket and opened the door to get out, when I heard a fellow on his mobile phone in the car opposite. He was having the kind of conversation that keeps a playwright in the car with the window wound down.

'When you're selling something, mate, here's what I do. You've got the bloke on the phone and you say to him, "Listen, mate, I don't want to scare you but the truth is … there's someone else interested in this one. So if you want it you should make an offer now. I'm just sayin' … because I don't want you to be disappointed, you know". You gotta do that, mate, or they muck you around, deciding, you know'.

There are two ways of seeing this. Is it the classic con – make like you're somebody's friend, doing them a real favour, when you're really hustling them for a quick sale? Or is it a tough-won understanding of human nature – people can dither around making a decision and you need to find a way to help them into it for both your sake and theirs? Well, as a writer you can see both perspectives.

Playwrights conducting interviews can learn something from upping the stakes and creating a deadline. You don't want to interview people for more than an hour. Maximum. Occasionally it will go over to about 80 minutes but really, once you're pushing the 90 minute mark you need to get out of there. You need to let them tell their favourite tales, hit them with some really curly questions, and then ramp it up to wrap it up. Why? Because you are going to have to sort through all of your interviewee contributions for your play and I have found that there is a limit to how much I can juggle in my brain on any one project (and I rarely have only one project in my brain at a time). In most cases you should be able to get your interviewee to articulate their perspective and experience in that time limit. I'm not saying there are not exceptions, but the one-hour interview should be your general rule. And like our canny salesman above, a time limit might help both your interviewee and yourself to get to the guts more quickly.

If you have been actively listening in an effective way, your interviewee is experiencing a potentially rare moment in their life where what they say is of consequence. As they've been happily exploring the inner workings of their own mind with your professional guidance, they've been surprising themselves with what they know and what they think. They may have thought things that they knew, but never put into words in quite this way before. It's been amazing, joyful, surprising and challenging in a good way. They just want to keep going. But you're not going to let them. You're going to say something like, 'Well thank you for so much of your time. It's been amazing speaking to you. Is there anything finally that you'd like to say?'

The shock of all of this coming to the end means that they'll probably say something like 'No, no, I think I've said enough'. Or they may add something that will really surprise you. But whatever you do don't stand up, don't move, don't go anywhere. It's not over. Not even nearly. Be generous and appreciative – they've given you the only thing any of us really have that's ours – our story. But once the recorder is off my experience has been that people may now tell you something that they haven't 'dared' to say 'on the record'. You may like to tease this out and persuade them to keep talking. And then, politely, but firmly ask if it's okay to turn the recorder back on because you've 'just got to get this'. If they say no, respect that. But more often than not *they* will be as interested as you are in what they might say next and will want it recorded.

Sometimes the best material will be caught after you thought the interview was over. I'm not sure what it is about human nature that stalls and then yields in this way. It's not that you are trying to 'trick' your interviewee, or get them to say something on the record that is going to get them into trouble. Quite the opposite, you are acknowledging that the previous hour has yielded new insights or revelations only now forming in their minds. Contradictory, unformed and preciously mutable insights which come from inside a lived experience. You are reaping the conversational harvest for your future theatre audience, bringing back the riches from this moment, a moment that is going to end, like theatre ends and so too, dare I say, does life. So you are valorising the time you have shared together and the connection you have made about this community.

It's not a science experiment – people aren't Pavlov's dog – so you won't get the same results every time. Sometimes the interview will end right there. Or they'll say more but nothing interesting or useable, or someone else has said it better and you're going to use them instead. Some people say the most interesting things in the first ten minutes and the rest is just padding. Every human being is different and can be slippery or cranky or evasive. No formula will work every time. Mostly you want to create a genuine, honest connection and let people have their head. Sincerity is a rarer quality than you might imagine and I would urge you to develop a true interest in your subject. Good technique can yield results even when your interviewee has been interviewed many times before. Because in the moment, in the thrill of an enthralling interview, an interviewee may want to be drawn out and will be grateful that you 'found' all this material hiding in the corners of their brain.

26

Extreme playwriting

I'm sitting in a padded seat, gripping the underside of the vinyl to convince myself that it makes me feel more secure. I'm midair, in the passenger seat of a helicopter, hovering over a Panamax class bulk carrier about 5 kilometres off the coast of Newcastle. In the back seat of the helicopter is the marine pilot for the Port of Newcastle. In a moment, after we land, I am going to follow him as he scuttles across the ship's deck and quickly climbs the ladder to the bridge to inform the ship's captain that he will now guide his ship through the narrow mouth of the harbour entrance and secure it to its berth.

I had to wait about a week for this helicopter transfer, and the subtleties of weather have become second nature to me. For days there has been too much wind or too much swell, or both, and they wouldn't take me out. One of the first things I learn is that for marine pilots every day is fluid and responsive to the elements. The weather affects everything about their job, to the point where the amount of fresh water in the harbour determines the speed at which they push a ship through the harbour entrance.

I've been co-commissioned to write a play for Tantrum Theatre Company in Newcastle in conjunction with the Australian Theatre for Young People (ATYP) in Sydney. I had earlier come to Newcastle to work with Tantrum's artistic director Brendan O'Connell and to mentor a young writer called Dean Blackford who was writing a play about his experience in the Australian Army Reserve. When I spoke to a number of other Tantrum participants I asked them, 'So if you had to tell people something about Newcastle, about what makes it distinctive, about why you like it, what would you tell them?' They said the beach, the lifestyle, the beach, the arts scene, the beach, the laid back lifestyle. 'The port?' I asked. 'No way', they said, readily sneering. 'I barely notice that it is even a port.' The largest coal port in the world to be exact. Barely notice it.

Partly because of this stated indifference, I deliberately created a tale at an intersection between the port and this Newcastle youth theatre. I have a genuine interest in all things on water and a passionate interest in shipping. My stepfather had worked his way around the world as a cabin hand on cruise liners and he still sails regularly to Antarctica on Russian-made icebreakers. I wrote a play for the Australian National Maritime Museum about Matthew Flinders and his black sheep of a brother called Samuel. Give me a sextant and the smell of a stiff breeze and I am happy. Later when I did my Museum Studies diploma, several of my assignments were set at the Australian National Maritime Museum (about the Welcome Wall where migrants engraved their names) and it was my first choice when I had to elect somewhere to do my compulsory three month internship. Shipping was (and remains) a great attraction to me, anything really that involves large machines or vessels of any kind, but I find ocean liners, tankers and bulk carriers an endless source of interest.

In every Australian port an Australian marine pilot brings in visiting container ships, bulk carriers and ocean liners. Each port around the country has upwards of twenty-three marine pilots depending on its size, so there are hundreds of them. To become a marine pilot you must first be a captain. When I was researching, there were seven female marine pilots in Australia including Captain Sandra Risk in Newcastle.

Grounded is about a young woman who wants to be a marine pilot and how the Pasha Bulker, the Panamax bulk carrier famously grounded on Newcastle's Nobbys Beach in 2007, affects her decision. The play contains several pure verbatim moments as well as a structured narrative that is based around my research about the port, the Pasha and the experience of being a young adult in a regional city. The grounding of the Pasha provides a dramatic crisis in the central character's notions of identity, future prospects and how the world works.

One of the first things that ATYP's artistic director, Fraser Corfield said to me when he read a draft of *Grounded*, was 'Alana, you've actually made shipping seem really interesting'. 'But shipping really is interesting', I exclaimed. 'Yeah', he bobbed his head left and right in doubt, 'But I'm still not convinced about why Farrah would be so obsessed with it. I mean, why would a young woman be so obsessed?' 'Just lucky I guess' is not really a response to such a dramaturgical question, but I had no trouble believing in my character Farrah's predilection for how she floated her boat.

Grounded was a great process – two magnificent workshops with the local young adults at Tantrum, and then a terrific cast for the production at the Civic and subsequently the Wharf. Cassie Tongue of aussietheatre.com.au reviewed it in Sydney, saying 'There's a truth to the dialogue that's rare, there's a truth to the dialogue that makes this play profound'.

I took several things from the experience – a report that the retiring harbour master was sitting in the audience crying with pride as he watched the show, the support of many marine pilots on opening night and through the season, the boundless enthusiasm and serious achievements of the cast, a splendid publication by Currency (now in its second print run), two AWGIE statues, an engraved leather bound notebook and a cheque for $25,000 for the inaugural David Williamson Prize for Excellence in Writing for the Australian Theatre. Then Suzie Miller, who took her young son to see it, told me that one day at the breakfast table he compared Farrah's obsession with shipping to one of his friends at school. He conjectured that, like Farrah, his friend's obsessions might be a psychological reaction to losing her father. That anecdote from a generous fellow playwright beat every accolade.

27

Beyond the fourth wall

Peter Bishop called me when he was the head impresario at Varuna the National Writers' House in the Blue Mountains outside Sydney to say they had funding to send writers out into the regions to conduct workshops. He wondered if I would like a Longlines Fellowship. 'How far out into the regions?' I asked. 'Katherine', he replied, 'in the Northern Territory, they've specifically requested a playwright'. I was interested for a couple of reasons. First, I had never been to Katherine and have an ambition to explore every corner of Australia, so this would service that desire. Second, they *specifically requested* a playwright? Unheard of. Regional areas were full of aspiring novelists in my experience, prose writers who could give urban upstarts a run for their money. But a writer's centre who requested a playwright? This I had to see.

I first visited Katherine in April 2006 and though they were into the Dry, it was still bloody hot. I was housed in a small apartment at the back of the Anglican church: 'Where they put women who come in from the bush to have their babies. Where they stay while they're waiting to give birth'. I liked it immediately. I get a lot of mileage out of a story I tell about cooking lamb chops one evening when the apartment filled with flies. I found a way to drive most of them out, and then the screen door was thick with them trying to get back in. 'Yeah, only with lamb,' said the locals, 'Stick to the beef.' They had their laughs with me as a Territory rookie. 'You're not a vegetarian, are you?' they said, as soon as I arrived. 'Everyone from Sydney is vegetarian, or gay.' Ah, no, not a vegetarian I assured them.

I decided to conduct the workshops about writing for radio, rather than to build up their hopes for an Australian mainstage production. I'm not saying that can't happen. But a half hour radio drama was genuinely within their reach. They could flex their dramatic muscles and offer the national broadcaster an all too rare view from the Top End. What's more, their fellow Territorians would hear it since Radio National broadcast in Katherine. It's an opportunity that's since been lost because of savage cuts to the ABC. Sound artists and radio dramatists must now find a way through podcasts, internet broadcasts and community radio.

I played the assembled group of twelve aspiring dramatists a radio work of mine called *Salvaged* about the devastation of New Orleans by Hurricane Katrina in 2005. I had visited the city months before the maelstrom had struck, to attend a museum theatre conference in the same conference centre that became the site of horrific suffering by the stranded residents. I also conducted interviews for a commissioned radio feature. When the city was flattened and flooded by the hurricane after I got back to Australia, I could hardly ignore it. So I made a work that reflected on what one does with memories and experiences from a place that no longer exists either physically or spiritually. How does one clear away the trash of nostalgia along with all the other things one junks after a flood?

It was an uncannily apt choice. Had I done my research I would have known that Katherine had been devastated by an 18-metre flood in 1998 and, as I soon found out, the psychological and physical scars remained. When I set an exercise for participants to write an internal monologue from the perspective of an individual of their choice, several stories focused on flood victims still suffering recurring nightmares and stress from the crisis. A coyness also emerged, a discomfort inherent in writing about small-town life – the ever-present danger that others in the group will know, or guess, your subject. The difficulty of wanting to dive deep versus the dangerous stakes of exposing people others might know. It wasn't something my anonymous experience in the metropolis could really help them with.

During this first workshop I heard that the group had plans to write a play to commemorate the tenth anniversary of the Katherine flood. That's why they asked for a playwright. I outlined the problems I anticipated with a group-devised and group-performed work. I suggested strategies for building in 'fringe' and 'alternative' perspectives, and instructed them on interviewing techniques. It was important that the work not only look through the sometimes rose-coloured glasses of hindsight, I told them.

In terms of Peter Bishop's stated aims for the Longlines Fellowship it was a slam dunk. It was a brilliant workshop process that created a durable, deeply-felt connection with a vibrant community of writers, genuinely reaching for literary and soon, I hoped, dramatic excellence. I was so inspired that when I returned to Sydney I convinced the ABC's Regional Arts Fund to commission the Katherine Regional Arts Centre (KRAC) and myself to produce a short feature with short stories by six members of the group. I returned to Katherine to record the writers reading their stories, sometimes on location, with some judicious editing and dramaturgy along the way. I also recorded some background material for sound environments and effects.

On this second visit, the problems I had forecast for the flood play were emerging. They couldn't find a way to wrangle someone to actually *write* the thing. It's funny how many times in my career I have heard someone say, 'I've done all the research and all the thinking and I know what I want it to be, I just haven't actually written it'. Yes, because that's what a writer does. So many people think that because anyone *can* write, writing is easy. Funny how many people don't see the next step as *the* writing gift. Funny how many people think that if only they could find the time and the discipline they could be a writer. And, apart from when there are cultural considerations, it is not really funny when they want a co-credit as the writer when they've never actually typed or written anything on a blank page – hey, they've done the research and the background and everything, that's almost like writing it isn't it? No, it's not. Co-writing is when you bring in pages and I get to pencil mark them, like you get to pencil mark mine. Co-writing is not me writing it and you changing it and me retyping it up. Not *really*. I once sat with a director–dramaturg and structured an entire play. Later, when we were talking about the credit, he argued that structure is dramaturgy, not writing. In the end I said to him, 'Put it this way, if you do it, because you're a recognised dramaturg, it's dramaturgy, and if I do it, because I'm a recognised playwright, it's writing'.

'Would you put it together for us?' KRAC asked me. I agreed because the profoundly well-connected and superb Katherine-based writer Toni Tapp Coutts agreed to be my research assistant. She would purchase a small MP3 player and, in consultation with me, record interviews with community members which she would email to me to transcribe and include in the play.

Writing for community performers or youth theatre performers is different to writing for trained actors. As the writer you can build work which supports amateur performers and uses their assets to their best effect – assets such as sincerity, authenticity and enthusiasm. In the case of *Watermark*, the play about Katherine's flood, I structured a long poem to embody the flood waters and provide a central narration for the work. The poem wound through the work, connecting the various perspectives gathered from the emailed interviews and others I'd done myself. I also wrote scenes that distilled some of the aspects of human nature displayed in the verbatim monologues included from the interviews.

I directed a public reading of *Watermark* in the Katherine cinema in January 2008, on the tenth anniversary of the flood. There were eighteen community performers and we decorated the stage with a line of blue silk cloths, to represent the flooding waters. As more than two hundred members of the community came into the cinema to see the reading, they were turned away from the front ten rows, told that they were 'reserved' for VIP guests. When the time for the reading neared and the front rows remained unoccupied I began to get quite antsy. The time ticked away and still no-one arrived to take up the prime positions. Eventually the seats were released to the general public and a few people moved into them but I still recall that evening, playing to a packed cinema, with the front stalls only irregularly occupied. The night started with speeches. And then, at last, the lights went down and the play was read to an attentive audience.

I will never forget the moment, almost towards the end of the play, commemorating the people who had died as a result of the flood waters. Using the transcript from the Territory parliament, it named the people and detailed the circumstances. At the time, the parliamentarian reading this had asked his fellow politicians to stand for a minute's silence. I included this as an authentic part of the record. We had asked a few people associated with the cast to stand at this moment, to see if it might encourage others in the audience to do the same. We needn't have bothered. Almost before the invitation to stand was issued, the entire house got to its feet and stood, silent, respectful, grateful to be able to respond to the pain and heartbreak outlined. It was a precious moment that anyone who works in community theatre will know well – that moment when the work of art becomes a conduit for spontaneous community feeling. It's not a moment you can plan or control or construct, but you can set up the conditions before you surrender to a phenomenon much bigger than yourself.

I have had that moment so many times in my career. The closing night of *Run Rabbit Run* when, at the very end of the work, the fans and audience at Belvoir went absolutely nuts as if Souths had won the grand final (as they were to do years later); the opening night of *Parramatta Girls* when the Indigenous and non-Indigenous ex-inmates came onto the stage together for a standing ovation; the opening night of *Dead Man Brake* when crash survivors and paramedics from the Waterfall train disaster joined the actors on stage for a final bow, the deceased train driver's mother making her way so slowly and so tentatively to the stage; the opening night of *Ladies Day*, arm in arm with gay men living in Broome; the opening of *Letters to Lindy* in Wollongong when Lindy Chamberlain-Creighton spoke her words of endorsement in the foyer after the play – so many others, *every* time I have worked with community big or small, every time there is a moment that sears onto your brain and your soul. The moments when people from the audience at a Blue Knot Day event, many of them victims of childhood sexual abuse, came forward to read part of my play *Swimming Upstream* in a public space; at the Q&A after *Comin' Home Soon* when the Chair of the Pejar Aboriginal Land Council, Alfie Walker, took control of the feedback later saying 'Alana this is no longer your play, this is ours'. The moment when the Outback Theatre for Young People performed *Eyes to the Floor*, the story of the Hay Institution for Girls, in the actual Hay Gaol in front of women who had been incarcerated there in their childhood; the public reading of *The Tree Widows*, inspired by an avenue of trees planted to commemorate Tasmanian casualties in World War One, with relatives of the soldiers in the audience, crying; the front row on the opening night of *Shafana and Aunt Sarrinah* occupied with hijab-wearing young women; Newcastle's only female marine pilot smiling as she sat through the production of *Grounded*.

Nothing I do on stage is ever as moving, as significant or as indelible as these moments of audience response. For me, perhaps perversely, the play is *not* the thing. It is the rare, unifying, utterly intangible response of the audience during or after the performance that keeps me coming back into the theatre. For me it's not *enough* just to sit in an audience and appreciate great artistry on stage from dedicated, talented or even spectacularly gifted artists. Maybe this is the nub of what drives me and, horror of horrors, perhaps my motivational engine is not purely artistic. I revere good art, I work to produce it; I resent bad art which is reductive or bland or merely a decadent set of distractions. But in the final wash my deepest motivation is a fascination with the behaviour of the collective, with the moment when the individual is subsumed into the group, when the crowd has power and purpose. My life's work has been to reproduce that moment in the controlled, almost lab-like conditions of the theatre. I work to participate in this moment over and over. It is why I can see a perfectly good production of a well-written play, performed capably, directed thoughtfully and received politely and go home empty and dissatisfied.

People often ask artists if they think about the audience and they mostly reply, 'No, not at all, I do what I want and then let the audience make what they want of it'. That is not me. I think about the audience all the time – how they will receive it, their potential response and what they might collectively be caught up in and reveal to me in *that moment* at the end. I stayed in Darwin for all ten public performances of the world premiere production of *Head Full of Love* and, at every one, audiences gave generously to a fund we raised for the Purple House, where I had done my research. The actors Colette Mann and Roxanne McDonald collected $15,000 for the Purple House and a further $45,000 from the Queensland Theatre Company run.

Actors in my plays often say that they don't want the run to end, that the experience of connecting with a 'real' community has changed their life. This is not me boasting, but articulating what I have worked my life to conjure into the theatre and it goes beyond what you might see on stage. Lee Lewis, the current artistic director of Griffin Theatre Company, watching the first night of *Head Full of Love* told me that she was always struck by the way in which I found a deep connection with the community of interest I was writing about. My work is not just about the artefact on stage. My plays are about what happens in the audience when you mix middle-class theatregoers with a real live subculture. My artistry is as much about what happens in the audience as it is about what happens on stage.

Watermark was such a success that Festivals Australia funded us to do a return production at the Katherine Festival in 2009. We borrowed a 3-metre fibreglass crocodile from a local retailer to put onto the front of the stage, where we also set a mess of all the debris, rubbish and other flotsam churned up by the 18-metre flood. The party of twelve readers then travelled to Darwin to present a reading of the play as part of the Darwin Festival. *Watermark* won the AWGIE Award in 2009 for Community and Youth Theatre.

28

Your truest self

In 2004 I was approached by Canberra director Camilla Blunden to write a play with music. An actor and singer named Julie McElhone had done a considerable amount of research about cross-dressing women in the Australian theatre around the turn of the 20th century and wondered if I would be interested in distilling the research into a play. Camilla ran a significant women's theatre company called Women on a Shoestring and she had secured a production spot at Canberra's Street Theatre to present the play. She just needed someone interested in working with Julie and musician Peter J. Casey to write it.

At the time I was writing plays with non-gender-specific casting requirements. My plays *Savage Grace* and *Love Potions* both specify that the gender of the cast is at the discretion of the director. My contention is that gender constructs can be used to advantage the status quo, by positing some people as 'different' and ticking a box about activism within the system. In the same way constructing a notion of diversity can reinforce an (unchanged) dominant paradigm by nominating individuals as exemplars instead of changing the system as a whole. In my work I was trying to establish alternate gender ideas integrated into a norm of changed consciousness. That phrase 'close work' comes back to mind since my experience with young adults, the queer community and the inventive curiosity of gifted actors had encouraged me to give directors multiple choices rather than selectively privileging alternative identities up front.

So initially I wasn't interested in Camilla's proposal. Cross-dressing is inherently theatrical and has been used as a tool of rebellion for the queer communities for years and yet I was struggling with the desire to write a work which celebrated the transformative power of clothing and the continuing questioning of gender politics through dress. I just didn't find it radical *enough* I suppose. Gnawing away at me was the notion that aesthetic choices in both the content and form of theatre can masquerade as signifiers instead of instigating real change. Historical passion had driven Julie to do the research but male impersonation wasn't a metaphor that resonated for me. I had no interest in writing historical documentary and I was now living in the 21st century where the freedom to dress in whatever you liked was so commonplace as to be unnoticeable. Indeed I think one of the hardest things to dramatise for an audience is what it is like to not have freedoms that we now take for granted. What could such research possibly have to say to women in 21st-century Australia? Why would I want to live and breathe this material for the time it took to make it into drama?

So I said no. Politely, regrettably, but no, don't think so. And then I went away and thought about it. What if I could construe a character who was a 'reluctant' cross-dresser? What if I could, using the research, look at the way women in theatre face a crisis of employment once they begin to get 'too old' to play the soubrette? What if I created a lead character, a performer called Mirabella, who had to compete for work with performers imported from overseas by theatre managements? What if at first she wears male clothes out of desperation but soon finds that she actually likes the liberation and freedoms they confer? Yes, I was finding a dramatic premise that linked me to the work. What would happen, I asked, if life could still find a way to surprise us, just when we thought we were jaded and faded and all washed up? What if your accepted version of yourself was suddenly challenged and you found a new one, a new 'me' that you actually liked? I rang back and said yes.

Now that could be a play I wanted to write. I would use the lens of 'cross-dressing women at the turn of the century' but the play would be about a concern not for that time or this but (I hoped) all time. A concern not just for women in theatre but women and men everywhere. And the question was real for me. Could life really surprise me still?

This was one of the first times I wrote lyrics for songs, nine songs in total, and thanks to the genius of Peter J Casey and Julie McElhone's compositions I found the show deeply creatively satisfying. I went on to put songs in many of my works, not least, *Dead Man Brake* and later *Barbara and the Camp Dogs*. *Butterfly Dandy* was my first production in Canberra and the beginning of an ongoing love affair with that city, an incomparable playground for a writer. A city full of interesting, well-informed people who are not scared of intellectual ideas, who are skilled at the nuances of making an argument and defending it, who *as a matter of professional competence* know that it is always worth considering alternative points of view, if only to learn how to destroy them.

Rosalba Clemente, former artistic director of the State Theatre Company of South Australia and a brilliant actor with whom I had the privilege to work on *Spool Time*, once talked to me about 'delivering the envelope but finding nothing inside'. What she was talking about, I think, was the artist's ability to change and shift and mutate into many selves and, in the context of the dominant paradigm, to become whatever is necessary to be able to work. To find an outward appearance and persona that can 'pass' you into multiple contexts but then, when it comes to digging down into the truth of yourself, into the grit and muck and glitter and motivation for being an artist, finding that who you are in the essence of yourself is not what is welcome. It's why you need to do the work and find colleagues who speak to the deepest part of you. Of course you need to have the ambition to practise your creativity in a range of contexts, the self-belief to see yourself at the pinnacle of your art form. But my advice is to believe it will happen for you when you have the colleagues and story, and an opportunity to tell the story that reflects your truest self. In short, you can fake it till you make it but if you keep on faking it, in the end you are faking it only to yourself.

29

Doing dawn

At 5am the day before Anzac Day in 2007, I am standing on a cobbled street in Istanbul, ready to board a bus for the Gallipoli Peninsula. The coach is full of twenty-something Australians and New Zealanders making the pilgrimage to the Anzac site. One of them says to me excitedly, 'Haven't you just *always* wanted to go to Gallipoli?' and I reply, evenly, 'No, actually I am only here to find out why you all are'. When we stop for a breakfast of hot cheese gözleme I slide up next to them in the cafe booth and ask them about their motivations. I am writing a verbatim play called *Doing Dawn*, about the contemporary phenomenon of tens of thousands of Australians turning up in Turkey to commemorate Anzac Day. They give me stirring, fascinating answers that go well beyond the commonly assumed 'Big Day Out goes to Turkey' scenario. There is a young Indigenous man travelling to the site to honour one of his elders; a Kiwi who has crocheted a wreath of woollen red poppies to lay at the site for a great-great-grandfather; and a whole bus full of others with moving reasons for being there. Because of drunken behaviour by a crass minority there are alcohol restrictions, but that is nothing compared to the security restrictions that will dominate in the years ahead.

When we get to the small fishing village of Gelibolu, they head straight for the fast food and burgers. I dash away for a break from their unreconstructed patriotism, seeking my own lunch in a little Turkish restaurant where I find kebabs and salad and a cold glass of wine.

Rising at dawn at the end of April is familiar to me. As a child, I remember putting on a short white gym outfit with a Legacy Torch patch sewn onto the front, and huge red bloomers drooping out underneath because my mother left it to the last minute to buy them and there were only XXL left. All this for the local RSL in return for their free weekly gym classes, an activity with its own ritual. At the end of every class, the lights would go off and the mayhem and chaos of a room full of teen and pre-teen children would suddenly quieten down as, like a crowd of hypnotised eloi in H. G. Wells' *The Time Machine*, we turned to face the Legacy Torch glowing red and solemn on the back wall. A recording of the Last Post would play, followed by a recorded recitation of the 'Ode of Remembrance', which we would repeat in unison:

> They shall grow not old, as we that are left grow old;
> Age shall not weary them, nor the years condemn.
> At the going down of the sun and in the morning
> We will remember them.

And then, in unison, sixty-plus children would say, 'We will remember them'. 'Lest we forget', the recorded voice would say, and we would respond 'Lest we forget'. And then the lights would come up and we would run around, shouting and screaming and forgetting why we were there and the sacrifice we had just commemorated. The young dramatist in me loved the ritual, the poetry, the suspense of the lights going down, the focus, and discovering a deep notion of the sacred that it conjured into my suburban Australian experience.

As the years went by, and my formal obligation to the RSL was no longer required, I still always went to Anzac Day out of respect and habit. I remember being excited in Canberra at the Australian National Playwrights' Conference for the chance to attend the dawn service at the Australian War Memorial. I kept it a secret from what I thought was surely a conference full of non–Anzac Day colleagues. But then a couple of the Indigenous actors confessed that they were going to the service and we could all sneak out together. In front of the exquisite architecture of the War Memorial, we watched each other and recognised something about the nature of class and commemoration that was common among our forebears.

I have never been offended by people who don't go to Anzac services. I loved Alan Seymour's *The One Day of the Year*, and told him so, years later, when I was on an Australian Writers' Guild committee with him. Of course it is not disrespectful, but deeply respectful to interrogate a profoundly-held belief. Anything that has real mettle can stand up to a robust intellectual and emotional questioning and Seymour represented all sides of the conflict with integrity and brilliance. The pilgrims on the bus with me were removed by a generation from the legacy of physically and psychologically war-wounded fathers, but they were reverencing this history in a different way. Verbatim testimony was the way to chronicle how and why.

When we got back on the bus in Gelibolu we were joined by a remarkable old Turkish sea captain named Captain Ali, who provided an elaborate historical commentary of the bungled landing, from both the Turkish and Allied perspectives. He knew enough about Antipodeans to know that his strongest card for the day would be British incompetence. When we got to Anzac Cove, I settled onto the rough grass in my sleeping bag. Without a plastic groundsheet my hips and back were taking some punishment, but a couple of codeine tablets eased the pain. And now the familiar features of the site were beginning to work an eerie magic on me. It is genuinely disorientating to be somewhere you have never been before whose topography you know *so well*. The Sphinx, the Nek, Lone Pine, Chunuk Bair. I recorded interviews with scores more young pilgrims who were effusive, overwhelmed and intense. I didn't sleep so much as doze fitfully. I didn't want to come all this way and snore through the service. Though with the PA and the huge screen constantly showing First World War documentaries, there was not much chance of that. I learnt about Māori battalions and Atatürk and the courage of the nurses.

And then at dawn the service begins. And I watch thousands of young Australians stand silently in their garish, fluorescent yellow and green beanies, and New Zealanders in their black and white. It is impossible to resist the psychological pull of participating in this ritual – out on a bleak, cold peninsula with ten thousand other people honouring an idea – even if you have questions about the compromises, the history, the culpability, the tragedy, the meaninglessness, the colonial ideology, the motivation or the mythology. There are tears streaming down the faces of every young adult I can see and there are tears streaming down my face too – the cold, the fatigue, the deaths, the courage, the carnage. Australians being solemn. Being profoundly serious. It's something to behold.

Later, Yalin Ozucelik's mother translated sections of my play into Turkish, something I have not seen in any play about the Anzac experience. Ten years later, fewer Australians travelled to Turkey because of security threats. The verbatim testimonies I chose try to capture the contradictions and the complex nature of the motivations for pilgrimage. Maybe, when the upcoming generation begin to wonder why so many people used to go to Gallipoli, this research will come into its own. And for you, the writer unable to get on stage the play you think has urgent relevance the lesson is this. Your bottom drawer is not an abyss, it is your library for the future.

30

All the beautiful students

It is May 2011 and I am in a foyer, surrounded by over a hundred international students – Indian, Chinese, Korean, Singaporean, and Malaysian. BOObook Theatre have just opened a production of my play *Student Body* at Melbourne University's Union House Theatre. There is wine from a cask and cheese and cabanossi on toothpicks and the students are responding excitedly to seeing versions of themselves on stage – the performers are Keith Brockett, Sheena Reyes, Ash Kakkar, Rachel Fong and Kelly Ryan. I am staying in the lounge room of the producer and artistic director of BOObook, Sue Lindsay, where her resourceful husband has made a fantastic 'spare room' for me by hanging sheets up to make a dark space to sleep in.

The entire first night audience of students stay back to speak to me after the production. They are frank and tough. They oscillate between wild praise and harsh criticism. They acknowledge that their response is more critical because they see themselves represented so rarely; they admit that they imbue their feedback with deeply subjective personal perspectives. They are animated to the point of hysteria, buzzing with opinion and possibilities and the unique energy of having seen their lives dramatised on the public stage. I am completely overwhelmed and utterly thrilled by the passion and fierce ownership of their response.

Almost without exception, they commented on the fact that each of the student characters spoke 'broken' English in a different, culturally specific way that reflected how their own individual language works. Too often, they told me, characters from an Asian or Indian background either speak perfect English or a kind of chopped-up patois that is simplified and uniform across all ethnicities. As if new English speakers all learn English in the same way and express it in the same tentative, broken style. In fact, as I found, and faithfully represented from my verbatim process, the Thai student spoke English in an entirely different way to the Chinese or Indian student – not simply with a different accent. For example, in Manglish (Malaysian English) sentences tend to be short and sharp and sound authentic when used with an accent. Chinese students have longer sentences but disregard the use of tense or plural: 'I do' instead of 'I did', 'tooths' instead of 'teeth'. Perhaps I remember this feedback most because this aspect of my play had, in fact, provoked a good deal of criticism when I showed it to industry professionals. Even though I had faithfully transcribed what the students had said to me, *on the page* broken English can look patronising and seem derogatory. So while teachers from RMIT and Melbourne University told me about teaching issues specific to the first language of their students, theatre industry professionals told me that when they read my script the characters came across as, well, a bit simple and my treatment bordered on offensive.

'But that's how they speak', I would try to explain, 'of course their English is broken, they're learning'.

'Yes, but you've made them sound … well, they sound … unsophisticated.'

'But isn't there a difference between how they speak and what we see them do? I mean, isn't the drama about their actions, not just their speech? Don't we see their complexity and dimensionality in their actions?'

'Maybe, but this is a verbatim play so it's all about how they speak.'

'I think you're misunderstanding verbatim and the use of broken English, and I think you're somehow ashamed of your own assumptions about these students.'

No, of course I didn't say the last line. Suffice to say that the more diverse the experience of people in positions of power in the theatre are, the more we will see the theatre genuinely reflect the world we live in. It's probably the most frustrating experience I have had of not being able to unpick the response to my work. Was the world of the play so unfamiliar to the industry readers that they could not appreciate the veracity of the characters on the page? Speaking in a dialect of English, appropriating words in surprising and comic ways – was it all too close for comfort? Is it uncomfortable to laugh at a Thai student, for instance, using the word 'seldom', in a way seldom used by English speakers, because it feels patronising, even though they would laugh at themselves when they discovered that their 'misuse' of English could make their expressions arcane or crude or comic? It's like people reading working-class characters and conflating the extent of a character's vocabulary with the sophistication of their analysis or experience of the world. Apparently only those who speak well have the deep, philosophical experiences of life worthy of the theatre. I do NOT think.

My first contact with international students was a decade earlier when I did a Graduate Diploma in Museum Studies at the University of Sydney. There were a lot of international students in the course and many seemed to get a pretty raw deal, fleeced but also ignored, because they weren't showing up on the cultural or even journalistic radar at that stage. I started sniffing around for a story that would go beyond a current affairs type exposé and applied to the Australia Council to write about them. No success. But they remained in the back of my mind as phantoms in our presence, thousands and thousands of them pumping billions and billions into the economy. These, potentially the next generations of leaders in business and politics in their respective countries, were taking back lasting impressions of Australia. In 2004, when Melbourne Theatre Company asked me to pitch them ideas for a play I included an outline for *Student Body* and secured a commission.

I began to research the play in earnest, hanging around the RMIT and Monash campuses, speaking to education providers, English teachers, counsellors, people in the Department of Immigration and students – from Indonesia, Singapore, mainland China, Thailand, Malaysia and India. I finished a draft of the play by 2007 but the MTC declined to produce it. It was agonising to witness the 2008 riots in Melbourne, to sit in front of the TV night after night and hear the voice of these students, making it into the cultural discourse because of repeated violence and perceived racism. All those years I had tried to find a way to bring their voice and concerns onto the public stage in a dynamic, dramatic and entertaining way and I still wanted to honour the generosity of those who had trusted me with their stories and their voices. I had to have another go. I sat down to rewrite the play, amid the continuing controversy over student attacks and was swept back into their fascinating experience – the stories of coming from all over the world to (in their view) quiet little Melbourne, where at nights the streets are eerily still, even in the city. The fiery activism fostered at the Union of Students, the intense problems with gambling, the fascination with adult shops and strip clubs, the tendency for students to 'stick' to groups of students with a similar background and the implications this has for their studies and socialisation in Australia. When BOObook agreed to produce the work I was elated. I was slightly awed at the generosity and passionate rigour of the students that now surrounded me in the foyer after the opening.

When you have the choice between representing your verbatim subjects with an authenticity that may be misunderstood or smoothing them out into a version that can be more easily digested, you know I am going to tell you to take the high road and the long view. Frankly, don't give any power to what the powerful want – write the world as you see it, as it is. That world will *eventually* come round to your version because it is truthful. Find a flaw in your characters and your community that they will reasonably acknowledge is the case. Give it a title that will attract the community of interest and intrigue your faithful theatregoer. Find a moment of inner conflict and genuine doubt in your characters and your communities – you're not a mirror, you're a writer, so have the courage to give your audiences your perspective. And if some find it hard to read on the page – remember that the page is not its ultimate destination.

31
The wounded public

In 2016 Mrs Lindy Chamberlain-Creighton generously invited me to her home to look through a batch of letters before they were sent to the National Library (NLA). They were sorted and filed in the usual manner, but rather than the archive boxes that I had previously seen in the NLA here they were in Sanitarium sultana boxes. It was infinitely easier to access them this way than via the relatively-simple but still protracted library retrieval process. I only needed to bend to the floor and select the files of interest, which I did. And that's when I felt an alarming tear in the centre back seam of the self-made dress that I was wearing. Lindy had already commented on a small gap in the side seam when I came in. 'Did you do that on the way up?' she asked. I had to admit that no, I noticed it when I got in the car, but I was fully dressed and 'didn't want to change'. Now, with the dress split right down the back, you can be sure that I deeply regretted that decision. My face flushed red with shame that Lindy, a qualified tailor, would notice.

I needn't have worried. Lindy of course noticed the gaping tear and I confided my horror of her disapproval. She talked for a short time about the likely source of the problem and then, as often happens when you expose a vulnerability, proceeded to tell me of a wardrobe malfunction of her own. It happened when she was on the flight to the second inquest, accompanied by her lawyer Stuart Tipple.

'I was all dressed up because I knew there would be reporters the minute we left the plane and I was sitting next to Stuart because we were going over stuff. He asked for grape juice and then he knocked it in my lap. Red grape juice, and I was wearing a white dress that was starched. I spent half the trip in the toilets down the back with the hostesses who gave me soda water to get it out. I had to wash it about eight times but I got it all out and somebody had a hair dryer and the hostess is pulling the fabric tight because we couldn't iron it.'

'Was it linen?' I asked.

'It wasn't linen but it was starched and now it just looked like it had been squashed in the centre, runched up. I mean, I felt self-conscious. It didn't turn up in any pictures. But the look on Stuart's face was priceless.'

We laughed and laughed. Lindy is, without doubt, one of the smartest people I have ever met. She doesn't misremember a detail. And she is fully alive in the present, able to see the funny side of turning up at an inquest, accused of murder, in a white dress with the ghost of a red-purple stain down the front!

I noticed an increase in my levels of anxiety from my daily contact reading these letters written to Lindy. I hesitate to use that word because it seems melodramatic. My anxiety was, I'm sure, specifically related to being in contact with her appalling situation, perversely and maliciously unjust. Cognitive behaviour therapists will tell you that 90 per cent of what we worry about never happens – but here every day I was exposed to a situation where, for the Chamberlain family, the worst case scenario comes true.

I don't think it helped that in recent years my work had been concerned with children of prisoners, child sexual assault victims, train crash survivors and incarcerated teenage girls. Then there were marine pilots negotiating a shipping disaster, gay domestic violence survivors, people grieving over the loss of relatives in war and the massacre of Aboriginal people in Western Sydney (working with Romaine Moreton on *One Billion Beats* in Tharawal country). But this project was the one that really sent my already wary nature into hyper-drive. The anxiety began to leak into the rest of my life. Turning off all the power points when I went out of the house. Making sure I knew where the insurance documents were kept. Putting a cover over the built-in camera in my laptop.

There is a legacy in doing work that involves daily empathy with the pain and suffering of others. This is the work that artists do for the community. We hear these stories again and again and again. People may think that I always involve the communities that I work with out of respect and certainly, respect is part of the equation. But the greater truth is that these community members are the people who can most safely and sympathetically guide you through it.

And so it was here. Without having long conversations or placing any more demand on her time than I thought reasonable, Lindy herself became my exemplar of strength with regards how to deal with the anxiety I was feeling. I never asked her, or told her of the effect on me. I simply watched how *she* coped with the material, how she reacted and responded, how she resolved to go on. In my copy of her autobiography *The Dingo's Got My Baby*, Lindy wrote a beautiful dedication. When I read it I thought to myself 'she will never know how much that means to me'. But the point about Lindy Chamberlain-Creighton is that she does know. She knows the value of a line or a verse or a thought. That is why she has filed them all so meticulously.

I once heard an Australian filmmaker say that in her office, in the edit suite they joke that 'You should never call the film important'. I utterly disagree. My work is earnestly, indelibly important. Otherwise I would not waste your time in asking you to come and see it. Indeed I would argue that theatre is one of the most enduring art forms because it allows us to come together as a community to reflect and decide on our civic responsibilities and responses. It presents an opportunity to show who we are by taking an action, not by mouthing platitudes.

We can go to the theatre as a community to reconcile our response, in this case, to Lindy – because as a community we not only did her and her entire family a great wrong, but we did a great wrong to ourselves. We wounded ourselves with shameful mob mindlessness and we belittled ourselves with crass, ill-informed spite. We need to understand that not everyone did that and some now take the time and trouble to make amends. Lindy told me how, when the 2012 inquest finally declared that a dingo took Azaria, the comedienne and writer Wendy Harmer apologised to her. Lindy said, 'I asked her why she apologised after all these years and she said, "Because I'm better than that"'.

I wonder if we too are better than that now. Are we better than demanding that all theatrical encounters are merely there to distract and entertain? I trust that we are not yet so decadent that everything we do must be motivated by what we will get, rather than what we might give. There *are* generous individuals who actively support the performing arts and public institutions, to enable their lucidity and diversity. Can we really not afford to better fund our culture, or are we short-changing ourselves for other reasons?

Professional artists in this county are called on constantly to justify the validity of the arts and the public money it is given. I do not resile from this – all areas of public funding deserve to be scrutinised and evaluated. But it can be a struggle to quantify the contribution that the arts and artists because it may take years to manifest. In my radio documentary *City of Glass*, about the National Art Glass Collection in Wagga Wagga, the curator Judy Le Lievre described how a teacher at the local school used to bring students in every year to look at and write about the collection. After some years the excursions were discontinued but, she said, that teachers at the school used to say:

> You can tell those children who went through that program, they are complex thinkers and problem solvers, they are curious about life and so they are more resilient against drugs and alcohol and food addictions. Of course, not all of them, but as a group they seemed to lift each other up as a whole, the smarter ones pulled up both the academic and ambitious average of the rest. Oh, you can tell that group of kids, you really can.

Such programs – in theatre, in the visual arts, in music – have proven again and again to be valuable ways of building community and instilling resilience in young adults and the general population. The arts can be a route to healing, to education, to empowerment and social change. But the arts must also be valued as gloriously non-utilitarian too, as simply a deep and revelatory way to experience pleasure and humour and joy.

32

Like learning a new language

MP, my play about women in politics for the Street Theatre in Canberra, has fictional characters and a dramatic narrative based on a compilation of interviews with female Members of Parliament (MPs), public servants, journalists and locals. My brief was to make a work which locals would find interesting, amusing and resonant in a town where wit and the ability to speak cleverly are at an absolute premium.

The idea of *MP* was not to trot out the usual clichés, prejudices and misunderstandings about life in politics and the public service in Canberra. Instead it was to get under the skin of Canberrans, and surprise them with an insight into their own community. To do that I had to be accurate, complex and subtle – something made possible by the candour and generosity of my interviewees. So I didn't write a political satire sending them up, I didn't present them as self-interested, power-hungry, ego-driven crazies. I presented a central character who gives us an insight into how idealism can sometimes be a political liability and how a woman in politics needs to be strategic and calculated.

I discovered in the process that if you wanted to divide politicians into two types you wouldn't do it by gender. There are politicians who are good at passing difficult legislation but find it hard to simplify complex things into digestible or understandable narratives; and others who excel at the simple narrative that the public can swallow but who are less skilled at the real work of political change. Julia Gillard had the political skills to articulate and pass legislation that would cause change in the real world and that's what made her a brilliant tactician.

When I was doing the interviews for *MP*, commissioned by the Street Theatre, I interviewed a lot of, well, slippery female politicians. The best interviews were with parliamentarians who had either left or were in their last term because, you know what, they want to spill. Or the MPs who were not the glamour stars – the ones the press gallery don't really rate. I think I did draw some fresh material from Julie Bishop and Tanya Plibersek but I imagine it helped that they weren't 'on the record' as individuals. The agreement that I made with all interviewees was that I wouldn't attribute words to anyone specifically. But the theatre program included a list of the people I spoke to, so there were still stakes for them in their disclosures. These women are good at their job and they've dealt with every weasel in the pack. But for a stage play I needed to get them to talk about their lives in new and surprising ways. I needed to coax out revelations and ideas that they have only *just* had. I needed to find some way to make them enjoy exploring new corners of their own minds, so that my audience also would as well.

Julie Bishop spoke in the most incredible way about why she went into politics and the moment she realised she wanted to. Maybe she had talked about it before but her sincerity and passions were real. Tanya Plibersek paid tribute to the influence of her parents, and Kay Hull was very candid because she was getting ready to leave politics. Still, if you listened to some of my verbatim interviews for *MP* you might think, 'Why does she interrupt people so often, and why is she so underprepared? Sometimes she sounds ignorant of some of the most basic facts. I can't believe she went to that interview without knowing such and such'. But strategic ignorance and strategic interruptions can be effective tools in your interviews.

Strategic interrupting is a technique you might like to try if your interviewee is media savvy and, these days, who isn't? These kind of interviewees can be hard nuts to crack but the way to do it is a combination of sometimes-deliberate naïvety, provocative interrupting to put them off their train of thought, and a strong instinct for what it is that they *do* want to talk about.

One approach you can take with the media savvy is to draw them out about their attitude to their own fame, public importance, respectability and responsibility. Another is to remember to let them be the expert on their own lives. You may know a lot of public information on them but it is *so* much more interesting to let them tell you their version instead of assuming what you've read is true. Of course this apparent naïvety is not a front for sloppy research. You have to know when to hold back and let them tell you something you may already know. As a playwright you are interested in character, not news.

The key is to step back. Stop trying to prove you know your stuff. Stop trying to prove that you're a good interviewer by being polite and listening quietly (though be that if you have to). Interrupt them. Fail to know something about their lives that they think everyone knows. Ignorance, clumsiness, even stupidity can be incredibly effective in an interview. People may underestimate you and let down their guard. But only use it once or twice and use it tactically. Being repeatedly ignorant or clumsy or stupid will become annoying and your subjects will shut down. Begin by seeming underinformed and gradually get more focused. I'm not going to resort to the overused metaphor about hooking a fish and hauling it in gradually because, well, whenever I've gone fishing I've just hauled the line straight up. But imagine yourself with your finger on the line, feeling for the slightest vibration.

When the play was produced in October 2011, *MP* attracted the Street Theatre's highest ever box office return for a text-based work (work generated by playwrights, as distinct from cabaret or music theatre). On the opening night the audience was riddled with peals of laughter and gave the play a standing ovation. Great reviews, great production, a stunning central performance from Geraldine Turner. So, why did I feel so conflicted and challenged by its success there and its inability to interest companies outside the ACT?

This was not the first time I had become aware of the contradictions of speaking effectively to the community at the centre of a work. During the previews of *Parramatta Girls*, especially after the supportive reactions of the ex-inmates, Neil Armfield cautioned me to continue to work on the script because, he said, 'their reaction is not typical'. Meaning, I needed to make sure the work would be understood by the theatregoer who was not part of the community. You want to portray that community to themselves but you don't want to preclude speaking beyond the community to the larger theatre-going public.

To say a work may be directed too strongly to its constituency is about much more than including too many in-jokes. As a writer, you become a kind of surrogate community member as you begin to understand the complexities and machinations of how it works, beyond the outsider's superficial viewpoint. But this can be a tricky position because you can begin to assume that your general audience knows more than they actually do. So you have to find the balance between giving us a true insider's perspective and also acting as a kind of 'go-between' that connects the community to a general theatre audience.

I was very conscious when I was writing *MP* that there was, and is now, a profound public cynicism about politicians and that by far the most effective Australian work about politics is satirical. Not for Australians the American love letter to the democratic process which is Aaron Sorkin's *The West Wing*, though I wonder if this brilliant work now seems to come from another time when there was still a widespread belief in the political process as an agent for change in the United States. I wanted to write a sincere play about the intricacies of the Australian political process, to write sympathetically not about a Labor politician but a Coalition one, about a woman whose worst enemies were in her own party, and whose maverick style and approach was part of her own suite of problems. I also wanted to write a female character who didn't mouth some kind of you-beaut feminism but was, instead, a fragile, conflicted woman who makes bad choices and suffers from her own mistakes. My priority was to make *MP* pass muster as accurate for a deeply sophisticated political audience in Canberra but to give audiences outside of the capital a dose of the serious compromises that are the daily reality of a politician's life.

You can write a play that is received well by its community but you may have a wait on your hands for the world to catch up, a wait for a mainstage audience who want to hear about unfamiliar worlds and points of view. That's when your prescient play will find its voice in a larger context. In the meantime, don't have a hierarchy of where you might want to work as a writer, but instead cultivate a consciousness of the audience you want to address. If you work in one of the mainstage companies you will be addressing a largely moneyed audience with certain cultural values and anticipated cultural norms. But there are so many other important audiences to which you can speak effectively and originally.

From Frank Moorhouse, whose novel *Cold Light* I adapted for the stage, also for the Street Theatre, I learnt the word 'thaumaturgy'. He uses it in his brilliant satirical work 'The Cabaret Voltaire', in the collection *Lateshows*. Thaumaturgy, loosely translated from the Greek, means wonderworking. Wikipedia defines it as, 'The use of magic for nonreligious purposes'. What a fantastic word. We playwrights are not only theatre workers but wonderworkers and we can work that wonder in any number of places, venues, hearts, minds, heights, depths, lounge rooms, public bars, theatres, cinemas, spaces virtual and concrete. Your job is not to get into bigger and bigger theatres (though you're gonna love the resources and audiences they can offer). Your job is to be a genius thaumaturge wherever and whenever you can. Believe me when I say that your fellow thaumaturges will be able to recognise you, wherever you conjure your art.

33

Savage reality

In 1984, when the world still did not know what Acquired Immune Deficiency Syndrome was, I went to visit a man named Phillip at Westmead Hospital. This was so early in the progress of the HIV pandemic that I was required to wear protective clothing to enter his isolation room: a full face mask, goggles and a protective outer garment. Phillip's room had a huge sign on the door which said INFECTIOUS HAZARD. He looked small in the bed, which was surrounded by plastic curtains. He was already showing many symptoms that I would come to know way too well – extreme gaunt thinness in the face and body and Kaposi sarcoma purple spots on his arms and face.

When I sat down beside his bed, fully protected in head-to-toe clothing, he looked utterly terrified. So scared, in fact, that he could not speak. No doubt my my presence, bizarrely covered like a HAZMAT worker, was confronting for him and made him feel even more isolated. After saying my muffled hellos through the thin fabric of the mask, he reached his hand out towards me and instinctively, I reached out my own gloveless hand and held his. His dark eyes looked at me with gratitude and love, a small moment of calm connection.

I knew Phillip only as an acquaintance from a Sydney gay and lesbian organisation, the Metropolitan Community Church, who were at the forefront of activism around heath care, public programs and social activism related to HIV/AIDS in the very early 1980s. When Phillip got sick they asked me to go out and see him. Like the rest of the world, I had little or no idea about HIV/AIDS. I had agreed to visit without knowing much about the medical implications of exposure, or the emotional implications of coming face to face with the illness that was starting to stir up discussion in clubs and bars. But since I had come all the way from the inner city to Westmead I wasn't going to leave without saying hello. I knew not to ask him how he was doing, and instead asked only if I could get him anything. He told me that he would like a chocolate milkshake. I am a little ashamed to say that it was a relief to make a fast retreat, strip off the eyewear, facemask and gown and go down to the hospital cafe.

I was surprised that the nurses had admitted me when I wasn't a relative. I was curious that they had let me hold his hand without gloves even though I was so suited up. I was confronted by his pallor, his sweaty, clammy skin, and, of course, by the unknown implications of his disease which now had a name but whose transmission was little understood. They didn't know yet that it was passed on via blood and semen, they didn't know it wasn't airborne (thus the face and eye masks), they suspected but weren't sure that it could not be transmitted via saliva. Strangely, I wasn't scared for myself. Not because I am unusually brave; perhaps it was a misplaced trust in the medical professionals though more likely it was a detachment that I will get to soon. I was not scared as much as I was embarrassed to be shuffling around in such an alarmist get up. I wondered if I could go through it again. I brought up the chocolate milkshake and gave it to the nurse who told me that Phillip was now asleep. Please give this to him, I said. Please tell him 'goodbye'. Please tell him 'Get well'. Please tell him 'See you soon'. I never saw him again. I know that he died. I didn't go to his funeral. But I went to so many others.

At some point in your life as a writer you will become aware that there is something uncomfortably self-conscious and strangely vicarious about your line of work. It will strike you more than once and you will push it down, repulsed and in denial about the cold detachment you feel. You will learn how to perform the expected noises of empathy and concern. But if you look back at an unusual situation you have been in, you may not remember the pain of another, although it is there, or the emotions one might expect from others in the situation. You will remember primarily your own feelings, fears and emotions, and you may recall a strange neutrality and objectivity, a perverse fascination in the uniqueness of the situation. You might be simultaneously repulsed and absorbed by your facility to step outside the situation to mine it for details. Later you might wonder at the depth of your humanity.

There is a kind of ruthlessness at the heart of being an artist which is sometimes distasteful, a capacity to look at the ugly truth about yourself and others. It will not always be appreciated or understood. It can be called exploitative, or seen as selfish; it may be misconstrued as voyeurism. When you recognise your facility for detached observation in a crisis situation you may be troubled by it. Certainly you should not retreat into an arrogant narcissism, seeing the rest of the world as a stimulant for your distraction or entertainment. But I have come to believe that this detachment, this cool ability to observe and absorb detail in an otherwise painful situation, is a creative gift which carries with it a responsibility to edify, describe, articulate and clarify the world around you. Embrace this aspect of yourself – you are fitted to the task of bearing witness. Writers, poets, dramatists can lyrically and lucidly describe the world in ways that others cannot, you can make startling, profound and intensely perceptive observations gifting to your audience or your readers, truths that would otherwise go unrecognised. For the friend, the lover, the companion or the acquaintance, the writer can sometimes seem aloof, but this is the way you take in the world. When you spit it back out it has an intensity and emotional depth that you don't seem to experience in reality. It's hard to describe but you'll recognise it. And if you have, well, you already know what I'm talking about, don't you?

My first friend to die of HIV/AIDS was fashion designer Adam Marriott. He'd taken me from being a confused, over-ironed, suburban girl to an inner-city fashionista but by 1986 he was gone. Like many people, the late 1980s and early 1990s meant watching my gay male friends go through months of hyper-manic behaviour, followed by deterioration into hollow-eyed, cadaver-like emaciation, isolation and then death.

St Vincent's hospital dedicated an entire ward to the HIV/AIDS patients and their hospice looked after many who were in the last stages of the illness. It was here that I first heard about the Plunkett Centre for Ethics, attached to the hospital. I began to visit it and read from their extensive library of books and journals about ethical issues, especially around the treatment of HIV/AIDS and euthanasia. I recorded an interview with Dr Bernadette Tobin, the director of the centre. I was not yet working in the verbatim style, but every play was becoming more and more research-informed. The politics of HIV/AIDS treatment was juicy ethical stuff but I was actually more interested in how an ethical dilemma might shape or misshape emotions.

I wrote a play about these ethical questions, initially called *The Sacred*, for the Sydney Theatre Company's New Stages project. It had a public reading in 1998 with Victoria Longley and Nicholas Eadie. Vanessa Downing, the brilliant actor, told me she loved the way that Nicholas' character 'seemed jealous of her relationship to her faith', which I still think a searingly perceptive take on the work. It was given a second public reading at Griffin in 1999 with Rachael Blake and Nicholas Eadie again, directed by Mark Gaal. It was shortlisted for the Griffin Award.

And then it went into my bottom drawer. Until one day my former agent, Nicholas Papademetriou, told me that he was looking for a two-hander to perform at FEAST, the gay festival in Adelaide and did I have something? I had conceived both the roles as gender fluid though it had always been played in the readings as male and female. I now suggested that it be played by two men and renamed the play *Savage Grace*. With Nicholas Opolski opposite Nicholas Eadie and Sarah Carradine as director, the play premiered in Adelaide in 2000. Later that year company gf (gorgeous faggots, good fun, get fucked), as the ensemble of myself, Sarah and the cast were now calling ourselves, did a reading at the Religion, Ethics and Art Conference in an exquisite little room full of stained glass windows in St Paul's College at Sydney University.

In 2001 Sally Richardson directed a production of *Savage Grace* in Perth at Steamworks with Humphrey Bower and Gibson Nolte. The production moved from the Blue Room to a second season at the Subiaco Arts Centre and then Performing Lines toured it to Sydney's Darlinghurst Theatre in 2002. Later Humph and Gibs did a brilliant version at La Mama, minus the rather large underpants that had caused so much derisive gay comment in Sydney, and Humphrey won one of his many Green Room acting awards for his performance. The play itself was commended for the Louis Esson Prize in 2001, co-winner of the Rodney Seaborn Award in 2002, and shortlisted for the Green Room Awards for best new Australian script in 2005.

Savage Grace is my most professionally produced work (*Eyes to the Floor* has had more amateur productions) and has been seen in most states. It was almost produced as a film by the cinematographer Geoff Burton, but the Australian Film Commission wouldn't give him the money to shoot it. It yielded some of the most important aesthetic conversations of my professional career with the actors and directors who worked on it. I got to have lunch with journalist Maxine McKew because of it. I still cherish it as a play not about ethics or euthanasia but about trying to love someone with whom you profoundly disagree.

The Australian gay community's organisation of health campaigns around the fight for people living with HIV/AIDS has now been acknowledged as the best in the world, with the public programs, tactics and radical management of health education subsequently copied internationally. The LGBTIQ communities in this country changed for the better the future of public education around HIV/AIDS, as well as all other health priorities, radically changed the doctor–patient relationship, and opened up debate about ethical areas such as euthanasia, research priorities, sexual liberation and diversity activism. The Australian public must be deeply grateful and profoundly respectful of these communities' ability to mobilise, enact and deliver public health outcomes and should embrace these years as a remarkable example of co-operative genius. So follow your passion and be honest about your doubts, be provocative and righteous and unreasonable and make other people angry. It's the only way anything has ever changed.

34

Fear of Kong

When it comes to sexism in the Australian theatre, I have spoken against it on panels, been quoted in newspaper articles, worked on the National Executive of the Australian Writers' Guild to fight it and attended many industry forums where female playwrights are expected to educate others on the complex ideas around gender bias. I call these forums 'Feminism 101' though others might call them 'Feminism for idiots'. When it comes to homophobia in the Australian theatre, I have spoken against it on panels, been quoted in newspaper articles, worked as the Festival Liaison Director on the board of the Sydney Gay and Lesbian Mardi Gras and written about non-binary sexuality, homosexuality, oppression and discrimination in my work.

In 2017 the Australian theatre's consciousness about acting on gender parity and cultural diversity is encouragingly prominent. I believe we are seeing a genuinely radical intervention by young artists which will translate into a sustained change in the kinds of stories and performers we see on our stages. What I have done in my life and my work has always been to try to smash gender and cultural inequity in our theatre – my casts, my subjects, my choices tell their own story. I remain deeply committed to these ideas in my own work and actions and celebrate the academics, theatre makers and philosophers who articulate these issues in a genuine way.

But here I want to write about my own vulnerability, about how these things have affected my career in the hope it will contribute something more nuanced to the broader debate. Because issues such as gender, sexuality and race manifest in much more insidious ways than the dismal statistics about female representation on our stages, simple quotas or the patronising effects of low expectation. The worst of it is the way that, despite years of activism, you internalise it *yourself* and it ambushes you when you least expect it.

In fact, it is so hard to be a playwright, to be a working artist in this country, that analysing the peculiarities of being a female playwright can sometimes seem reductive. Combine that with the fact that you are punished for speaking out about it (absolutely no question), and artistic directors who mouth generalities about women not 'being pushy enough' (which is such execrable shit it doesn't merit rebuttal), as you try to resist people categorising your work in a way that will ossify it (especially when the other monikers of young and/or political are starting to fade like a badly spray-painted graffiti tag) and you can find yourself intellectually fatigued and even semi-silenced about the relevance of identity politics to your own career.

The landfill-sized mountain of internalised self-hatred inside me became searingly clear, perversely, the day after I won three huge accolades at the 2013 AWGIE awards night for my Community and Youth theatre work, *Grounded*. Sitting in the Melbourne audience on the night of the awards, with the sound of the production of *King Kong* playing in the theatre downstairs and George Brandis on stage presenting the inaugural David Williamson Prize for Excellence in Writing for Australian Theatre, I suddenly heard my name called. In a state of genuine shock and not a little dismay at how unprepared I was, I staggered to the stage. Senator Brandis handed me a cheque for $25,000 and I, awed into silence, held it up to the assembled crowd of writers, as if he had pulled from within his jacket lapels a breathing thylacine.

Now I love public speaking. At least I have taught myself to love it. Early on I was motivated by not wanting to concede the public space to panellists of uniform gender. So I learnt to push down my fear and try to enjoy speaking in public, until what I told myself became an actual reality and now I positively crave it. But I love it with a written script. Let's face it, we writers can at least fashion ourselves a mean monologue. Now, here I was, in front of my peers, unprepared. I spoke genuinely about being proud to be part of a guild who valued telling

Australian stories, I thanked the young adults who had worked with me in Newcastle, I sputtered a bit about David Williamson and his generosity in providing the funds. And then, relieved, I returned to my seat.

But it wasn't over. I won again in the Community and Youth Theatre category. By then I was calmer and told a funny anecdote about getting the helicopter out to the bulk carrier, similar to the one in this book. Phew. That was it. And then at the end of the night, bam, my name was called again, when *Grounded* won the major award for best script of the year. At last I thanked my agents and my partner and espoused the virtues of the guild valorising community theatre in this category (the major winner was usually from film or stage), and I sang the praises of working with young people who would lead us into a dynamic future. Afterwards my peers all joined in buying me champagne and with the generosity that people find hard to believe really does exist between playwrights (because it is easier to imagine we are narcissistic, covetous and competitive) they celebrated this career-defining triumph with me.

Around 4 am I woke in the midst of a full blown panic attack. I had trouble breathing, I was shaking, moaning and sweating. I balled myself up into a foetal shape on my hands and knees and rocked backwards and forwards in an agony of self-doubt and self-flagellation about the inadequacies of my speeches. And then about the ridiculousness of being like this when I should *for God's sake* be celebrating. Alana, please relax, please lighten up, please, please, please change the way you think. This is a good moment. It doesn't matter what you said, you could have been blind drunk and slurring your words and it would still have been okay. You won. It's enough.

I went back to sleep and dozed in and out of anxiety. The next day my partner and I had booked to see *King Kong* at the Theatre Royal, as an aprés-awards treat. I was still shaken – beginning to be pleased, of course – but also confused by the night time horrors. Too much to drink, I thought, or too much excitement, maybe a fear of success, the unfamiliarity of being the centre of attention without a community member to deflect the recognition.

And then in the middle of the first act, soon after the incredible genius of the Kong puppet appeared, it struck again. The blood drained from my face and I went white with terror. An inability to really believe that I could have won. I left the theatre and Vicki came out to find me sitting in the bar rocking and crying, unable to articulate anything resembling a good reason for this totally inappropriate reaction. We bought two large glasses of the best French champagne they were selling and went out into the street to get some air. We said nothing, I breathed. We went back into the theatre and enjoyed the second half. As time passed I began to take pride in my achievement, to dismiss the anxiety as a bad hangover, overtired, overexposed and overthinking it all.

I couldn't talk about it for a long time. Who can credibly complain about being knocked sideways by three big awards? We all should have such problems. Today I am profoundly grateful and humbled by the win. But I expose the journey of the win to other writers, most especially to writers of difference – gender, sexuality, disability, culture or race – because success can (at least initially) be a destabilising shock and an unbalancing disincentive in some perverse, obscure and unpalatable way that, even now, I find hard to confront. I can hear a scalding voice heckling 'Fine, we won't bother you with another win any time soon', or the voices of peers who have never been adulated sputtering about 'the faux-horrors of recognition'. But my reaction to this multi-award approbation was, in part, nurtured by a lifetime of internalised cultural derogation, a sense that deep down I didn't deserve this triumph. Don't let it be the case for you. You who will write the stories of the future, you who will triumph and succeed and make us proud of our humanity and our generosity and our respect for the arts and artists. You, the great queer writer, the gifted writer of colour, the genius of language, the innovator of physical theatre or dance, the visionary feminist writer to come, make sure you grab with both hands any statuette they thrust your way.

35

Bodies in space

The kind of playwriting that I do, often based on interviews and verbatim transcripts, or archives and manuscripts, aims to reflect a community back to itself, trusting that a theatrical community 'selfie' may both amuse and intrigue; that the observations of an outsider might compel self-reflection and self-knowledge in an interesting, sometimes uncomfortable, but hopefully enlightening manner.

But you do not make drama out of information. You do not make drama out of facts or fallacies or even out of a pile of the most beautifully filed and annotated pages. You make it out of the conflict and contradictions and hidden, unexplained motives of being a human being. And so when I wrote *Letters to Lindy*, I conjectured a premise, a theory, a notion about the 199 boxes in the National Library. If I could explain that premise in prose I would not have to write it as a play. It is no perverse sales pitch to say that if you want to fully understand the way I see the relationship between Lindy and these letters, you will have to see it played out in bodies in space in the moment in a room full of others on a night when the gift of inspired insight flows out of the performers. Because as a playwright, I have given my life to the belief that we do not understand something because someone explains it to us in words, but when we experience it for ourselves in a moment of insight. We need to be artfully led into this moment.

Any great teacher will tell you that true pedagogy happens when a student makes the connection themselves. Any neurologist will describe the synaptic leaps the brain makes across the tiny nerve cells, or neurons, in that moment of realisation. Synapse, derived from the Greek *sun* 'together' and *haptein* 'join' – means the space across which nerve cells can join together. In the theatre, we join together as a community and embrace that synaptic leap. It's the moment when the audience suddenly realises what the playwright and the creative team have been doing, what they have been building. When you are in a theatre and that revelation dawns on you, you see that insight, that perception. You can't put it into words. When theatre is good it kicks inside you like a second heartbeat. It overwhelms your rational experience, like awe, like joy, like love. It takes you out of your preconceptions and individuality and joins you to something larger and more purposeful than yourself.

A public school teacher once told me about teaching *Run Rabbit Run*. Johnno, one of the students, came to her before the class, 'It's not a very good play, Miss', he said, grumpily. The teacher assigned the boys roles and they read them out in a classroom performance. 'It was interesting to watch their attitude towards the play transform as they read it', she reported. 'One of them started saying, "That's you Johnno, you're just like that, you talk like that". He smiled because he recognised himself and he enjoyed the others recognising him.' By the end of the class they apparently thought that verbatim was the new black and wanted to write their own verbatim play. They had even developed the new convert's hardline attitude to verbatim authenticity and questioned the validity of anything that wasn't strict transcript.

I have repeatedly witnessed a similar 'conversion experience' with actors who are new to effective verbatim. Some people's experience of topical theatre has consisted of actors who are basically teachers in funny hats (or other 'entertaining' apparel) who stand and exposit facts, theories and 'everyday' anecdotes. There is little subtext, little dramatic action and the transaction with the audience is that they are being 'educated' about a subject of particular interest to their demographic or geography. But this is not effective drama.

As a writer, I acknowledge that I have a palpable desire to entertain and wring a laugh, a gasp, a tear, an abiding moment of deeply silent realisation from my audiences. What am I talking about – a tear? I want people to have trouble breathing because they are sobbing with wild abandon, I want audiences to laugh so hard that they indecorously break wind beside their well-heeled companions, I want such a shocked and astonished silence that audiences forget to move their hands to clap, the world stops spinning on its axis, people leap to their feet and embrace their neighbour with forgiveness and understanding. I want them to do it right in this moment, in my presence, in a room where I can watch them.

The crucial difference between dramatists and prose writers is that our work remains unfinished, unrealised, unmade until it is embodied in the mouths of our greatest collaborators – theatre professionals. The ambition of our art form is to create a structure in which actors, designers and directors can play, and most rapturously liberate their imagination to wonder and invention. As playwrights our deepest most sincere belief is in the sacred nature of play, in the transformative abiding faith that empathy is the most enduring form of radical compassion, and one of the most effective motors for change in the real world. For all the façades and masks employed to render our craft, playwrights are ruthless judges of human nature, because playwrights do not believe what people say. We do not draw with costume or description or even dialogue. The substance of a play is action – not what the community or the characters or the society say, but what they do. If writers are the lie-detectors of our culture, then playwrights are the polygraph takers, sieving the words and thoughts of our contemporaries through the body, the brain and spirit in action to see what holds fast and true.

When I workshopped *The Tree Widows* in Tasmania in March 2013 with four experienced actors – Guy Hooper, Iain Lang, Jane Longhurst and Jane Johnson – they told me they enjoyed how my process moved beyond the pure transcript-driven verbatim style they knew, to reveal a poetic, dramatic and more surprisingly emotional form of theatre. Indeed, Guy Hooper confided to me that when he first read the monologues on the page before the workshop he was sceptical of their efficacy. Yet during the workshop, in performance and in the audience feedback sessions, he was one of the most vocal advocates for the project, revealing to the audience that this work often made him cry in a way that was 'unusual' for him. In fact, he said, he had to guard against over-emoting during the performances. This was a great honour for me from one of Tasmania's most respected theatre makers.

Many great actors develop a unique and distinctive voice. They transform how they use that voice from role to role of course, but they retain a 'manner' of speaking, attacking the words in a style which is recognisably their own. It is the way they choose to play on the instrument that is their body, the way they employ their tools of projection and rhythm and sonorous oration to draw the audience under their spell. I have found that the more 'distinctive' the performer is in this way, the less successful they sometimes are in 'giving themselves over' to the service of verbatim. In conventional drama they breathe life into a fictional creation by blowing the rhythm of their own breath into it. But in verbatim work, where you are embodying the words and cadence and thought patterns of another *real* person, sometimes a distinctive voice can hobble the performance. It's not that the actor needs to impersonate the real person. I usually don't let the actors meet or hear recordings of the real people before the opening night because – well because it isn't imitation that they need to find. It's their version of the real person as presented on the page, but it echoes the original through staying true to its vocal patterns.

Since I am not a professional actor I am prepared to countenance that there is little or nothing I can contribute that will be of use to actual actors. But I have seen verbatim in performance often enough to recognise those who perform it most effectively. Actors speak about the difference in film performance where you just have to 'be' rather than 'play' the character. Perhaps this is always true. But there is a form of effective surface embodiment of the roles in film that seems more similar to what works best for verbatim performance. Jack Nicholson apparently told another actor that as the Joker in *Batman* he just had to 'work the costume'. That might be a spectacularly talented performer in a rash of understatement or it might be a useful way to approach verbatim acting. At some point you have to surrender and 'let the text do the work'. Again, and this is more often the case than not, verbatim seems to be more effective not when actors 'add' something onto the words, but rather when they 'get out of the way' and deliver the words with deep authenticity.

Why do you need to know this as a writer? Because you need to be able to pick the difference between a problem with the text and a problem with its performance. You might have to fight for a line which looks nothing on the page but is deeply affective once the actor knows both why and how they are delivering it. Many people, too many professionals, cannot read work on the page. Scenes that look good on the page can be as thin as tissue when you put them up in three dimensions; scenes that at first may seem dense and complex can be the cornerstone of the play's originality after four weeks' rehearsal. You may be asked to cut something when the actor can't 'sustain' the speech and you need to know whether that is a fair call or not. There is a point in the rehearsal process where I, quite deliberately, go from being approachable, amenable Alana with the infinitely malleable text to intransigent, near-deaf Alana who won't change another word. I haven't had a personality transplant but I do it *because the actors will keep trying to make you solve problems for them to put off solving the problems themselves*. You will need to know the difference. How do you know the difference? Experience. Trust yourself. The mystery of creativity.

Does the process we theatre makers try to conjure sound mystical? Of course it does. It is an ultimate act of faith in our audience that they will make that leap, concentrate that perception, go with us and reach for that kind of involvement. When I went into the rehearsals of *Letters to Lindy* I found what usually happens at the midpoint of rehearsals, namely, doubt and barely-contained terror. In the middle of rehearsals the actors and director must close down some of the myriad possibilities that loomed at the beginning of the process and commit to decisions, and so they are literally mad with the volume of choices. My profound esteem for actors has many dimensions but chief among them is their ability to believe in another's work and to take it, bodily, into their voice and their heart. It takes courage for actors to face down their own demons, not only on the playing stage but through every part of the process. Much is made of the narcissism of actors – George Bernard Shaw said once that the trouble with a certain player was that he was 'in love with his wife and an actor can only afford to be in love with himself'. Personally I think that a very healthy dose of self-love may be a precious antidote to the daily practice of putting on the voice and soul of others.

36

The ecstasy of Italy

In April 2011 I travelled to Rome as part of my research for a radio documentary and stage play called *Ear to the Edge of Time* about the world of radio astronomers, specifically pulsar scientists. I had an appointment with Brother Guy Consolmagno at the Vatican Observatory in Albano who gave me detailed instructions on how to get to the observatory from the Roma Termini, a fifty-minute train ride that promised views of Castel Gandolfo (the Pope's summer residence), vineyards, tunnels and an incredible blue lake.

My appointment was on a Wednesday so I had arrived on the Monday to explore Rome a little and deal with the jet lag that always hits me pretty hard when travelling to Europe. I was staying in a monastery, the Casa Caterina Volpicelli. The first day I went for a walk along the Via XX Settembre and came upon the basilica of Santa Maria della Vittoria which contains the Bernini masterpiece, *The Ecstasy of St Teresa*. It is the most remarkable sculpture I have ever seen. Not only does it have two astonishing central figures – a swooning nun and a cherubic angel – but it is set up as a kind of theatre show, with the male members of the Cornaro family, who commissioned the work, sculpted in boxes at the side.

St Teresa of Avila wrote about the ecstasy of religious experience that Bernini immortalised in his statue:

> I thought that he pierced my heart with this dart several times, and in such a manner that it went through my bowels, and when he drew it out it seemed as if my bowels came with it, and I remained inflamed

with a great love of God. The pain thereof was so intense, that it forced deep groans from me, but the sweetness which this extreme pain caused in me was so excessive that there was no desiring to be free from it, nor is the soul then content with anything less than God. This is not a corporeal but a spiritual pain.

I'm not a Roman Catholic but that week I went to the eight o'clock mass at the basilica every morning so that I could see the sculpture and sit with it for an hour or more. It compelled me because female religious experience is so rarely valorised and celebrated in the Christian tradition. As a work of art it had me entirely in its thrall. On Wednesday I tore myself away from St Teresa and took the train to Albano where I met with Br Guy, whose life's work is the analysis of extraterrestrial comets donated to the Vatican by a Roman prince. Pulsars rather than comets were my main scientific focus, but I wanted access to the Vatican records, which contain every paper on astronomy ever published in any language for the past five centuries. That's exactly what Br Guy showed me and as we leafed through these documents – in German, Italian and English – the evidence for my thesis in both the documentary and play was clear. My contention was that scientific work, particularly in astronomy, was being done in increasingly larger groups, thus skewing attribution and 'discovery' credits and busting a rather sizeable hole in the idea of the individual 'genius'. In the documentary this would be a factual premise; in the subsequent stage play I focused on the consequences and human drama of such 'confusions'.

It was a strange week for me. I was unusually timid in the Italian capital, at pains not to speak English or reveal myself in a way that would offend. I felt conspicuously common in my clumsy Australian tourist identity, as though I was one of the endless stream of gawping English-speaking tourists that Italy has endured for centuries, and it unbalanced me. Perhaps my ritual of daily mass and singular focus on the Bernini sculpture gave me a sense that I was somehow more thoughtful, refined or sophisticated than your average traveller, but it was just an illusion. I found it hard to go into restaurants, and silently bought supplies from the local supermarket. I spotted a lovely nightdress and dressing gown in a local retail outlet and it took all my courage to actually go in and purchase them – I walked past for two days before I plucked up the necessary audacity to enter the shop and parlay with the glamorous Italian assistant.

The reason I have gone into so much detail about my contemplations and seemingly unassociated distractions with St Teresa is to acknowledge the fact that sometimes the road to creative writing for the stage is a straight line and sometimes it is not. Perhaps in previous chapters I have given the impression that you can, by rational logic and patient application, go straight to the work that needs to be done, find the people you need to speak to and write the drafts that need to be processed. But in the case of *Ear to the Edge of Time*, my time in Italy, in a monastery, alone and feeling conspicuously alien had a foundational effect on the writing of the play that I can't articulate and probably don't really understand.

The missteps, the random research, the getting up and working on stuff that doesn't end up in the play, the drafts that are aborted half way through, the times that feel like you are getting nowhere are, invariably, part of it. You might procrastinate to avoid work and ultimately you will know when that is the case. But there are also times when sitting alone in a Roman monastery breathlessly admiring a religious sculpture can be the key to the next creative step. The only thing you can do is keep sniffing around, keep making choices. When you realise a choice is wrong you go back to the drawing board. Making close work theatre is as creatively challenging as any other artistic act and requires antennae that cannot be completely taught; it is more than boiling down or editing your source material. You follow your nose and your heart until you get a revelation, sometimes suddenly, that this is the way to go, this is the direction to move. It's mysterious and impossible to put into words but also strangely familiar. So often it feels like 'this time I really can't crack it, I can't crack it, I really can't crack it. Oh, maybe. Yes. That's it!'

When I was daydreaming in Italy, I thought back to my two-week residency at the Parkes Observatory, also known as the Dish, where I made a radio feature called *The Sound of the Universe Singing* (available online if you search under that title), the starting place of *Ear to the Edge of Time*. I reflected on the commitment and contradictions of the radio astronomers I had met there, among them several Italian astronomers. At Parkes I had fascinating conversations about authorship and accreditation, often a vexed subject in contemporary theatre, especially in highly collaborative physical and multi-media collaborations. So it was interesting to find a science culture which, to an external eye, had been happily working in groups and sharing attribution for many years. Some time later, my interest was piqued when I witnessed an impassioned discussion over the case of Dame Jocelyn Bell Burnell, who had discovered pulsars as a PhD student. Her supervisor Dr Antony Hewish received the Nobel prize in 1974 for the discovery and while he acknowledged her in his speech, they did not share the prize. The passion this aroused among astronomers, and my suspicions about human nature, convinced me that there was, lurking in all this collaborative camaraderie, the possibilities of a very human drama about science.

After Parkes, which was partly supported by a small grant from the Commonwealth Scientific and Industrial Research Organisation (CSIRO), I received an Australia Council Fellowship to do further research which included the Vatican visit and a series of interviews in the UK with really estimable pulsar scientists. I interviewed the grande dame of the pulsar world herself, the academic and professor Dame Jocelyn Bell Burnell in Oxford, as well as Dr Marek Kukula and Dr Rebekah Higgit at London's Royal Observatory in Greenwich, and Professor Andrew Lyne at the Jodrell Bank Observatory near Manchester.

Radio astronomers are a unique group of individuals – obsessive, driven, funny and a little peculiar. A perfect group of characters for the stage. I have fictionalised some of the main characters in the play because, while I secured the trust and permission from all the scientists involved, I wanted to push the plot elements to better investigate my central dramatic premise. The conundrum at the heart of the play is about the nature of truth, what might happen when artistic truth and scientific truth come into conflict. When I discovered that Jocelyn Bell Burnell had co-curated a book of poems, brokering partnerships between scientists and poets, I had my premise.

Ear to the Edge of Time asks questions about the culture of contemporary science and the progress of change within the politics of that culture. Astronomy is the subject of the play, but the theme and concerns of the drama are as much about the fascinating machinations of astronomical physics as they are about the dilemmas, compromises and culture that are part of the discovery. The play asks questions about a reluctant activist, and interrogates assumptions about who should speak up and when. It looks at the ways in which the humanness of scientists affects the outcomes and discoveries that are made, and the truth that the 'genius' scientific discoverer has long been an anomaly rather than the norm. I hope the play will give its audience a glimpse into a world where unspoken understandings about authorship are part of the scientific process. *Ear to the Edge of Time* does not use verbatim transcripts but it has deep connections to real life physicists and world observatories and contains many of their words and opinions.

The play won the 2012 STAGE International Playwriting Award, a prestigious award for a play about science or technology that attracted over 200 entries from nineteen countries. In 2012 the judges were Pulitzer Prize–winning playwrights Tony Kushner, David Lindsay-Abaire and Donald Margulies, and Nobel Laureates Robert C. Richardson, Frank Wilczek and David J. Wineland. I travelled to Dublin to Trinity College to receive the award and see a reading of the play in the Samuel Beckett Theatre. I was presented with a holographic glass award and a cheque for 10,000 American dollars. In late 2018, Sport for Jove will produce the play as part of the Seymour Centre's Reginald Season.

37

Shudder in the city

My first play on the Belvoir stage was a short play called *Shudder* about the erotic possibilities of vomiting. In 1994, Belvoir presented a short play festival in the Upstairs Theatre and I wrote a work in which two people aroused themselves by making each other ill. It was, of course, a metaphor for all the couples I met, including sometimes myself, who stayed together even though they seemed to hate each other; a witty little work about the perversities of attraction. Diana Denley, who directed it, created a small rectangle of light on the Upstairs stage which corralled the action to a small brightly-lit bathroom. Terry Hansen and Julia Johnson, who performed it, wore white bathrobes. The Sydney Tap Centre, right at the end of Belvoir St, sponsored it by lending us a pristine, modern and beautifully sculptured porcelain toilet bowl for them to vomit into.

Robyn Kershaw, Belvoir's general manager at the time, called me in for a meeting and asked me if I had any longer plays. I gave them a copy of *Southern Belle*, my play about the early life and career of southern American playwright and novelist Carson McCullers. This play has been a brilliant 'calling card'. It won me the New Dramatists' Award to travel to New York and secured me my American agent Peregrine Whittlesey. I sent the play to Carrillo Gantner, who wrote to say he had tried to move things around in his Playbox season so he could produce it, but it wasn't possible at that late stage. Janis Balodis wrote a glowing letter from the Melbourne Theatre Company, and it garnered admiring feedback from all manner of American companies. May-Brit Akerholt, who was Literary Manager at the Sydney Theatre Company (STC), gave me huge encouragement to keep writing. In fact it wasn't produced until 2006, after I changed the name to *Singing the Lonely Heart*. Alex Galeazzi bit the bullet and put the most wonderful production on stage at the New Theatre with Jane Phegan (as Carson's muse Frankie), Abigail Austin, Elaine Hudson, Rebekah Moore, Jason Montgomery and Peter Flett. Brendan Cowell told me that his mother had gone to see it and loved it. She then came to see my staged reading of *The Sex Act* at the STC, which Brendan directed, performing in it with Rose Byrne, Heather Mitchell, Damon Herriman and Vanessa Downing.

But back to Belvoir and my regurgitating lovers. The company declined any interest in producing *Southern Belle*. Instead they offered to include me as one of the writers on a project called *The Sydney Vanities* which was to be a kind of cabaret / short play / pastiche evening with some of the best comedy writers in Australia. They put us up in a luxurious hotel down near the Rocks and we sat around in a room much like the teams of writers you see in fictional versions of *Saturday Night Live* or Aaron Sorkin's *Studio 60 on the Sunset Strip*. We were asked to write a provocative answering machine message. I fashioned a message involving four Rottweilers and a feminist goth. I wrote another piece about a man who turned into a half man – half insect by having some sort of congress with his ironing board. The project did not make it to the stage.

After the success of *Shudder*, Diana Denley invited me to write another short play to present as part of a showcase called Queer Fringe with playwright Alex Harding for the 1995 Sydney Gay and Lesbian Mardi Gras Festival. Diana was then artistic director of the Lookout Theatre, a tiny venue over a pub in Woollahra which seated about eighty people and had distinguished itself under her artistic vision.

I wrote another two-hander, an absurdist play called *Swellings* about two women who go in for cosmetic surgery and come out with perversions of their bodies; they submit to repeat surgery to correct the first mistake, and so on and so on. I did not formally interview anyone for the work but relied on newspaper and other archival research, anecdotal disclosures from friends and acquaintances, and my absurdist imagination. It was performed by Julia Johnson and Alice Livingstone and there was nudity, a washing line and sustained laughter when it was presented.

Not that I got to see the opening night. Because the opening had been overbooked and there were only eighty seats, Alex and I elected to sit in the foyer. 'We've seen it before', we said, laughing, and then spent the next ninety minutes with our ears pressed against the theatre doors, listening for laughter and applause through the heavy wood of the door. When we heard the plays had ended but there was no sound, I turned to Alex and said, 'Oh well, there's always next year', and he laughed. Then the audience broke into applause and we realised we had pre-empted the end. They flowed out into the foyer and their congratulations flowed out to us. Given my predilection, I may even say addiction, to watching an audience respond it was a quiet form of torture to be locked out of the opening night of my own play, but it makes for a suitably absurdist vision considering the absurdist form of the show.

I would add Alex Harding, and his gorgeous partner David Thompson who died in July 1990, to my list of early theatrical mentors. Before he died of HIV/AIDS, David gave me books by H.D. (the pen name of the American poet and novelist Hilda Doolittle) and others I had never heard of but soon acquainted myself with so I didn't appear ignorant in his sophisticated eyes. I wrote a stream-of-consciousness monologue for him called *h is for homo* that was shortlisted for the Nita Dobbie award in 1994.

38

Bullied with words

Joanna Golotta, a teacher at Presbyterian Ladies' College (PLC) Croydon, emailed me in 2010. Her drama group was making a verbatim play about cyberbullying and the students had conducted interviews with other students, teachers and parents. Cyberbullying is a subject that provokes extreme moral panic on one hand and ignorant indifference on the other. With Gregory Friend, PLC's Head of Drama, Joanna invited me to the school for a cup of tea. Now that they had gathered the material together, could I show them how to put it all together? Well, no, and yes. I couldn't show them how to put it together in an afternoon, or a week, or even a couple of weeks because this is the kind of thing that takes months for a writer to do full-time. The best way to show them how to put it together, I suggested, would be to observe and participate in a process which I would facilitate. Well would you be interested in a commission to do that, they asked me? I quoted them the Australian Writers' Guild commission fee for a one-act play and they readily agreed.

I took home the transcripts of their material. The interviews between the students beautifully caught the voices, language, values and ways of thinking of their generation. They hadn't, however, pushed their fellow students to reveal the darker, more vulnerable, more confronting inner thoughts lurking under the bravado and flippancy that emerged when the discussions got tough. To get the sort of dense, complex, revealing and subtext-riddled material that you need to sustain a monologue on stage, I would have to conduct some more interviews myself and embroider some of their material with more profound insights and perceptions. Not so much about cyberbullying but about the challenges of being a young adult in early 21st-century Australia. Which, let's face it, is similar to, but not exactly the same as, the challenges of being a young adult in other ages, or, indeed, being any human being alive in a world of choices and challenges.

There was one sublime interview that I included as pure verbatim. You usually strike one of these in every project: a brilliant speaker who is interesting, lucid and articulate. All you have to do is turn on the recorder and point it in the right direction. The trick is to recognise the gold as it comes out so you don't stop the flow. You don't need any interviewing techniques and tricks – you only need to listen, nod and not interrupt a ready-made monologue. This interviewee was a mother whose child had been a bully. Her exquisite self-analysis – complete with the complexity of her reaction, her shame, her tough-love tactics, her courage in allowing the bullying to be revealed and corrected – made for compulsive drama. She elucidated her own dramatic character journey complete with turning points, a crisis of confidence, the recovery of moral authority and a resolution. And all I had to do was put it in the show.

The rest of the process was more complex and required the sort of work that a playwright does that is hard to describe, teach or mentor. It's about an instinct for delicacy, boldness, character, and originality of thought or expression. I am always looking for nuance, particularity and specificity of character. The miracle of the fact is that there is so much difference in humanity that even in a large group of people you will find something weird and strangely contradictory about each person. I compiled a selection of monologues and took them into the school, to rehearse them with Miss Golotta's drama group and get their feedback for rewrites.

One section is extremely vulgar and uncomfortably crude. It describes young men making a mockery of female bodily fluids and expressing themselves in a provocative and distasteful way. There may sometimes be a moment when what you write could repulse and even horrify you. You will think, 'No, I cannot go there, I cannot put that in'. But you must. Sometimes you will realise that what initially horrified you is necessary for the play. That is your job – it's what makes you an artist, not a publicist. You may need this determination to overrule your modest and conservative self and take your drama past the limit of respectability, even though you cringe from the noxious nature of humanity that it portrays. This is why writers need courage, because they have the ability to look into the abyss of humanity, into the places and aspects of life that are genuinely unpleasant. The upside is that there is hope in that kind of honesty, in acknowledging those painful lacks in human nature and having the integrity to portray it. You go there because if you don't your audience, in this case young adults genuinely in the crossfire of cyberbullying, will sniff you out and write you off as a fake, a squib, a coward. You will take your play to the worst possible scenario because if you don't you will betray the deepest contract an artist has with the society they live in – to be painfully, often controversially, real.

For a respectable Christian school to commission and allow that sort of brazen honesty is as much a measure of the integrity of the PLC staff as it is of my determination in getting it past the teaching and management structure. Before the play went on stage, the PLC Headmaster Dr Paul Burgis emailed Gregory:

> I have read through the latest version of the play and am happy for it to go ahead. It is still raw and crude in parts but this is the culture that exists. I think we display this culture effectively without it being seen as gratuitous by families. Please plan for me to contextualise it by my saying a few words before each performance.

Joanna Golotta directed a dynamic and genuinely shocking production, complete with stunning effects for the 'matador' sequences – a fantasy element of the play in which the central character fights bulls as a metaphor for cyberbullies. Many of the parents, warned that the work would be confronting and offensive, shrugged a little afterwards and said that it was mild compared to what they might have expected. On stage, the girls were authentic, inventive and profoundly affecting in their various roles. It was a night of young women speaking about things that really concern them, that affect their lives right now and the ownership and investment in the work was compelling and immediate.

Before the play began, Dr Burgis stood on stage and said something along the lines of:

There are many, many students in our school who are resilient and hardy in the face of painful cyber hatred. But we commissioned this play for the *one* student in our midst who cannot cope, the *single* student for whom this play will be a lifeline to speaking up or asking for help. In this school we believe that leadership is about protecting and looking after the fragile minority, the vulnerable individual, the person on the edge who is most in need of understanding. We believe, and we invest with both our money and our time, that our school community is only as strong as our weakest member.

I remember these words because the thrust of so much public discourse is about representing the majority opinion and taking action for the 'sensible centre'. As a writer, if you are going to try to do something new, or real or provocative you will need to work with understanding and skill with others who are genuinely prepared not only to listen to your perspective but are as committed to protecting the fringes and loners and mavericks, as they are at this adventurous school.

Cyberbile was published by Currency Press in 2013. It was nominated for an AWGIE award in the Youth and Community category in 2012 and has since been produced multiple times.

39

Humble pie

When I went into Junee Correctional Centre I began my writing sessions with the inmates by playing a couple of theatre games. The first one was to have the group stand in a circle and one of the participants would say, 'I'm thinking of football teams' and then we would go around the circle and they would have to say a football team not previously mentioned. It can be varied with 'I'm thinking of colours' or 'I'm thinking of types of food' or 'I'm thinking of suburbs in Sydney', etc. The idea is to choose a subject that has plurals. It actually gets the brain going, especially when the person before you 'steals' your item just before you say it. If you don't say the item on the beat, that is, if you pause or hesitate, you are out and you have to start the next round with a new subject.

When I did it in Junee it worked a treat, as did other more physical trust and coordination exercises. So when I went into Goulburn Correctional Centre to conduct writing classes, I thought I would start with the same set of games. When I think about it now, I laugh out loud. Junee is private and minimum-security. Goulburn is a medium, maximum and super-maximum facility run by the Department of Corrective Services. It is reputedly the toughest jail in Australia and after visiting, I can believe this to be true. The prison officers told me that when prisoners 'played up' at other jails they were sent to Goulburn. This was the jail with, purportedly, the most life-hardened men in the country.

So picture it if you will. Here's Little Miss Theatre Games, in a room with a group of Goulburn prisoners, asking them to stand in a circle and play mind games. I can hardly write about it without gasping at my folly. I say, boldly, 'What is a group of things you could start with?' 'Ah, I dunno', comes the reply. 'Okay', I say, 'I'm thinking of football teams' and there are one or two teams named before we get to a gruff, off-the-beat 'I dunno'. I try again: 'I'm thinking of types of food'. Apples, oranges and then they are snorting and looking at each other askance. For an opening gambit, it's a disaster. One of the inmates lopes off saying 'This is bullshit'. The others sort of shrug and one says, 'What's this supposed to prove?' Great. My first foray into the workshop process and every single one of them see it as pretentious nonsense.

But despite the alienation, five of them do stick with it (because the alternative is utter, mind-numbing boredom) and I abandon the idea of playing trust games. We move to tables and I talk about my verbatim theatre process, then ask them to write about an area of the jail in a set of exercise books I have brought in. This goes a little better because it is more recognisably a 'writing' exercise. I keep pushing through every obstacle, whether of personal shame, or of a more practical nature. I refuse to be intimidated, I refuse to give up on them or the workshop, I refuse to fall into a little spoilt princess heap. Okay, I misfired badly with my first offer. 'You don't come to Goulburn to play games', sneers one fellow as we draw up our chairs to the table. So yes, I've taken my dressing-down and I'm displaying resilience. And they can respect that. Yes, I fell flat on my face, but after I smeared myself with metaphorical excrement, I got back up and got on with it. They had no regard for me for my mistake; but what I did afterwards, how I recovered, the sheer take-no-prisoners (excuse the pun) determination of it really did win them over.

So my distilled mentoring message for working in unfamiliar or challenging situations is not a list of bullet points but one rather rare and difficult quality: humility. The humility when you get egg on your face to keep a straight face while you wipe it off and move on. The humility to know that because you are working with communities and individuals whose values and culture you don't know, you are certain to make humungous blunders, cringe-inducing miscalculations and insanely poor judgements. Those 'sensitive' subjects may give you a sobering dressing-down, a firm kick up the ass or even immediate rejection. Keep trying, keep asking for forgiveness, keep being interested. Persistence will be your stock-in-trade in this kind of work and humility may, at times, be your only friend.

40

The delights of discipline

Well, I call it the delights. Others call it the difficulty or the drudgery or the demands. Whatever you want to call it, I often get asked about how to have it as a writer. Often directly, but it is also the real question that lurks behind the enquiry about your routine – do you work in the morning or at night, do you write with a pen or a computer, do you imagine the context of the scene or not, do you talk out loud to yourself performing all the parts – all of these are questions about discipline and time management. For those who don't have the gift of discipline, and for those who want more, here are some suggestions for knuckling down and getting it done.

I write in the morning. Someone once asked me in a Q&A why that is and I said that it's because there is a mystery to what I do and I'd rather engage and realise that mystery in the morning and have it affirmed for the day. What metaphor might be useful? It's like a compulsion to jump off a building and every time you do, somehow, mysteriously, you land in a way that doesn't break your ankles. But before you jump your rational mind is telling you, convincingly, that you won't just break your ankles, but kill yourself. And given that you don't really know how you've achieved it on the previous leaps, you become increasingly seduced by the impossibility of the task and the certainty of failure. Only the lingering memory of the pleasure of landing with your ankles intact propels you to leap again.

That's almost it. It feels like you never quite know what is going to happen on the page, no matter how much you have prepared for it. You do have a vague idea of what is going to happen, but then something unexpected comes through you and exceeds what your rational mind anticipated. Almost. It's like diving into the sea and being shocked by the cold every time until you acclimatise and swim around comfortably and then eventually tire of it and get out. A bit like that.

It certainly gives me a thrill to write a scene – for a scene to suddenly work on the page – but it is impossible to describe how and why you know it does. There's a letting go somehow. But the only way you're going to get to it is through the discipline of doing it regularly. I'm big on daily schedules, approximating hour-by-hour what I am going to work on and, if I miss the deadline because I feel unmotivated or slack, then I set a new schedule. Say I was supposed to write a scene between 9 and 11, but I don't, then I reschedule myself to start at 10 and go till 12. I set my own rolling personal deadlines through the day.

The thing that people don't realise about writing is that you have to factor in time to be bored, time to faff around before you knuckle down and write the thing. And in a world that has social media, television, books and newspapers to fill your time, working yourself into the restless boredom from which writing springs is tough. Zadie Smith's best advice to writers is to write on a computer that is not connected to the internet.

We all know how to procrastinate, but what can drive you to work? Only a rusted-on, merciless fear of being unproductive, not only with your life, but with your day. Where does that come from? I don't quite know but I know that when I do the work I have scheduled I feel great about myself, really resolved. But when I don't or can't write every day (which is rare) I feel a kind of despair that infects my ability to enjoy anything else in my life. If you haven't filtered the world somehow through the creative sieve of your mind you might find that you rapidly feel sad, bad, divorced from the universal spirit, disconnected from your surroundings. You might find that when you create you can be just about anywhere, but when you don't, nowhere is enjoyable.

My agent is not allowed to call me before midday. Ever. I try to schedule all my administration – finding things in my files, emailing, phoning, looking at social media, having meetings – in the afternoon. It's funny how many people think that getting a literature fund or theatre fund grant is like winning the lottery. It's not, because guess what, you actually have to turn around and do the work. I'm big on cutting things into small chunks of do-able work. Especially since verbatim involves a lot of transcribing, I am ruthlessly disciplined about requiring myself to transcribe at least two pages per day. Why? Because I'm unable to work 24/7 for days at a stretch to get it all done on deadline. I know and admire people who can work like that but I don't have their stamina. Perhaps my Chinese astrological sign of the Ox is kicking in here – I have to pull a little weight every day. I am not nimble like the Rat or flamboyant like the Tiger. I have to transcribe a couple of pages a day, type up a letter a day, produce three pages of script a day. Then I cross it off and go for a walk, do some sewing or some screen-printing or something that engages my rational mind so that my subconscious can do the work I'm going to draw on the next morning.

I meet a lot of people who say they could be great writers if they could knuckle down and do the work, but they never do. And you know why that is? It's because they're not writers. When there's just you and the blank page, the person who wrestles the work to the page in a logic that can be deciphered later by others has a legally-acknowledged right to be called the copyright holder.

41
Eyes full of grit

The story of the Hay Institution for Girls is one of the darkest chapters in my own writing history and, I believe, in Australia's treatment of its young adults. This calculated, systematic, institutional brutalisation visited upon Australian young adults reminds us that the state, in all its forms, can be responsible for enacting the worst crimes of human history upon its own citizens.

I was researching the stories of women who were incarcerated in the Girls Training School in Parramatta, formerly known as the Parramatta Girls Home, when I first began to hear stories of Hay. Women in their fifties, sixties, seventies and even eighties would sit across from me, having revealed the most gruesome and horrifying recollections of their time at Parramatta, and then they would say the word: Hay. After what I had heard, it did not seem possible they could fear a place even more than Parramatta. But they spoke of Hay in hushed and fearful tones. They had been there, or had been threatened with it, or had seen its effect on other inmates who returned to Parramatta. And where the stories about Parramatta flowed out of them – jagged, brutal, struggling into the light often after many years of silence – the stories about Hay were harder to speak aloud. Often it was just a look of utter pain and despair, a quiet shaking of the head as if the horror of the recollection was too incomprehensible, too appalling to form into syllables. But then these astonishingly courageous women, these women whom I have come to respect with such deep and abiding awe, these strong and beautiful survivors, gave voice to their memories and trusted me with their feelings and their stories. And a picture emerged of an injustice so grotesque that

I could only sit open-mouthed and weeping that such treatment had been meted out to Australian children until as recently as 1974.

It also sent me into a difficult quandary as a writer. Women had told me about the riots at the Parramatta home in the 1960s, and I was intending to make Marlene Riley-Wilson's verbatim account of ascending to the roof and dislodging roof tiles to throw at the superintendent a central monologue in *Parramatta Girls*. But what to do with the stories of what happened afterwards? How a men's jail at Hay, deemed uninhabitable and shut down, was converted by the Department of Corrections into a virtual concentration camp for ten girls who had rioted and were assigned the mantle of 'worst in NSW'. It was too big a story to crush into *Parramatta Girls* but too horrific to go untold. This may happen – you uncover research that forces you to decide just how big the play you are writing is. Perhaps your work needs to become a trilogy, or perhaps you need a sequel. Or perhaps you decide to leave the untold stories for another writer, another time.

I'm grateful that Parragirls founder Bonney Djuric suggested to Amy Hardingham, then the artistic director of the Hay-based Outback Theatre for Young People, that she should commission a play about the Hay Institution for Girls. This was conceived as an entirely separate work from *Parramatta Girls*, compiled using different strategies. It would be performed, importantly, by people the same age as the incarcerated girls. While *Parramatta Girls* was designed to display the virtuoso acting skills of its trained cast, here I would highlight the assets of the young actors – their authenticity, sincerity and most of all their age: using people the same age as the original inmates would have a visceral impact in portraying the treatment of young women at Hay.

In *Eyes to the Floor*, the play which emerged, the characters are composites from stories I was told by survivors of the Hay institution, as well as from material on the public record in newspapers, the Senate *Forgotten Australians* report and from interviews with counsellors and psychologists who treat the aftermath of such incarcerations. All of the characters are fictional, but all of the stories are true, drawn from one or another of the above sources. I was especially grateful to the former employees of the Hay Institution for Girls, some of them still living in Hay, who told me their stories with candour and sincerity. I wanted to include their perspective because a central thesis of this play is that a brutal state institution like this leaves a painful legacy – most especially on the former inmates themselves, of course, but also on their families, the guards who worked there, the town of Hay, and, in ways too numerous to calibrate, on the complexion of Australia's past and its future. I have profound admiration for the town of Hay for confronting and supporting this examination of old wounds and painful histories. I commemorate the women who died carrying the burden of a childhood broken by violence and abuse in institutions such as Hay. I dedicated the play to those working with Australian children today, under enormously difficult circumstances, to provide some better way forward for neglected and troubled young women and girls.

One response was particularly interesting. I have mentioned that many people you might work with in verbatim projects know little about theatre, may never have been in a theatre and are not familiar with its conceits. One woman I rang up when I was researching told me that she didn't want to speak to me about her time in Hay or support me to make a stage play because 'it couldn't be done'. Her experience could not be 'recreated' on stage. This woman came to see the play when it was produced in Hay and said to the director after the production: 'Those girls on stage weren't suffering the way that we suffered'. The director, shocked, asked her if she would really want that and she replied: 'No, but then they shouldn't pretend that it is about what happened here'.

Fundamentally, this woman rejected the central premise of theatre: that, in this case, the writer will recreate and the actors will simulate as realistically as possible, the historical experience of the subject of the play in order to elicit empathy and understanding. For her this vicarious experience was invalid – you could not understand it without going through it. Art was only artifice, not a means to experience a deeper truth or even, sometimes, a more harrowing truth than someone inside an experience can understand. For me, art can sometimes explain or elucidate an experience by crushing a narrative into two hours when, in the full rush of life, you might not understand or examine such a story. But that was not her view. In her opinion, the entire premise of art, of theatre, of a simulation that substitutes in a deep and compelling way for 'real' life was nothing but frippery and play-acting, it was a pretentious presumption that safe, middle-class performers in a theatre company or their audience could know what she had suffered.

I understand her perspective, though I profoundly disagree. If art cannot help us to empathise with others and more deeply understand their experience then doesn't that leave us marooned on islands of individual consciousness? If we cannot come together as a collective and try to understand things that are foreign to us, how can we create a society which respects diversity, that legally and socially privileges difference? And if we make art that only reinforces our orthodoxies, and complies with a narrow set of criteria for excellence, doesn't that corral art further and further into a niche cul-de-sac? There's more than one way to represent this woman's truth about her past – maybe in the future, virtual reality will bring it into vivid relief. But even that most immersive of mediums is still a metaphor for reality, a simulation of experience to potentially produce an empathetic response, not the thing itself. I am not speaking about insensitive or inappropriate depictions of trauma which may rightly attract criticism as vicarious titillation, or the more pejorative 'trauma porn', but as a writer you will need to be sensitive about how you are balancing the honest portrayal of your subjects experience against blithe indulgence.

Before the play reading of *Dead Man Brake* in Wollongong, the local newspaper (*Illawarra Mercury*) forwarded me an email it had received, allegedly from a survivor of the Waterfall crash. The letter was in reaction to a provocatively-phrased newspaper article about the play. The community member, who had not seen the play, said it was ill-informed, degrading to the memory of those killed, and in very poor taste. I was described as disrespectful, insensitive to others and ghoulish. The *Mercury* asked me to comment.

They never published the full letter, though the paper did print an article saying that an anonymous survivor objected to the play and thought that it was was too soon to dramatise the tragedy and that it would be better to wait fifty years to write about it. They ran a response from Simon Hinton, Merrigong's artistic director, who had commissioned the play: 'Theatre is a fundamental human way of not only making sense of the things which happen to our fellow human beings, but also of honouring their memory or hard work or ongoing suffering'. Privately to me, Simon was completely supportive and said that he knew stirring up local stories would provoke or uncover strong reactions. In fact Simon was intrigued that the play was already provoking a reaction. He told me that many people had told them not to do *The Table of Knowledge* with Version 1.0, but changed their minds after seeing the production. For my part I wished that the person had contacted me directly or come to the play reading to make her feelings known so that I could talk to her about what she would like to see in the play. Many, many community members came to the production and the theatre company and I received an overwhelming number of letters, calls, texts, Facebook posts and personal responses, several saying that the play was the best Merrigong had ever produced. There was not a single complaint.

When I did *Watermark* in Katherine on the tenth anniversary of the floods, I was told that a prominent member of the town council in Katherine was of the opinion that it should not be made, that the flood should simply be forgotten. The huge community support for the work kept me going and a number of people came up and said that it was a healing experience. The play made some people realise how far they had come, and made others aware of how much they still lived in fear. People who had not been in Katherine at that time said it gave them an understanding of some of the post-traumatic stress behaviour that they saw in the Katherine population even now.

In any community there are those who heal by remembering and talking and those who heal by nursing a private grief that they don't want made public. There are many different ways to grieve and, as an artist, you are among those who weigh in with the verbalisers, the expressers, the processors. Both approaches need to be respected. My position, ultimately, is to acknowledge that public tragedies happen to both the individuals involved and the communities who respond and rebuild, and if there is a community wanting to speak up and commemorate, to air their continuing grief, your job as an artist must be to privilege their voices back to the community themselves.

But as a close work theatre maker, you should always use community meetings or community newspapers or the community grapevine and make every effort to give *everyone* a chance to have their voice heard. Sometimes, even with the best ethical intentions, some people will object. The best you can do is make sure you can say, 'I gave everyone a chance to contribute, I listened to as many people as I could and in the end this is how I use my labour as an artist to give back to this community'.

Eyes to the Floor has been published as a companion work with *Parramatta Girls* and it remains one of my fondest achievements, even if it was the one that drilled the biggest and most indelible hole in my soul.

42
Courage in every fibre

In October 2011, I conceived and presented a visual art and verbatim theatre work called *Swimming Upstream* at the Orchard Gallery in Redfern. The project concerned adult survivors of child abuse, and I worked with the organisation ASCA (Adult Survivors of Child Abuse, now the Blue Knot Foundation) to guarantee it would be authentic, accurate and healing. For three years, Heather Robinson and Reverend Andrew Collis (chair and minister of the South Sydney Uniting Church) had presented a memorial service for adult survivors of child abuse. *Swimming Upstream* became part of their long-term commitment to this important community health issue.

The first part of the project was an artwork designed to engage the community by creating a safe space where women could come and participate without the pressure of immediate disclosure. The artwork was created by survivors, community members and supporters who wove thousands of origami fish by hand from small blue ribbons over many months. The idea was to take the tangled knot of child abuse – the symbol of ASCA – and give abuse survivors a sense of control as they wove the story of their abuse into the larger fabric of their lives. That each fish was individually handmade and unique was a metaphor for the individual pain of each abuse survivor. The care, dedication and concern taken over each fish also symbolically honoured the individual stories and experiences of people who have suffered childhood trauma.

After many months of bi-weekly weaving sessions and many more hours of participants making fish at home, we had between four and five thousand coloured fish from which we created an exhibition. Each fish carried the pain and hope of the estimated four to five million Australian adults who have suffered some form of childhood trauma. Like fish swimming upstream, adults recovering from trauma are always, metaphorically, swimming against the current. But despite struggling against powerful forces that push them the other way, they can make it upstream and recover from their ordeal.

When visitors walked into the Orchard Gallery they were greeted by hundreds of small blue origami fish swimming above them as if in mid-air. The lines of suspended fish continued as they proceeded into the main part of the gallery, thousands and thousands of them. Strung up on invisible fishing lines, predominantly blue but with occasional flashes of other colours including red, green and yellow, it gave the effect of being underwater. Caught by the breeze, the fish seemed to move. As people walked around the gallery, the individual character and charm of the fish changed with the aspect, the angle and the visitors changing proximity. The exhibition of small, delicate, highly individual fish swimming up the walls, some of them tangled by the wind, offered many important symbolic metaphors. The predominance of blue – ASCA's colour – symbolised that adult survivors are not alone. The makers of the exhibition hoped that visitors would share other metaphorical intepretations with the weavers and curators.

The second stage of the project was a public reading of individual verbatim interviews with abuse survivors. I sourced participants from the Redfern community, through the ASCA website and from recommendations after attending sessions for health professionals working with abuse survivors. I travelled from Summer Hill to Waterloo, from Bowral to Hornsby and beyond to interview them. Many of the abuse survivors had contributed to the exhibition and I knew they would attend the showing. I structured the script so that four community narrators read sections of poetry, jingles and songs woven through the narrative. Between these sections, a procession of readers from the audience would read the stories taken from the interviews in the words of the survivors.

It was a daring but also affirming experience to conceive a public performance when the reader is unknown and you cannot control how they will perform. Of course the audience knew that it was spontaneous, that it was up to them to 'step up' and this created an astonishing tension and unity. I have seen a similar effect in the theatre when an understudy, sometimes holding script in hand, has to replace the usual performer for some reason. The audience collectively wills the substitute performer to do well; they actively participate in carrying the understudy, washing the stage with waves of encouraging laughter and even applause.

In this Redfern gallery, it was a small miracle of healing to watch people come up from the audience to read the stories of survivors – to sometimes cry a little, to find the courage to use their voice, to feel the support of the audience, to become bolder and bolder, to participate in their own healing and to gain courage and self-esteem in collective truth-telling. After the presentation, one reader said, 'I didn't think I could do it, but then, each time I got up I felt stronger and stronger about being able to participate'. Another found, 'When it first started I began to cry and thought, I have to get out of here, but then as it went on, and I stood up to read a couple of times, I felt myself really able to do it'. A third said:

> My therapist told me I should come along to the presentation. When people from the audience were invited to read I went up to take a turn, not knowing what I would be confronted with, but then so many of the aspects of the story on the page resonated with my own story. It was amazing to read someone else's story aloud that was both not mine and so much mine at the same time. It was really amazing.

When making this kind of community-sourced and participatory work, I am always looking for creative solutions to the problem of not exposing individuals to intrusive public scrutiny, but also making the work authentic and vivid; in other words to find a way to both protect participants and expose their stories. Allowing abuse survivors, their supporters and family, and other community members to read these verbatim accounts was an effective way to allow for both anonymity and authenticity. The act of getting up and reading publicly at the event was a statement of solidarity and support, a leap of faith into the unknown of what might be on the page, and a reassurance that the community were all in this together – the reading and the healing.

And not knowing whether the readers were abuse survivors or not was a powerful metaphor for the way in which child abuse lives all around us, unseen and unacknowledged for the most part in the lives of adults, while having its destructive, debilitating effect.

At the end of the presentation, during thank yous, I asked if any of the survivors who had contributed stories would like to stand and take a bow. One brave woman did so and then addressed the audience saying, 'I can't tell you how important it was for me to sit there and hear my story read … and just be believed'. The power of her confession in that moment will, I'm sure, resonate with the assembled audience for a long time. Another audience member said, 'I wanted to come today to bear witness. I believe that if, at ASCA, we want people to listen, then we first have to be listeners. I came today as an act of solidarity for those who need their truth to be listened to'. A week after the reading, the prime minister announced the federal Royal Commission into the response of various public and religious institutions to child abuse.

Swimming Upstream was a small but definite step towards healing for the audience who gathered at the Orchard Gallery that day, against the backdrop of a thousand acts of ribbon woven into fish, on their way to recovery. For me it was a revelatory model for extending the verbatim process out past the fourth wall, a way to make the audience participants in the performance. The play concludes with a chanted final line:

> Alone we are smallish and churlish and bullish,
> Together we replenish and nourish and astonish.

43

Wait to be asked

During my childhood, my stepfather Roy used to take my brother and I on oyster-gathering expeditions down near Tom Uglys Bridge on the Georges River, Sydney. At the tender age of eight, I was handed a short-handled oyster knife and told to cherish it like a prize which, indeed, it turned out to be. In this environment it was no knife, no oyster and no oyster, no tucker. If you didn't learn quick smart how to shuck the oysters spread before you on every rock, well, tough luck. Everyone else had their own mouths to fill.

Between 2010 and 2016 when I had the privilege to work with the supremely gifted Goenpul / Jagara / Bundjulung poet and filmmaker Dr Romaine Moreton, I learnt that her knowledge about, respect for, and enjoyment of eating freshly shucked oysters is fundamental to her creative genius and the power of her original vision. This can be seen through her brilliant short films *The Oysterman* and *The Farm* and her astonishing collection of poetry, *Post Me to the Prime Minister*. We worked together as co-writers and co-directors of *One Billion Beats*, which shows how the representation of First Nations people in Australian cinema intersects with Romaine's lived experience throughout her years. We liaised with Tharawal elders about the introduction and context of the work, which meant engaging with the massacres that took place on their land; and the poetry sits in a musical score by Yorta Yorta / Dja Dja Wurrung musician Lou Bennett which is so beautiful that it used to regularly make my eyes water with wonder and tears. As part of the development of *One Billion Beats*, I listened to Romaine yarning about her life, sharing her philosophical and cultural perspectives and her artistic ambitions. We structured the transcribed material together and collaborated on the presentation style and content. But although I have a credit as co-writer, this is Romaine's story and ICIP (Indigenous Cultural Intellectual Property).

Cultural appropriation is an ongoing and passionately contested debate in Australia in 2017. Who can write what stories? How can you authentically represent diversity and humanity in literature and theatre? In my experience close work enables you to work respectfully and sincerely with people who have a profoundly different identity to you as long as you are willing to offer your creative energy to their service. I am a woman and a lesbian, which gives me access in some sense to the exclusions and discriminations that are practised on women and lesbians in our culture. But it would be wrong for me to presume that those identities allow me to understand other forms of oppression or discrimination. To do that I have to do what any good writer or theatre maker must do – research, listen, research, listen, listen.

I worked in a similar way on the development of *The Fox and the Freedom Fighters*. I spent time yarning with Aunty Rhonda Dixon-Grovenor (Dharug / Yuin) and Nadeena Dixon (Wiradjuri / Dharug / Yuin) about their lives and experience as the family of activist Charles 'Chicka' Dixon and their consummate work of researching and documenting his legacy. During our discussions I encouraged them to dig down not just into their father and grandfather's story but also their own. We structured the material together around filmed and performed segments, but the content was intrinsically personal and the intellectual and cultural integrity of the work resides with these two remarkable and resilent women.

Working with Romaine and Lou, and Rhonda and Nadeena, and on a variety of dramaturgical projects with Andrea James, was a wonder – a mystery. I am strenuously resisting the temptation to reference the notion of finding pearls. It might be an apt description of how much I cherish my time with these unique individuals but, well, how many of you have ever found a pearl inside an oyster and *really* know what it is like? In a world where it's rare to eat an oyster that is not pre-shucked and rinsed in chlorinated tap water, working with these women was like tasting the intense flavour of a living oyster – unrefrigerated, raw and deeply nourishing to both the body and the spirit.

I first worked with Stephen Page at Bangarra Dance Theatre on *ID* (part of *Belong*) in 2011 and then on *Patyegarang* in 2014, when I researched the notebooks of William Dawes, an astronomer and soldier, who set up an observatory on what is now called Dawes Point in Sydney. Dawes' notebooks, unearthed in London in 1972, give an insight into the humour, tension, intimacy and depth of his friendship with Patyegarang, a young Dharug woman. They provided a starting point to the process of imagining the story of *Patyegarang* presented by Bangarra. Yet even more potent was Stephen's cultural knowledge gifted from the many elders, countrymen, artists and ancestors with whom he has worked. In our discussion of 'incidents' from the notebooks, Stephen would frequently draw parallels with his knowledge of other cultural instances which might explain why the Eora reacted in the way that Dawes observed. I found it inspiring to witness this 'transfer' and 'translation' of cultural knowledge, as if Patyegarang was speaking directly to Stephen through the notebooks. It was like a contemporary Dharug elder recognising significance in the details of a colonial painting that the artist was perhaps unaware of capturing. I watched and documented as Stephen drew from Dawes' meticulous, scientific chronicle a rich and playful and deeply authentic language of movement and land and spirit, to embody Patyegarang's world on stage.

I wrote in the program note about kā´ma, a Dharug word in the William Dawes diaries, which means 'to dig', and noted that although we used the German word 'dramaturgy' to describe my work with Stephen, I thought it would be much more appropriate say that I was the kā´maturg on this project because I was Stephen's digging tool and reflecting pool and sometimes his Shakespearian fool in the creative journey to honour and imagine into breath the respected ancestors, Patyegarang, the Eora and William Dawes.

In 2017 I again worked with Stephen as dramaturg on the acclaimed narrative dance work *Bennelong*. In this case I explored the work of historians and others and sometimes sent Stephen information as poems, to infuse his day with beauty and artistry as well as for brevity. Although they were intended only for his eyes, I was intrigued that some of these poems inspired sections of the narrative – composer

Steve Francis and the remarkable Bangarra dancers made them their own. In this way they were sieved through the bodies and voices of a living culture – claimed and changed, just as Stephen transformed the historical Bennelong and conjured him to life, to breath, to honour, in this landmark new dance theatre work.

I first met Ursula Yovich's alter-ego at the the Helpmann Awards in 2008 when I was having a few consoling champagnes on an after-party couch after my nominated play *Parramatta Girls* did not win. Ms Yovich began to regale us with a 'persona' named Barbara who was pissed off, ramped up, foul-mouthed, wickedly funny, shamelessly sexual, flirtatious and dangerous. She was wild-eyed, hip-shaking, loud-laughing and brilliant good fun. Ursula is a gob-smackingly talented performer and as I watched her between tears of helpless laughter and howls of disbelief, I saw a version of First Nations female power that busted the stereotypes. This was Ursula as raw and real as it comes, a version of herself that she said she had no opportunity to expose on the stage at the time. It was one of those moments when you open your eyes to see what has always been there – and you can never see that person in the same way again. Producer Vicki Gordon began managing Ursula's muscial career in 2010 and she encouraged Ursula and I to work together on a show for Barbara. Stephen Page joked that Barbara could have her own band called the camp dogs, after the dogs that hang around camp fires in the Territory and elsewhere. The Australia Council funded development workshops with Elaine Crombie, Jeremy Brennan and Casey Donovan and Leah Purcell directing. Adm Ventoura and Ursula and I would go to Adm's studio to write songs as Ursula brought the remarkable instrument that is her singing voice to cohere the words and melodies. Eamon Flack came to a rough draft showing of the work on a rainy Saturday in 2013. With Belvoir's support we continued to work on *Barbara and the Camp Dogs* and, nine years later, Barbara is as much of a spit-fire wonder on Belvoir's stage as she was on the first night I saw her. In 2017, Leticia Cáceres and her team, especially Stephen Curtis and Karen Norris and the astonishing band – Michelle Vincent, Debbie Yap, and Jessica Dunn – transformed Belvoir into a rock gig music event that conjured Sydney Theatre Award nominations for Best New Australian Work, Best Original Score and acting gong noms for both Ursula and Elaine. Troy Brady was the magic ingredient of brother love and Luke McGettigan was the stage manager extraordinaire. I'm very grateful to have been able to ride with Ursula's profoundly unique spirit in Barbara's motorbike sidecar.

If Romaine Moreton wants to collaborate with me as a co-writer and co-director, that is her prerogative. The same is true for Aunty Rhonda Dixon-Grovenor and Nadeena Dixon. If Stephen Page finds it useful for me to work as a dramaturg and trawl through the historical record and brief him on accounts of colonial history to make the best possible art for his living culture, that is his choice. If Ursula Yovich and I bounce off each other in fun, sparky, tough, combative ways to write songs and scenes for *Barbara and the Camp Dogs*, that is a great privilege for me. People have asked me how non-Indigenous writers can help tell Indigenous stories and the short answer is 'Wait to be asked'. The artists I've discussed here have the primary creative roles and I contribute my imagination, skills, informed advice and professional perspective to collaborate in *their* artistic vision.

I've found that sharing my close work theatre experience in these collaborations is like learning to shuck an oyster. It takes instinct and experience to know where to place the oyster knife on the lip of the shell, in order to leverage up the top of the bivalve. It requires sensitivity and expert wrist action – a sublime combination of strength and delicacy – to twist the oyster blade *just so* until the lid of the oyster comes up cleanly and whole. It takes concentration to keep the salty liquor in the living oyster without spilling it all over yourself. Then it takes a certain ruthless decisiveness to cut the oyster away from the adductor muscle. Too often dramaturgy fails because of the application of too much force – just like when you're shucking oysters.

44

Best process for best practice

I have worked with several organisations that deal with especially vulnerable and sensitive people – among them Parragirls, Adults Surviving Child Abuse (ASCA, now the Blue Knot Foundation), Purple House and Shine for Kids. At the end of my process with both the ASCA and Shine organisations, I conducted formal interviews with their respective CEOs – Cathy Kezelman from ASCA and Gloria Larman from Shine. It was illuminating to hear their take on how to deal with their clients without psychological injury to either party and to fold them into my own experience, to come up with a short set of guidelines. This is essentially list of do's and don'ts – to protect both the subjects and the artists from unnecessary psychological damage.

Some of them are so obvious and natural that they should go without saying, but I have been surprised at anecdotal reports from clients of these two organisations concerning inexperienced, well-meaning or just plain exploitative artists 'blundering in where angels fear to tread' so I have tried to spell these principles out as clearly as possible.

- A participant should be able to assess and check an interviewer's bona fides via contact with people or organisations that they already know (and implicitly trust). This is necessary for both the interviewee and the interviewer. If any issue, bad effect or trouble arises they will both have an intermediary who can assist them. When

I was looking for subjects for a Blue Knot Day presentation about adult survivors of child abuse, I advertised in the *South Sydney Herald*, a community newspaper, via the ASCA website and via contact I made with treating therapists at ASCA workshops for health professionals. Potential interviewees contacted the *Herald* editor, who is also an ordained minister, as well as ASCA and their therapists before speaking to me.

- Be alert to the vulnerability and sensitivity of speaking to traumatised people. In the case of child sexual abuse, for instance, don't go straight to a request for gory details about the abuse experience. You need to express interest in their entire story, and approach it gently. Be mindful it is a privilege if they decide to tell you about the abuse, not something to 'take for granted'. In essence, don't be tabloid in your approach, imagining that the most voyeuristic details are the most compelling ones. Instead focus on the more subtle, complex and even contradictory aspects of human nature. How is this person revealing that to you?
- When or if you are told something shocking, strike a careful balance between 'not too scandalised' but 'not too blasé'. I hope I don't need to advise against melodramatically clapping your hand to your mouth, shaking your head or tsking your tongue, though a discreet gesture of any of these may, in the right circumstances, be appropriate. In your questions it might be useful to mention in passing some of the things other interviewees have told you, not in a way that breaks confidentiality, but to reassure the person at hand that you won't be scandalised or judgemental. The Parramatta girls often told me that they preferred speaking to other Parramatta girls about their experience because they 'understand in a way that if you haven't been through it you don't'. So you have to convince them, that, in a vicarious way, you have 'been through it' via your experience of interviewing others. Try using generalised statements: 'some girls have spoken about blaming themselves' or 'some people have

told me that it took them years to even name it as abuse because at the time they simply didn't know the words'. You need to bring an intimate and sophisticated knowledge of the psychological effects of abuse to the table. Don't act like a shocked ingenue but don't be afraid to show your own emotional response – many times I stopped my interviews with the Parramatta or Hay girls to have a little cry with them. But I emphasise 'little'– give yourself to an authentic moment of empathy, not the full cathartic thunderclap. Don't make them have to look after you. Don't lose control and indulge in your own response so that the interview suddenly becomes about you. But don't be a cold, unaffected automaton either.

- At regular intervals ask them if they are okay. Do they need to stop, would they like a glass of water? This is about both making sure they *are* okay and also reinforcing constantly that they are in the driver's seat, that they are controlling this.
- Tell them that you are going to call or text them the next day to make sure they are still okay. And if you have told them this, for pity's sake DO IT. Don't make promises that you don't keep. They have generously granted you their story. Show some respect, show some continuing concern for the effect the interview might have on their lives. So retain the connection that you have established. Don't suffocate or smother them with over-kindness. Just text them if you say you're going to.
- Before you leave the interview, check that there is someone they can call in the unlikely event that they feel dreadful and alone after the interview. Don't make a big deal of it, act as if a rough night, or the need to talk to someone, would be quite normal. I never mention the 'need to have a glass of wine' because so many survivors struggle with alcohol or drug addiction issues. But if they mention a glass of wine, affirm that. Strike a balance between inappropriate controlling and utter indifference – don't just waltz in and rip their story from them without qualms, but don't become their mother

or their best friend. They are adults after all.
- That is, unless they're not. Interviewing children needs a whole different set of strategies. When I worked with the children out at Shine for Kids I didn't ask them direct questions but set exercises and games and workshop ideas. In one exercise I told them that I knew (because 'other children have told me') that they might sometimes make up a small white lie about where their parent was, rather than reveal they were in jail. I then asked them to write a bona fide lie – 'the biggest, most outrageous, most unlikely lie you can muster'. When one little girl called Mona, aged 8, wrote that her father was away on a Greenpeace-like ship saving the world and the planet for six years, all the adults in the room swallowed hard. Mona had revealed that, just like any other kid, she wanted her father to be someone to look up to and admire, rather than the stigmatised, jailed criminal he was. It was something she could probably never put into words. So find a way to extract children's feelings without directly asking them. Then again, I had a laugh with one of the Shine workers at the end of one session. She said, 'You spent all that time subtly softening them up to tell you about their experience through exercises and games and then when you asked them they just told you straight out. The thing with our kids is that because you're here, because you already know the secret (that they have a parent in jail) they speak to you as openly as they would to each other or to us. It's the people who don't know the secret that they won't talk to about it'. So sometimes a direct question is not the worst course you can take. It's all about feeling your way. Have strategies up your sleeve to respond to what occurs.
- Be aware that hearing, reading, being exposed to ugly story after heartbreaking story after tragic, infuriating injustice will affect you. Sometimes when I was transcribing the letters to Lindy Chamberlain-Creighton, I could hardly see the screen for sobbing – just the mind-boggling, breathtaking cruelty and sadistic injustice of it. There is a cost to working with this

material and you need to count the cost. ASCA CEO Cathy Kezelman calls it vicarious trauma or transmitted trauma. From my first meeting with her she insisted that I put in place strategies to look after myself as I gathered stories from abuse survivors. Be aware that it can have a bigger effect on you than you realise. Don't wait until you are screaming at your partner before you recognise the trauma from the interview you did that afternoon. If you have a bad dream, think about giving yourself time out to absorb it. Go for a walk, go for a swim. If you've spent the morning transcribing super confronting material, spend the afternoon doing something that makes you feel good about the world and other human beings.

- Often community organisations have long associations with your interviewees. They can see the different effects of storytelling on individuals. One person may be quite good at first but later have poor consequences, another might have the opposite experience. A client may find the interview hard and challenging but later report they feel a sense of completion or relief. Organisations may have the knowledge to judge the likely reaction of their clients or even quantify the best 'prospects' for interviewing and storytelling. So use their recommendations where you can, and, if they require it, let one of their counsellors or staff workers sit in.
- At the same time, be aware that many community organisations are understaffed and time-poor. Gloria Larman at Shine for Kids prioritises her staff to sit in on any interview or encounter between 'outsiders' and clients. This means that media or artist demands for stories puts a heavy demand on her organisation. Gloria Larman supported me because:
    a) I worked with her and her staff to make sure the time frame was suitable for them (and it changed quite frequently);
    b) I was fine when some clients dropped out and rescheduled (which they did often);
    c) I attended many events where I could mix with staff and

        client families and gather my own information and didn't need to be 'looked after';

    d) I offered the children an activity and an opportunity for fun and entertainment that took some pressure off their staff, so I was giving back to the organisation as well as asking something of it.

- You may be asked to undergo a police check or other process before working with children. Do it without complaint or resistance. Yes, bureaucracy can be tedious and protracted but it is unreasonable to take your frustrations out on people who are, simply, part of the system. It took me five months to get permission to go into Goulburn Correctional Centre and work with the prisoners there, it also took me five months to get permission to get into the Royal Archives at Windsor, and it took more than eighteen months to get an interview with the COO of News Corporation. You need to be patient and persistent and actually compliant when it comes to bureaucracy and gatekeepers. You will need to be water wearing away at stone.

45

Inconvenient behaviour

When I was undertaking my bachelor degree I supported myself by working for twenty to thirty hours per week at the Oriental Variety Store in Enmore (and also at its outlets in Bexley North and Rockdale). The degree had only fifteen face-to-face hours per week, with practical projects and assignments to fill up the rest of my time. But I didn't have the financial luxury to focus solely on the course, so I worked in the Oriental Variety Store – an early combination of a two-dollar shop and an expensive gift shop or import emporium in Chinatown. Mr Gordon Lin sourced embroidered and crocheted tablecloths of the highest quality, as well as embroidered handkerchiefs, crocheted doilies and runners; but he augmented these gorgeous items with folding paper fans, affordable black clothing (very popular with the grieving Italian matrons) as well as all kinds of homewares, trinkets and costume jewellery.

Enmore was a welfare-class suburb in the 1980s and the Oriental Variety Store offered their customers lay-buys. Lay-buys, which were widespread before credit cards became commonplace, allowed people to pay off an item bit by bit before they took it home. You'd enter the customer's name into a small exercise book and every payment was calculated manually and entered in this 'lay-buy book' for reference. The item itself was stored under the retail clothing displays until it was fully paid. Most people paid in instalments of ten or twenty dollars. One woman, though, paid off her small purchases one or two cents at a time (they were still in circulation). The practice infuriated Mr Lin since it was unprofitable to take so much time to service the customer. I think he would have preferred to give the items away rather than tolerate the absurd scheme. But Mrs Lorna Davidson, the store manager, believed it was better to let the woman pay in small tender, with dedication and commitment, than to offer her charity.

Over the years of my life I have often thought about this one-cent-at-a-time purchaser. I can vividly recall her face and her features, whereas I can barely remember a single other customer in the store. It was inconvenient, unprofitable and sometimes infuriating behaviour, a kind of retail drip-torture. Yet the day she finally paid off the last single cent was remarkable. The staff talked about it for days – we all knew the customer had picked up her purchase and we rejoiced in her achievement.

I'm not suggesting that you replicate this behaviour as a consumer. You certainly couldn't convince any large department store or even a small corner store to allow you to do this in the early 21st century. But I'd like to use this story as a metaphor for adopting the long view of your progress as a writer. It is easy to say don't judge your achievements, don't compare your achievements, don't relativise your achievements. It's all very well to say that but we work in an industry where the status of having work at the big theatres – on the main stages, at important venues and festivals – is a ticket to greater opportunities. But I would encourage you to consider your achievements in relation to who you are, your own circumstances and the kind of work you are undertaking. Like the woman paying off her purchases one cent at a time, there may be times when you are working with a community and you feel like you have to do so much work to get a tiny ninety minutes on stage. So much placating and politicking and transcribing stuff that never gets used – an entire mining lease of material to get barely two hours of diamonds.

The other conclusion to draw from this story is to celebrate being difficult, inconvenient, ornery and impractical. Or maybe the best moral to draw from it is an even gentler one – about the satisfaction of doing things yourself no matter how long they take. For me, this one-cent-for-every-visit woman, this have-a-twenty-minute-chat for a two-cent payment woman, this person who found ways to factor what she needed into the limitations of where she found herself remains a strong, archetypal inspiration. The tortoise for our hare-loving times perhaps. I've never forgotten her and I don't suppose I ever will.

46

More than words can say

Have you been to a local dump recently? Let me recommend it as highly as possible when you are working with a regional community. Or just as an artist brain excursion of infinite fascination. Yes, truly, a visit to a rubbish tip can be an imaginative bonanza, a snapshot literally and visually of what the community does and does not value, how it sorts, what it chooses to preserve and attempts to re-use. When I visited the town dump in Katherine, during my research for *Watermark*, I was overwhelmed by the sorted mounds of disposed materials – the tangle of electrical goods in the whitegoods section, the large pieces of artfully rusting metal in the metal section, the piles of beautiful furniture in the wood section and so on. Golf clubs, welders, lawnmowers, picture frames, boats (yes, truly, whole boats!), plus all manner of materials that could be refashioned into works of art, or simply plugged back in and reused.

Wandering around this paradise of discarded bounty brought back intensely happy memories of childhood adventures with my brother and stepfather when we would get up early to reconnoitre the piles of junk thrown out in the semi-annual council clean-ups. Oh, the furniture that we pushed back to our house in our specially-adapted pram on wheels with its top removed. I vividly recall finding a whole box of unbroken Christmas decorations once. Imagine, if you will, my delight when I continued to dig down and found a fully intact 3-metre plastic Christmas tree underneath. It is no exaggeration to say that I was high on the ecstasy of this find – it is one of the sweetest memories of my young life. Is there anything better than finding something valuable for free? That year was the best Christmas ever and, I confess, I still evoke that find every year by methodically putting up a green plastic Christmas tree, decorated with my grandmother's fragile Christmas decorations. No amount of shoulder rubbing with the fresh tree buying aesthetic, no amused contempt for my plastic tree, will ever deter me.

The Katherine dump is especially wonderful – they have a terrific tip shop and now boast a regional festival of junk arts – but I have replicated the joy at other well-organised dumps too. But let me return to the issue of how all this can help, especially for a close work writer. We are all familiar with the term 'found materials' in contemporary visual art. It has been useful to sometimes think of myself as a 'found materials' playwright. The term implicitly understands that the visual artist must *transform* the found material to make it art. From as far back as Duchamp's urinal we have understood that the act of putting this object in a gallery and calling it art makes it revolutionary. The act of taking 'found dialogue' and transferring it into a theatre is rarely understood in the same transgressive way. I believe this reflects a misunderstanding that verbatim is all, and only, about words and not also about images – indeed the term 'verbatim' itself underscores this. It is another reason why I have moved towards describing my work as close work theatre.

The point of this story about the Katherine dump is to encourage the fledgling writer to do more than interview people when working with a regional community. Walk around the place and look for a central visual metaphor to help structure and direct your material. Interviewees in Katherine frequently talked about how the flood generated so much waste material it filled the dump several times over, forcing the creation of an entirely new site. Although the dump I saw was well-organised, the piles of broken and discarded materials, intertwined and unnaturally merged with incongruous companions, gave me a vision of the tangling, swirling floodwaters, animal bodies, sediment, building materials and household belongings described to me in the interviews. This informed the design of the stage when the reading was performed, and also the way I was drawn towards images describing piles of waste in people's front yards and elsewhere when I was editing the material.

Like a great work for radio, meaningful drama, whether using verbatim material or not, needs to create visual images in the mind of the audience. In close work drama especially, the world of your characters and the context of their experience will be intrinsic to your understanding of community behaviours that (to an outsider) may appear to be exaggerated or improbable. My trip to the dump fundamentally deepened and shifted my priorities as a writer on *Watermark*, so that things I might have ignored or perceived differently resonated when I analysed what was said. In a similar vein, accompanying the Parragirls to the site of their incarceration was a revelation in provoking empathy and, more importantly, prompted the dramatic premise of *Parramatta Girls*, namely, that place affects memory. I began the play *Dead Man Brake* with physical descriptions of the site of the train accident precisely because the site was inaccessible to grieving relatives, an inaccessibility that underlined the commemorative responsibilities of the stage set and the theatre itself as a place of sacred memorial. For *Shafana and Aunt Sarrinah* the hospitality, warmth and generosity offered to me during the research process was distilled dramatically into the stage business of two women preparing a meal together on stage, complete with visceral and sensuous smells, and metaphorical notions of nurture. Theatre is, of course, a visual medium. Staging it should be acutely visually conscious. Let your research and writing process inspire and shape the visual symbols in your work, so you interface with more than the verbal representations of community.

47

No shoes, no divas

In 2012 the Sydney Festival and the New Zealand International Arts Festival commissioned a collaboration with producer Vicki Gordon and six Indigenous singer songwriters. *Walk a Mile in my Shoes* is a work of musical theatre that combines spoken word poetry, storytelling and song, performed by Barefoot Divas, six multi-award winning First Nations female singer-songwriters: Emma Donovan (Gumbaynggirr), Ursula Yovich (Burrara / Serbian), Ngaiire (Papua New Guinean / Australian), Merenia Gillies (Māori / Roma / Welsh), Whirimako Black (Māori) and Maisey Rika (Māori). I interviewed these six divas and structured the piece so the performers could reflect on their lives both as individuals and First Nation women, and describe their experiences in both word and song. All of the story excerpts were scripted and, even though I used their material verbatim, the artists had to learn their lines for performance. They spoke about their lives, their songs, their life in the industry and the importance of their cultural practices to their songwriting. I also directed the work, along with Adm Ventoura as musical director. In Australia it sold out three days before we opened, and in New Zealand it twice sold out the 1000-seat Wellington Town Hall as well as two other regional performances.

Central to the work is an astonishing monologue written for Ursula Yovich. It was one of the highlights of my career to shape Ursula's extraordinary passion, fury, frustration and longing into this speech. When Ursula, unarguably one of the most gifted performers in the world, rose to give this monologue during rehearsals, the other divas encouraged her with 'You say it, girl, you tell it for all of us'. In it Ursula laments:

I've worked for fifteen years and I'm really proud of what I've achieved. But I've only ever been asked to do one film role that wasn't Indigenous. And that was for a stop motion animation. And you know I think all of us say this thing to ourselves, 'it doesn't matter', 'it's okay', 'I'm okay with it' and then one day, and this is so scary for me to talk about ... one day I realised that I just can't say 'it's okay' any more. I can't keep the door closed on all this ... rage you know, all this fury that I'm living now and I'm only allowed to be ... this much. And there's this knocking on the door of my heart, saying 'It's not okay', 'I'm not okay with how it is'. And the knocking becomes a long low thumping on the door, bang bang bang. 'You're not going to lie to yourself any more that it is okay'. And you know ... what happens when I answer that door? Well first thing that happens is that I realise that it's not a door at all but a dam wall. And that water is ... the colour of a slammed fingernail, covered in churned up ocean scum, and sniggering cold. Knife-point cold. I'm moving to try and stay warm but living in fear of what slime is down there, the angry scrape of all my grievances and pain. My legs just pistons below a cramped up belly. I want to just let go completely and open right up and share who I am ... but deep down ... this time, this place, the world I live in right now ... on tough days ... on the really tough days, the world says to me, we don't really accept you as equal, not right deep down.

Ursula's deep passion, structured to flow in *complete service* to the indescribable beauty of her spirit, was made breath and flesh in that moment on stage. Ursula and I were so inspired by this collaboration that we began writing songs for a full show, giving birth to *Barbara and the Camp Dogs*. In the Barefoot Divas project I was a willing tool to fashion the experience of these women for the stage and had the wisdom to get out of the way, to step back in order to bring their stories forward so that my skills, professional opinion and experience were liberated by the generosity and creativity of the six performers.

Later in the year I made a radio documentary for ABC's *Into the Music* that you can find online if you search for Barefoot Divas and *Into the Music*. I had initially interviewed the divas and shaped the festival script before they got together, but the interviews for the documentary came from rehearsals for the show, which gave them a connected authenticity. I'd had to manufacture the connections and relationships from the first interviews, whereas the documentary material was pulled from genuine interactions in rehearsal. When the show was subsequently remounted for the Queensland Music Festival, I pulled in some material from the documentary and the quality of the storytelling jumped – it was more natural and flowed better. The work continues to grow. *Walk a Mile in my Shoes* toured North America and Canada in 2014 with more modifications and rewrites and yet again in 2015 when it sold out the 2000-seat Hong Kong Concert Hall, as part of the Hong Kong Arts Festival.

The Barefoot Divas collaboration, with the performers singing in six-part harmony in their own and each other's languages, is a powerful metaphor for the value of each individual in diverse communities across the planet. Beyond the tunes of their individual voices, Barefoot Divas sing a song about the possibilities of mutual respect and exchange between cultures – a song whose time will come, whose time must come.

48

The king's man

In October 2014 I secured the privilege of access to the Royal Archives at Windsor Castle, a short rail journey from London, where Queen Elizabeth II holds copyright on all the papers of her royal predecessors. It had taken me five months and the imprimatur of a fellowship from the Australian Prime Ministers Centre at the Museum of Australian Democracy to be granted this special access. Playwrights are infrequently allowed in to review these archives; even academics have selective purview. I was excited to be granted the rare opportunity to have a look into this remarkable storehouse of regal administration . My request was to see the papers and diaries of King George V, specifically those relating to the 1930 visit of the Australian Prime Minister James Scullin, when Scullin insisted, against the king's wishes, on appointing Sir Isaac Isaacs as Governor-General. Isaacs was our first ever Australian-born – or 'native-born' as they said in those days – representative of the Crown.

The Royal Archives are located in the Round Tower, a magnificent 12th-century mediaeval keep. They open precisely at 9 am, not a moment before, as I found one chilly morning when I arrived at 8:30. I began to walk around the grounds of Windsor Castle but after one too many suspicious glances from security personnel whispering into their Motorola radios, I gave up and sat on a slatted wooden bench waiting to be 'let up'.

At the appointed time you are escorted from the security gatehouse to the base of an imposing flight of some two hundred stairs up to a door with a brass plate which simply says 'Royal Archives'. There you wait for an assistant archivist to come and escort you to the researchers' room.

The National Library of Australia holds few of Scullin's prime ministerial papers, and most of the five boxes in their manuscript collection relate to his work after World War II so you can imagine the thrill that moved down in me to a molecular level when I discovered the Royal Archives held original telegrams and memorandum from Prime Minister Scullin which did not exist in the NLA cache. There were also memorandum from Lord Stamfordham, the king's private secretary, to King George V detailing briefings they took on the option of abolishing the position of governor-general altogether rather than defer to Scullin's preference. Can you imagine me reading the originals of this incredible historical exchange seated in a small room in which you are compelled to be reverently quiet as you write out these memos in pencil? Abolish the office of governor-general rather than concede an Australian to the position? I knew that Professor John Waugh, a legal academic, had already published this little known fact but, as many of my fellow researchers and archive lovers will attest, there is nothing like holding in your hand the same document that the king held as he contemplated this option. I had trouble stilling my limbs to prevent myself from jumping up and embracing the archivists.

I visited the archive on four occasions. *Crossing the King*, my play about Scullin and his defiant act of Australian nationalism, has been co-commissioned by the National Theatre of London and the Sydney Theatre Company. It is a fifteen-actor epic history play. I have high hopes it will grace a stage in Australia and/or the UK sometime in the near future. In that manner I may reach thousands of people with a story of courage, duty and vision and, I hope, compel an interest in the history of constitutional change and the mechanics of the magnificent Westminster system of democracy. I encourage you to make your own pilgrimage to archives all over the world.

The hour I spent interviewing Professor Bob Carr, formerly NSW Premier and Federal Minister for Foreign Affairs, about the legacy of James Scullin in the Federal Labor Party was as valuable as my visit to the Royal archives and my fellowship at the Museum of Australian Democracy. He spoke freely about the perception in the party of Scullin as a bit of a 'bore', explained how he was economically compromised by the financial woes he inherited in 1930, and confirmed that, as I had found in my research, very little is known about his wife Sarah Scullin. Aside from two remarkable photographic portraits in the National Library, I found only scraps in letters and accounts of the times. To be honest this can be an asset to a dramatist since it means you can make informed speculations based on research of the period and the situation of the character without being creatively strangled by authoritative biographies and family legacies. Scullin and his wife had no children, but one day when I was at the Museum of Australian Democracy James Scullin's great-great-niece happened to come into Old Parliament House. She was just beginning her own family research and had taken a bus trip out to Scullin, the ACT suburb named after him. I enthusiastically went to speak to her and she was delighted to find me writing a play about his bold legacy. The synchronicity of this encounter, as well as parlance with a Labor Party elder about the life of this remarkable Australian leader, gave juice and pith and muscle to the characters that I was seeking to fold out from ideas and achievements into corporeal proportions for the stage. So, however remarkable and revelatory you find the archives, and however long the passage of time, I would urge you to augment your research by speaking with people who may give you a taste of the bruising culture of their profession, or the cruel poverty of their situation, or the unspoken understandings of their family – all the intangible details that can slap the still heart of a play into beating, vivid life.

49

Scientist as sentinel

In August 2016, I attended a public forum at the Charles Perkins Auditorium, 'An Evening with Dr David Katz', presented by the Australasian Society of Lifestyle Medicine. It was a fascinating insight into the current science around obesity and its causes, and the public health approaches a variety of scientists and lifestyle medicine practitioners bring to their work.

I have already talked about how the Charles Perkins Centre (CPC) commissioned me to write a play called *Made to Measure* about wedding clothes and their relationship to body image, fat-shaming and the Instagram-obsessed practices of the contemporary marriage ritual. CPC commissioned *Made to Measure* to give voice to people who live with the conditions associated with metabolic syndrome so they can inform, educate and change minds around them. So instead of a 'top down' approach where medical and health professionals 'tell' people living with these conditions what they should do, or worse, scold and bully them to change, the centre hopes to encourage people affected by and living with metabolic syndrome to connect as a community in order to influence and bring about change themselves.

I have brought to the CPC commission my close work writing practice and interviewed a large cross-section of wedding dress couturiers and their clients to bring the provocative nature of their experience, of fat-shaming and public discrimination, to the page and the stage. The Australian Medical Association declared obesity a disease in 2012 but entrenched public attitudes, including from the current Deputy Prime Minister Barnaby Joyce, can be dismissive: basically an 'eat less, move more' response.

I went to the David Katz seminar because I wanted to keep abreast of the science informing obesity research, hoping I would find a way to weave it into my play. But when I was there, I was struck by the psychological and motivational struggles of scientists and health professionals working to contain an epidemic and yet, both nationally and globally, losing the battle. At the seminar, the entire panel of experts gave a sense of being unable to hold back a tsunami of diabetes, fatty liver disease, heart attacks and tooth removal in younger and younger children. I was intrigued and moved to pity. It struck me as a fertile area for a stage play.

'It's the individual successes that keep me going in the game', said Professor Amanda Salis from the University of Sydney when I spoke to her. 'You see success with an individual and they tell you that the help you gave them has changed their life. It's incredibly frustrating. It's the frustration of an environment that makes eating and drinking too much really hard to avoid.'

To me, these scientists seem reluctant to talk about themselves or to reflect on the difficulty of their own position. They focus on the public problem, the enormity of the challenge, the imperative to 'get the message out' and the need to have a noticeable public impact. This naturally predisposes them towards public projects. But I suspected that a stage play that depicted their struggles, dilemmas, frustrations and enormous challenges might effectively communicate their research to the general public. Indeed, turning the spotlight onto the scientists might yield greater interest by mitigating the blame and guilt that audiences can feel in relation to health issues.

I have now secured a Charles Perkins Centre Fellowship to research and write a work with a dedicated female scientist as the protagonist. *Dr Cassandra* will draw a portrait of the science community of obesity researchers, activists, and lifestyle medicine advocates, both at CPC and beyond. The CPC is a centre for world class science, but it is also an ecosystem of richly connected, interdisciplinary 'project nodes' that form a complex, evolving system of research and educational activities spanning all sixteen faculties of Sydney University.

In Greek mythology Cassandra was a daughter of Priam, the King of Troy. Struck by her beauty, Apollo provided her with the gift of prophecy, but when Cassandra refused Apollo's romantic advances, he placed a curse ensuring that nobody would believe her warnings. Cassandra was left with the knowledge of future events, but could neither alter these events nor convince others they would happen.

The plot of *Dr Cassandra* concerns the frustration when scientists repeatedly, but unsuccessfully, try to have investigations validated in the media and heard by the public. The characters in Dr Cassandra are neither entirely selfless nor selfish, neither heroines nor villains – but fascinating metaphors for anyone who finds they cannot make their truths heard. The play is provoked by my close work practice of working with communities, to talk about the culture of their life – in this case the inability of scientists and other health professionals to impede the obesity epidemic – to each other, to their communities and to the general public through the medium of theatre.

So right now I am aiming to be a 'spy in the herd' of scientists, researchers and others at the CPC and create a sobering work about the profound pain of having your truth ignored. Theatre is a community-building exercise, unique in its creative ability to reflect a community back to itself. In the case of *Dr Cassandra* I would like to present readings at the CPC itself, involving staff scientists in the roles (there will inevitably be undiscovered talents among them!). I hope that this can suggest a vivid future for writers – their skills and expertise harnessed by people outside the arts in new and productive ways, their storytelling expertise valued across diverse sectors of society.

50

Balls in the air

In 2010 I pitched an idea to Mind's Eye, the development arm of Bell Shakespeare, for a play about lesbian sex workers putting on a show using Shakespeare's long poem *The Phoenix and the Turtle*. It was not commissioned but I spent time in a King's Cross halfway house talking to sex workers trying to get out of the industry and wrote the play. In 2012, I removed the Shakespeare and adapted it for radio so I could submit it to the BBC's International Radio Playwriting Competition. *The Ravens* won the prize for English as a First Language drama and was produced in the BBC studios (and on the streets of London) with Australian actors. Subesquently I returned to the stage version and rewrote it too without the Shakespeare, and sent it to the Venus Theatre, based in Washington DC, who staged a rehearsed reading at the Lincoln Centre in 2016 and also produced my play *Shafana and Aunt Sarrinah* (using the title *Soft Revolution*). Only later, when Venus decided to produce the play in 2017, did I realise that I had sent Venus the earlier version of the script with Shakespeare's poem still featured. I sent Deborah Randall, their artistic director, the later script, but she wanted the earlier version. In a season programmed to honour an actor friend who had been murdered, she saw it as 'our nod to her Shakespearian work'. When the play opened on 2 November 2017, seven years after I first conceived the idea, reviewer Amanda Gunther on TheatreBloom was enthusiastic, describing it as 'a visually poetic and evocatively moving new work' that 'should be seen by all'.

Some plays take the long way round to get the stage. In the performing arts there is an inherent illusion of making work appear spontaneous and effortless when it is actually the result of long, careful attention to detail over time. Indeed excellence is often directly proportionate to the amount of time you can work on a project. The public who see the two hours' traffic of the stage – simplified, polished, rehearsed to infinite precision – may think 'how could it take several years to make that?'. But it does.

If you are planning to eat while you work in the performing arts you will inevitably need to have several balls in the air at once. You will want to carve out periods of time where you focus on one particular project, exclusively, even obsessively, but you will also *learn to juggle*. Some projects can take *many* years to get to production and some involve huge amounts of administrative checking, community liaison and research work. Sometimes several projects come together at the same time, and people will think you are prolific when really you are just persistent and profoundly *patient*.

So I always have several works in progress, some of which I have discussed elsewhere in this book. Of the projects I initiated in 2017, one of my most beloved is *Wayside Bride*, inspired by the second marriage of my mother Janice Wainwright at the Wayside Chapel in 1969. The Wayside Chapel was started in 1964 as a social experiment and has, over the decades, married celebrities such as Jane Powell, Andy Gibb, Kerri-Anne Kennerley and Ita Buttrose, as well as many of the 'street people' it helps and thousands of other Australians. It remains a radical organisation with celebrity ambassadors (David Wenham, Dick Smith, Leah Purcell, Teddy Tahu Rhodes and Ernie Dingo among them), a continuing outreach to the destitute and disadvantaged of the Kings Cross area, and it has a unique cultural legacy as a religious and political agent for social change.

Reverend Graham Long, the pastor of the Wayside Chapel, supported my idea and with the help of several Wayside Chapel staff, I received a small grant to develop the project in 2016 from the City of Sydney, auspiced by Griffin Theatre Company. I have since gathered some incredible stories of inspiring, radical, current and former Kings Cross residents, who often married against their family's wishes or the social taboos of the time. A large number were Catholic–Protestant marriages, but others include Catholic divorcees and other cross-faith marriages.

Many simply liked and supported the values of the Wayside Chapel and its 'alternative' approach to religion. Reverend Bill Crews of the Uniting Church talked about the toll on Reverend Ted Noffs when his own church charged him with heresy. City of Sydney historian Dr Lisa Murray told me she believes that 'the relationship between Australians and religion is one of the most underwritten about, under-documented areas in our history'. *Wayside Bride* is the first time I set up and used a web portal (www.waysidebride.com) to attract contributors because the project was conceived to create and cohere an online community in tandem with the theatre project. Wayside has also advertised their support of the project through Facebook, and ABC Radio ran a terrific story directing people to the website and many listeners rang in to talk to me live on air.

Another new project in 2017 involves working with composer Sandra French and director Caroline Stacey on *Flight Memory*, a jazz song cycle based on the development of the black box, which was conceived by David Warren in 1953. The work charts the difficulties that Warren and his team encountered trying to convince indifferent bureaucrats of the value of a tool which, by recording the cockpit voices and instrument data of a plane, would provide concrete data of what went wrong in the event of a crash. I have already completed an extensive interview with the last living member of the black box team, Ken Fraser, and hope to conduct interviews with members of the Warren family.

The project will stretch me in new ways. Sandra's compositional focus and intensity inspired me when I saw *From a Black Sky* in Canberra in 2013. She has an intensely original musical vision and expression and it has been a revelation to work with her on the jazz form, which values words both for their meaning and for their sound and shape. As a director, Caroline's remarkable knowledge about the possibilities of staging jazz and opera in a way that liberates an intellectual and emotional journey for an audience is deeply creative, nurturing and revelatory. So while music has long been a part of my plays, *Flight Memory* will expand and diversify my practice. I want to contribute an instinct for dramatic expression and structure as well as glistening words – hard and sharp like tiny stones, round and sensuous like river pebbles, painful and bruising like rocks thrown in anger and rage.

One advantage of working on several projects at once is that it allows time for plays that take a more circuitous journey to get up. *The Ravens* is not the only play that has jumped onto the stage after a hiatus. I've already talked about *Student Body* and *Southern Belle*. And in 2018, Belvoir will present *The Sugar House*, a play they commissioned several years ago but never pursued. Set in Pyrmont about three generations of a local family, *The Sugar House* concerns aspects of law. It is not a verbatim play but, as with my close work plays, the diversity of language as it relates to the class, profession, age and attitude of my characters is the bedrock of the performance text. The play benefited from an interview with Justice Terence (Terry) Sheahan, an Australian judge and former politician, as well as extensive online reading of Hansard, several parliamentary acts and some Royal Commission reports.

Of course it can be tricky juggling several projects at once. My humble suggestion is that you find another creative activity that is not as intellectually demanding as writing, one where you get to make all the creative decisions. What I do is sew. After a day of wrestling words and action to the page I don't want to read or watch other narratives. Sewing is task-orientated; you can complete a garment in a couple of days, a week at the most, and best of all no-one is going say you put the zipper in wrongly or the bodice is crooked. You might cook or might play music, you might walk or swim or dance or play some kind of sport, anything you like. In a life of being open and collaborative and conciliatory it helps to have something creative in your life which is utterly your own. Plus if I am wearing something that I have made myself and someone comments on it, I think of my mother and say a small thank you to her for teaching me to sew. It is a way of keeping her with me, almost every day.

If you can find a way to deeply respect that your creative work is still *actual work*, then you will find a way to accept that sincere creative work is ongoing – changed and possibly even improved by time.

51

Now versus posterity

The Australian Writers' Guild once asked me to pen an article about 'writing for now versus writing for posterity'. The subject intrigued me but the deadline was impossible. Now, though, it seems appropriate to finish with some observations on the subject, particularly given that theatre using verbatim techniques is so often seen as 'of the moment'.

None of us know the future so to try to write *for* posterity would be foolish. But, as a writer, thinking about where your work might sit beyond the present involves articulating values that are central to your long-term artistry. Once you commit to more than just the next play idea, you start to develop a set of moral, social and theatrical values. These can shift from play to play but they tend to solidify over time. This is not writing for posterity, but articulating your vision as a writer – what your body of work might say about you, and how someone will interpret it, in relation to contemporary fashions and other Australian theatre writing of the period; and what might happen in the future.

Like all individuals, artists are subject to their times. One of the sobering moments for any artist, but particularly for a playwright, is to realise that you become the kind of artist that society allows you to be. As a society we get the artists we deserve and/or empower. Some artists are separate and forge careers outside of these constrictions, and certainly I've always believed in finding the company to support me to do what I want. But as a theatre maker you can only survive on that for so long. A playwright has to get bums on seats. You need to be a multi-armed octopus to get a play up and one arm must be squarely set in the contemporary theatre zeitgeist. You have to try and get your work up *now*. Critical success is not in itself enough either, you need to engage an audience. It's no good having a great play two months ago that people *meant* to go to. It's about getting them in *now*.

Someday when someone looks back on early 21st-century drama they might see things in your work that perhaps you cannot see yourself. The hope of the future, and its great marvel, is that we cannot forecast its priorities. Future writers might be attracted to aspects of your work you never imagined. As a writer you hope to corral things that reflect your commitment to being truthful, authentic and felicitous to your characters. Since language is one of the fascinations of the close work playwright, I am confident that my plays will serve as time capsules for the language of these communities.

The close work process busts the usual feudal hierarchies of theatre that sometimes perceives performers as interpreters without the authority of the director, writer or other creatives. Close work theatre calls the whole creative team into honouring the community at the centre of the work. The future of Australian dramaturgy and theatrical collaboration has the potential to be shocking and wonderous as new theatre makers and workers insist that theatre culture must open its eyes and and see the abundance of the potential contributors all around it. Not just on stage but in all the production and technical and management staff there must be expectation-busting, innovating new people of vision. We need to privilege diverse voices to powerful and central creative roles by asking members of diverse communities what *they* want from artists working with them, what *they* consider authentic. As a writer of close work theatre I am aware of an implicit contract. If Makiz Ansari and her aunt Laila Daqiq are generous and honest enough to allow me to tell their story on the Australian stage in *Shafana and Aunt Sarrinah*, my responsibility is to bring their story to the stage authentically and with as little intervention as possible

In the end, that's the core of the close work process. It's relational. It is premised on the idea that love, ideas, art, humour and life itself is about the relationship between people and the energy created when any community of people – small or large – get together to make meaning out of character in action. Like the ever-rotating pulsars of my play *Ear to the Edge of Time*, this relational joy and pain is a clock that will tick inside you for an artistic lifetime.

If I have used my work to interrogate a point of view, it is that our capacity to act together as a community, to be steadfast in our purpose and our will, offers real hope. We must be emboldened and infuriated and committed to action to defend artists and culture and learning and scholarship and history. Much of the work I have done looks at the tension between tradition and change through the lens of a community rather than a single individual and I am trying to argue that a reason for optimism, a sense of solution, can be gained by working together as a community. I still believe this deeply and I think this a worthy thing to use a public space to interrogate and demonstrate.

If a writer is perceptive and original about the human condition in theatrical ways, their play should, given sufficient directorial imagination, endure for decades or beyond. But the immediacy and urgency of a play also makes it relevant for its time. Theatre asks people to sit in a space and respond and reflect as a community. There is great value in looking at contemporary issues in this way.

Yet I know that in future visionary directors will have the imaginative capacity to see close work theatre as more than 'of the moment', to reinvent it in a different context. When *Parramatta Girls* was produced at Riverside in 2014, seven years after the original production at Belvoir St, the Royal Commission into child sexual abuse was still sitting, and stories about inter-inmate abuse were emerging. The passage of time shifted the audience focus from the culpability of the institution to the collaboration of 'dominant' inmates within that culture. It was all there in the play. In another ten years what new aspects of the women's relationships might be highlighted in a new production? We playwrights live in hope.

We put our work into the world with as much integrity, beauty and sincerity as we can, and the world will do to it as it pleases. But we can challenge the idea that 'plays that last' have the greatest value and importance. Who says so? No-one can know the value of a play produced only once in a small regional community. No-one can definitively assert that the play that makes it to the stages of London and New York is more important. More important to whom you might ask? To your vanity as a writer? To your estimation by the establishment as a writer of 'significance'? Some stories need to be told globally, some history needs to be revised worldwide; other stories are profoundly important to one community at a particular time. Don't be bullied by conservative notions of 'excellence', but strive for it at all times.

An interior designer once came to my home for dinner. He looked around my apartment and declared it a comfortable space. I relaxed. 'But', he said, 'I go to a lot of houses and I've never seen a room like that one through there'. In a tone which implied that he had seen something akin to an 11th-century torture chamber, he was referring to my study. 'I can't believe you sit in there', he continued, 'let alone do any work'.

I immediately jumped up from the table and took him into the room, which to my eyes was stocked with all the comforts a writer needs – books, files, a desk and a computer. 'But there's nothing of you in here', he said, desperately. 'Nothing that makes the space particularly speak of you.'

I love the idea that an actor is never so much herself as when she is being someone else. And I think this is the case for writers too. My decorator friend didn't realise it but he was paying me a great compliment. I'm not suggesting that all writers need monk-like, austere cells to do great work; that elaborately decorated writing spaces cannot house writers with a mutable interior space and life. It's not about the space so much as the metaphor. He brought my attention to who I am.

I have faith in the great writers, in the gifted young playwrights who will come after me. They will know that they can see the future as a hopeless prison or a beautifully blank page depending on what perspective they take. My friend despaired at the lack of 'self' in my work room, unaware that artists, particularly dramatists, write from our many selves. We write the shifting perspectives that come as we inhabit a range of possible skins. Indeed, part of our artistry is attempting to lose our 'self', while at the same time distinctively define it.

I am reluctant to trust phrases like 'At no other time in the history of the world ...' and 'Faced with issues unprecedented in human history ...' because it seems to me that civilisations continually repeat issues that they have faced in another form. The threat of the end of the world, for instance, is a recurrent one. Consider the collapse of the Roman Empire, or the publication of Darwin's *On the Origin of Species*, or the nuclear insanity that culminated in the bombing of Hiroshima and Nagasaki among innumerable other historical acts of war, colonisation and change. In each case the world, as people had come to know it, collapsed. Let's not flatter and delude ourselves with rhetoric: we are writers, not politicians. We are trying to examine our lived experience unsentimentally, not write verses on a global birthday card.

The film director Jean Renoir has a notion that the world is divided into horizontal levels rather than national ones. In his theory, a cleaner or a specialist nurse or a dictionary compiler in Australia has more in common with their counterpart in another country than they do with their compatriots in other professions. There is nothing quite so seductive as global generalisations. They give you an illusion of an informed overview; you think, just for a minute, that you can see the big picture. There is no doubt in my mind that our job as writers is to have something to say about the big picture as we understand it.

We work to harness the skills of our craft to articulate something bigger than ourselves, something that is about the changes we want to see and the beliefs we want to reflect. I am less interested, however, in conjecturing the future when it descends into a buzz-word infested guessing game. As a writer I am charged with the excitement of writing a play for our times, a play which speaks to audiences and resonates with their current experience. But the questions I ask can be remarkably similar to those asked by my writing forebears. For instance how can you make the sexual exploitation of children matter to audiences? How do you dramatise for an Australian – and perhaps international – audience, the personal stories that will move them to consider the experience of the many different people sharing their world?

This is what writing is finally about for me, both for now and for posterity. It is about creating work for an audience who wants to see itself reflected on stage but who can also be moved to see its other selves on stage –cultural identities, sexual identities, gender identities, national identities. But it is important that our cultural industries, including theatre, encourage more than servicing particular niches, and that playwrights continue to develop a voice which speaks across identity categories and chronological set dressing to investigate something profound about the human spirit.

We charge our artists, our writers, our dramatists with the burden of tearing the veil away from our collective delusions, to reaffirm our striving to make our communities equal to our belief. And you, the aspiring playwright, are essential to this future. You must have faith and vision and hope for yourself and for the challenges that will be placed in your path. My interior decorator friend offered to lend me a whole lot of things to break the relentless austerity of my home office as he perceived it. I hope that future playwrights will be creating works that speak of both now and our collective futures, and not merely putting up a new set of curtains. The theatre can be a ruthless, competitive, ignorant arena for the indulgence of personal egos and petty jealousies and cheap thrills. It can also be the cradle of empathy and the platform for thaumaturgy – wonderworking – the most ancient of pleasures and the most spectacularly contemporary. Theatre makers know that it is one of the greatest art forms in the world. I can't wait to see what you conjure to the stage.

Acknowledgements

Some material in this book has previously appeared as part of my Alex Buzo Memorial Lecture (2009), in the AWG Newsletter (*Tune of the Spoken Voice* 2011), the Ray Mathew Lecture at the National Library of Australia (2016), keynote addresses to the HSC drama event OnSTAGE, as part of the Griffin Theatre Company blog (2016), and in workshops for the ERUDIO Education series. Some reflections on writing *Letters to Lindy* also appear in the NLA publication *Dear Lindy* and I have cribbed and edited throughout some notes that first appeared in printed theatre programs that accompanied productions. All the material has been collected, rearranged and adjusted.

The Theatre Fund of the Australia Council for the Arts in 2012 granted me a Cultural Leadership Fellowship to work with Adults Surviving Child Abuse (ASCA, now the Blue Knot Foundation) and Shine for Kids and I am grateful for their support and personally thank Dr Cathy Kezelman and Gloria Larman for helping me to develop my own take on some 'best practice' guidelines mentioned throughout the book. Claire Grady, Emma Rose Smith, Rachel Ford, Sharne McGee, Victoria Chance and Vicki Gordon have offered many valuable insights into the writing and editing of this book, as have the many teachers who have participated in verbatim workshops I have given at the Sydney Theatre Company, Belvoir St Theatre, ERUDIO Education, and many individual schools, conferences and public panels. Thanks also to Deborah Franco at Currency and my love and thanks to Virginia Madsen, Tony MacGregor, Lina and Nathalie MacGregor; Phillip Ulman; Debra Horton, Ian, Alana and Jesse Greig; Bec Allen and Kathryn McCabe; Catherine Skipper and Maidie Wood; Helen Grasswill and Bruno Jean Grasswill; Matthew Curlewis and Mart van

Drunen; Darren Yap and Max Lambert; Peter Gordon and Michael McGrath and Alastair Carruthers and Peter Bezuijen; Donna Gordon, Tracey Gordon, Roe Ritchie, Kai Gordon Ritchie, Timmy Shaw; Chiaki Ajioka; Max Middleton and Terry Hurrey; Shaun, Emma and Carter Sullivan and Helen Ulcoq; Anna Cater; Martin Portus and Martin Smith; Alan Maurice, Raymond Holmes, Greg Smith; Andrew Collis; Heather Robinson; Nikhalylah Workman; Priscilla Yates; Bill Harding; Wendy and Peach Reid; Maxine Morris; Peter Valentine; Roy Powell and Anna Rauls.

Every year since 2012 I have given a lecture to Margaret Davis' theatre students at the Australian Institute of Music (Dramatic Arts) in Sydney and their questions and passionate interest in verbatim has helped me to articulate many of the insights and reflections in this book that I hope fledgling writers will find useful. In 2013 Katie Pollock wrote to me and asked me if I would be willing to mentor her through the Australia Council JUMP mentorship scheme. After a lot of cogitation and fear about potential hubris, I agreed and we went ahead with the submission to the Australia Council for the Arts. Unfortunately they rejected her application but, as is often the case, by the time I agree to apply I had already psychologically and emotionally committed to the process and began writing a kind of mentorship memoir which gradually widened out into *Bowerbird*.

I have mentioned a number of colleagues in the context of anecdotes or examples in the book but there are literally hundreds of others, actually thousands of actors and creative crew with whom I have worked, whose generosity and intelligence and creative inventiveness has been an inspiration and a revelation. If it takes a village to raise a child, then it takes a vast network of theatre professionals and practitioners to burnish a playwright, a network that might rival the intricacies of the mound-building termite mounds I saw in the Northern Territory. All of us, playwrights and other theatre makers, exist in a co-dependent ecology in which individual success is ultimately subsumed to the golden days – when theatre is thriving, the arts are valued, intellectual debate and creative response is flourishing and equality, justice and compassion are enacted in both our hearts and our laws.

I have not chronicled a history of verbatim theatre, nor a broad analysis of verbatim in the context of 21st century contemporary theatre. There are others who can give a more extensive, academic and generalised view of the genre and they may be found on the website of Currency Press and elsewhere. Read anything and everything about the form you can get your hands on. In contemporary practice, close work projects have been at the forefront of breaking the traditional boundaries between art forms so that artists and communities can express themselves across a variety of digital, visual and conceptual platforms in tandem with theatre and performance programs. I have chronicled in *Bowerbird* times where my playwrighting has intersected with visual art and digital projects that I have conceived with communities to accompany the theatre work. Because of my desire to focus on verbatim and close work style practices I have not written here about my commissioned work in adaptation of novels, my film work which includes a screenplay for a waterscreen installation in Darling Harbour, plays which are predominantly fictional, my work in numerous cultural institutions and my journalism and prose work, all of which have informed and creatively fed my close work for theatre. Artists, and all people really, are simultaneously limitless and uniquely individual and should seek to find expressions of their own and others creativity in the many ways our precious world offers.

Index of plays for stage and radio

Barbara and the Camp Dogs
Co-written with Ursula Yovich
Creative Development showing presented 2013 at the University of NSW, produced by Vicki Gordon Music Productions (VGMP), funded by the Aboriginal and Torres Strait Islander Arts Board (ATSIAB) Creative Development. First produced 2017 by Belvoir St Theatre and VGMP (dir. Letitia Cáceres, with Ursula Yovich, Elaine Crombie, Troy Brady, Michelle Vincent, Debbie Yap and Jessica Dunn). Published 2017 by Currency Press. 5-song CD released 2017.

Black Friday
Broadcast 1998 on 'Radio Eye' (ABC Radio) (with Angie Milliken, Anthony Brandon Wong, Robert Alexander, Celia Ireland, Don Reid, Tony Poli and Kate McLennan).

Butterfly Dandy
First produced 2005 by The Street Theatre, Canberra (dir. Camilla Blunden, with Peter J. Casey and Julie McElhone).

City of Glass: A Portrait of Wagga Wagga
Broadcast 2001 on 'Radio Eye' (ABC Radio).

Cold Light
Adapted from the novel by Frank Moorhouse
Presented in first draft at The Street Theatre, Canberra, as part of the Centenary of Canberra celebrations 2013. First produced 2017 at The Street Theatre, Canberra (dir. Caroline Stacey, with Sonia Todd, Craig

Alexander, Nick Byrne, Gerard Carroll, Tobias Cole and Kiki Skountzoz). Published 2017 by Currency Press.

Comin' Home Soon
First produced 2013 by the Lieder Theatre Company, Goulburn (dir. Chrisjohn Hancock). Published 2013 by Snowy Owl Press. Awarded a 2014 AWGIE Award (Community and Youth Theatre).

Cool Hunter, London
Broadcast 2015 on 'Radiotonic' (ABC Radio).

Covenant
First produced 2005 by Powerhouse Youth Theatre, Fairfield (dir. Katrina Douglas).

Crossing the King
Awarded a 2004 research fellowship at the Prime Ministers Centre, Museum of Australian Democracy, Canberra. Commissioned 2016 by Sydney Theatre Company and National Theatre, London.

Cyberbile
First produced 2011 at Presbyterian Ladies' College, Sydney. Nominated for a 2012 AWGIE Award (Community and Youth Theatre). Published 2013 by Currency Press (in a double volume with *Grounded*).

Dead Man Brake
First produced 2013 by Merrigong Theatre Company, Wollongong (dir. Anne-Louise Rentell, with Alicia Battestini, Nicholas Brown, Gerard Carroll, Phillip Hinton, Drayton Morley, Katrina Retallick and Sabryna Te'o).

Doing Dawn
Shortlisted for the 2009 Griffin Award.

Dr Cassandra
Awarded a 2017 Charles Perkins Centre Fellowship, University of Sydney.

Dusted by Pindan: Tales from a Pilbara Sojourn
Broadcast 2000 on 'Radio Eye' (ABC Radio). Published 2001 in *Tangent*.

Ear to the Edge of Time
Broadcast 2011 on '360documentaries' (ABC Radio). Staged presentation

2012 at Samuel Beckett Theatre, Dublin. Awarded the 2012 STAGE International Script Award. First produced 2018 by Sport for Jove at Seymour Centre, Sydney (dir. Nadia Tass).

Elderflowers
Public reading 2009 at the Orchard Gallery, part of Older and Wiser week.

Eyes to the Floor
First produced 2008 by Outback Theatre for Young People (dir. Amy Hardingham). Produced 2009 by Sydney Theatre School at Sidetrack Theatre, Marrickville (dir. Luke Rogers). Produced 2010 by Wentworth Falls School of Arts and Ravenswood School for Girls. Published 2014 by Currency Press (in a double volume with *Parramatta Girls*).

Flight Memory
With composer Sandra French
Commissioned 2016 by The Street Theatre, Canberra. First produced 2018 by the Street Theatre, Canberra (dir. Caroline Stacey).

Grounded
First produced 2012 at the Civic Theatre (Newcastle) and Australian Theatre for Young People (ATYP), Sydney. Received two 2013 AWGIE Awards (Major Award, Community and Youth Theatre). Published 2013 by Currency Press (in a double volume with *Cyberbile*).

Head Full of Love
First produced 2010 at the Darwin Festival, Cairns Festival, and Alice Springs Desert Festival (dir. Wesley Enoch, with Colette Rayment and Roxanne MacDonald). Nominated for the 2011 Queensland Premier's Literary Award (Stage). Produced 2012 by Queensland Theatre Company and broadcast on 'Airplay' (ABC Radio). 2015 national tour (with Annie Byron and Paula Delaney Nazarski). Awarded the 2016 APACA Drover Award for Tour of the Year.

Holy Homes
Broadcast 2002 on 'Radio Eye' (ABC Radio).

Journeys
First produced 2001 for the Centenary of Federation Celebration, Sydney (dir. Andrew Walsh). Awarded the 2003 Centenary Medal.

Katherine Characters
Broadcast 2007 on ABC Radio.

Kimberley Queerboy
Broadcast 2015 on '360documentaries' (ABC Radio).

Ladies Day
First produced 2016 by Griffin Theatre Company, Sydney (dir. Darren Yap, with Matthew Backer, Lucia Mastrantone, Wade Briggs and Elan Zavelsky). Published 2016 by Currency Press. Nominated for the 2017 NSW Premier's Literary Award (Playwriting).

Lavender Bay
Shortlisted for the 2012 Griffin Award.

Letters to Lindy
Public research presentation at the National Library of Australia as part of the Harold White Fellowship. First produced 2016 by Merrigong Theatre Company at Illawarra Performing Arts Centre (Wollongong), Canberra Theatre Centre (Canberra) and the Seymour Centre (Sydney) (dir. Darren Yap, with Jeanette Cronin, Jane Phegan, Glenn Hazeldine and Phillip Hinton). Published 2017 by Currency Press. 2018 national tour.

Lost Illusions
First produced 2010 as a graduating play at NIDA.

Love Potions
First produced 2006 by the New Theatre, Newtown (dir. Jessica Symes, with Florette Cohen, Lucy Waldron-Brown, Aimeé Falzon, Alexandra Vaughan, Geraldine Timmins and Matt Edgerton). Published 2006 by Snowy Owl Press. Produced 2007 at Newcastle University.

Made to Measure
Commissioned 2016 by the Charles Perkins Centre, University of Sydney. Staged reading 2017 at the Seymour Centre (with Megan Wilding, Heather Mitchell and Sam O'Sullivan).

Moses Joseph
Monologue, produced 2008 as a video installation at the Sydney Jewish Museum (prod. Gary Warner, directed by Alana, with Brian Lipson).

MP
First produced 2011 by The Street Theatre, Canberra (dir. Caroline Stacey, with Geraldine Turner, Leah Baulch, Soren Jensen, Stephen Barker and Andrea Close).

Multiple Choice
First produced 1985 by Australian Theatre for Young People (ATYP), Sydney (dir. Colette Rayment). Re-staged 1986 by Australian Theatre for Young People (ATYP) for Sydney Festival (dir. Colette Rayment).

One Billion Beats
Co-written and co-directed with Romaine Moreton
First produced 2016 at Campbelltown Arts Centre, Sydney (associate producer Vicki Gordon Music Productions).

Oysters at the Paragon
Broadcast 1994 on ABC Radio (with Miranda Otto, Rosalba Clemente and David Wenham). Nominated for a 1995 AWGIE Award. Broadcast 1997 by the Icelandic National Broadcasting Service (translated into Icelandic!).

Ozone
First produced 1998 at Brisbane Festival (dir. Mike Dickinson, with Deborah Kennedy, Patrick Dickson, Scott Witt, Barbara Lowing and Sam Fitzgerald). Published 2008 by Snowy Owl Press.

Parramatta Girls
Awarded a 2003 NSW Writers' Fellowship. First produced 2007 by Belvoir St Theatre, Sydney (dir. Wesley Enoch, with Leah Purcell, Genevieve Hegney, Valerie Bader, Annie Byron, Jeanette Cronin, Lisa Flanagan, Roxanne McDonald and Carole Skinner). Published 2007 and 2014 (in a double volume with *Eyes to the Floor*) by Currency Press. Nominated for two 2008 Helpmann Awards (Best New Australian Work, Best Play) and for the 2008 NSW Premier's Literary Award (Playwriting). Produced 2011 at the New Theatre, Sydney (dir. Annette Rowlinson, with Elaine Crombie, Kylie Coolwell, Di Adams, Amanda Marsden, Abi Rayment, Christine Greenough, Kym Parrish and Sandy Velini). Produced 2014 at Riverside Theatres, Parramatta (dir. Tanya Goldberg, with Christine Anu, Sharni McDermott, Tessa Rose, Holly Austin, Annie Byron, Anni Finsterer and Sandy Gore). Numerous amateur and school productions nationwide.

Radio Silence
First produced 2003 at the Australian War Memorial, Canberra (with Mary Rachel Brown).

Rats and Shillings
Broadcast 2004 on 'Radio Eye' (ABC Radio).

Ratticus and Reidar
First produced 2009 at Hyde Park Barracks, Sydney (directed by Alana, with Gibson Nolte and Arabella McPherson).

Redfern Heights
Broadcast 2003 on 'Airplay' (ABC Radio) (with William Zappa, Anthony Phelan, Lydia Miller, Kerrily White and Lancho Davey). Shortlisted for the 2008 Griffin Award.

Row of Tents
First produced 2001 at the New York International Fringe Festival (dir. Sarah Carradine, with Jenny Vuletic and Nicholas Papademetriou).

Run Rabbit Run
First produced 2004 at Belvoir St Theatre, Sydney (dir. Kate Gaul, with Wayne Blair, Joseph Ber, Roy Billing, Tyler Coppin, Julie Hamilton, Jody Kennedy, Russell Kiefel, Eliza Logan, Georgina Naidu, Alex Sideratos). Published 2004 by Currency Press. Awarded the 2004 Queensland Premier's Literary Award for Drama Script (Stage). Broadcast 2005 on 'Airplay' (ABC Radio). Nominated for a 2005 AWGIE Award (Stage).

Savage Grace
First produced 2000 for FEAST Festival, Adelaide (dir. Sarah Carradine, with Nicholas Papademetriou and Nicholas Opolski). Produced 2001 at the University of Sydney (dir. Sarah Carradine) and by Steamworks Arts, Perth (dir. Sally Richardson, with Humphrey Bower and Gibson Nolte). Received a commendation at the 2001 Victorian Premier's Literary Awards. Awarded the 2002 Rodney Seaborn Playwrights' Award and shortlisted for the 2002 Griffin Award. Produced 2002 at the Subiaco Arts Centre, Perth (dir. Sally Richardson). Produced 2003 by Darlinghurst Theatre Company, Sydney (dir. Sally Richardson). Broadcast 2003 on 'Flix' (ABC Radio). Produced 2005 by La Mama Theatre, Melbourne (dir. Sally Richardson).

Published 2006 by Snowy Owl Press.

Screamers
Broadcast 1990 on ABC Radio (with Tony Sheldon and Raj Ryan [Raj Sidhu]).

Shafana and Aunt Sarrinah
Nominated for the 2008 Kit Denton Fellowship. First produced 2009 by the Alex Buzo Company at the Seymour Centre, Sydney (dir. Aarne Neeme, with Sheridan Harbridge and Camilla Ah Kin). Broadcast 2010 on 'Airplay' (ABC Radio). Published 2010 by Currency Press.

Shudder
First produced 1994 at Belvoir St Theatre, Sydney (dir. Diana Denley, with Alice Livingstone and Julia Johnson). Produced 1995 at Queer Fringe, Sydney (dir. Diana Denley).

Singing the Lonely Heart
As *Southern Belle*, rehearsed reading 1992 at Belvoir St Theatre, Sydney, for the Sydney Gay and Lesbian Mardi Gras (SGLMG). Rehearsed reading at New Dramatists, New York City (with Martha Plimpton and Frances McDormand). First produced as *Singing the Lonely Heart* 2006 by the New Theatre, Newtown (dir. Alex Galeazzi, with Peter Flett, Jane Phegan, Rebekah Moore, Elaine Hudson, Abigail Austin, Jason Montgomery). Published 2008 by Snowy Owl Press.

Small Mercies
Presented 1992 as a work-in-progress at Performance Space, Sydney (with Maroochy Barambah and Lydia Miller).

Spool Time
First produced 1998 by Vitalstatistix Theatre Company, Adelaide (dir. Catherine Fitzgerald, with Rosalba Clemente).

Student Body
First produced 2011 by BOObook Theatre at Melbourne University Theatre (dir. Dione Joseph, with Ash Kakkar, Rachel Fong, Sheena Reyes, Kelly Ryan and Keith Brockett).

Swallowing Communion
Broadcast 1997 on ABC Radio (with Deborah Kennedy and Angela Toohey). Nominated for the 1998 AWGIE Awards.

Sweethearts
Broadcast 2007 on ABC Radio.

Swellings
First produced 1995 at Queer Fringe, Sydney (dir. Diana Denley).

Swimming the Globe
First produced 1996 by Freewheels Theatre Company, Newcastle (dir. Bryan Joyce) and nominated for a City of Newcastle Drama Award. 1997 tour of Northern NSW and Queensland. Produced 1998 at the Civic Theatre, Newcastle and Kuali Works, Malaysia (part of the Commonwealth Games Cultural Festival) (dir. Brian Joyce). Published 1999 by Currency Press.

Swimming Upstream
Public reading in 2011 as part of a Blue Knot Foundation event at the Orchard Gallery, Redfern.

Tales of Galileo
Performed at the ABC Centre, Ultimo (with Peter Flett, Annie Byron and Drayton Morley). Film version (with Peter Flett, Annie Byron, Brian Adams and Drew Fairley).

Tarantula
First produced by Tredwood Productions at King Street Theatre, Newtown (dir. Nastassja Djalog, with Zoe Carides and Michael Whalley).

The Bookshop Job
Rehearsed reading 1987 at Belvoir St Theatre, Sydney.

The Conjurers
First produced 1997 by Playbox Theatre Company, Melbourne (dir. Kim Durban). Published 1997 by Currency Press. Nominated for the 1997 NSW Premier's Literary Award (Playwriting). Produced 1998 by La Boite Theatre Company, Brisbane (dir. Sue Rider). Nominated for a 1998 AWGIE Award.

The Fox and the Freedom Fighters
Co-written with Rhonda Dixon-Grovenor
First produced 2014 at Carriageworks, Sydney (dir. Lisa-Mare Syron, with Rhonda Dixon-Grovenor and Nadeena Dixon).

The Glass Monologues
First produced 2019 by Canberra Glassworks.

The Keys
First produced by the Queensland Theatre Company (Oz Shorts) (dir. Jennifer Flowers).

The Mapmaker's Brother
First produced 2002 at the Australian National Maritime Museum (ANMM) (directed by Alana, with Christopher Tomkinson and Michael Cullen).

The Modest Aussie Cozzie
First produced 2009 at St Ignatius College Festival, Riverview (directed by Alana, with Jacqui Livingstone, Chloe Dunn and Jarrod Crellin).

The Monkey's Mask
Adapted from the novel by Dorothy Porter
Broadcast 1999 on ABC Radio (dir. Libby Douglas, with Deborah Kennedy, Jeanette Cronin, Kelly Butler, Jessica Napier, Neil Fitzpatrick, Nicholas Eadie and Steve Vidler).

The Prayers of Mary
Broadcast 1997 on ABC Radio (with Kelly Butler and Glenn Hazeldine).

The Prospectors
First produced 2001 at the Australian National Maritime Museum (ANMM), Sydney (directed by Alana, with Christopher Saunders and Nicholas Papademetriou). Nominated for a 2001 AWGIE Award (Theatre for Young Audiences). Produced 2005 by Monkey Baa Theatre Company (Sydney, regional tour) (dir. Sandra Eldridge, with Tim McGarry and Mark Constable).

The Ravens
Awarded the 2013 BBC International Radio Playwriting Award in the English language category, winning from 1000 entries from 86 countries.

Produced 2014 in London (dir. Rosalynd Ward, with Sophie Ross, Josie Taylor, Vanessa Hehir, Ben Lewis and Vivien Carter). Nominated for the 2015 AWGIE Award (Radio). Produced 2017 for the stage by Venus Theatre, Maryland, USA (dir. Deborah Randall, with Suzanne Edgar, Ashley Zielinski, Erin Hanratty and Alison Talvacchio).

The Sex Act
Shortlisted for the 2006 Rodney Seaborn Playwrights' Award. Produced 2011 at New Theatre, Sydney (dir. Augusta Supple, with Odile le Clezio, Kate Skinner, Stephen Wilkinson, Luke Carson and Bridgette Sneddon).

The Sound of the Universe Singing
Broadcast 2009 on '360documentaries' (ABC Radio).

The Story of Anger Lee Bredenza
Broadcast 1988 on ABC Radio (dir. Ron Blair with Lydia Miller, Pat Thompson and Evdokia Katahanas). Awarded the 1988 Ian Reed Prize for Radio Drama. Awarded the 1989 NSW Premier's Literary Award (Radio), and nominated for a 1989 AWGIE Award (Radio). Produced 2002 at Chapel off Chapel, Melbourne (dir. Julie Waddington).

The Sugar House
Shortlisted for the 2010 Griffin Award. First produced 2018 by Belvoir St Theatre (dir. Sarah Goodes, with Kris McQuade, Sacha Horler and Josh McConville).

The Tree Widows
Staged presentation 2013 at Backspace of Theatre Royal, Hobart, by Tasmanian Theatre Company at Ten Days on the Island Festival. First produced 2016 by Tasmanian Theatre Company, Hobart (directed by Alana, with Guy Hooper, Iain Lang, Jane Longhurst and Jane Johnson). Awarded two 2017 Errol Awards (Best Writing in a Professional Production, Judges' Award), with Alana also nominated as Best Director.

The Word Salon
Broadcast 1998 on ABC Radio (with Aidan Fennessy). Awarded a 1999 AWGIE Award (Radio). Nominated for the 2000 NSW Premier's Literary Award (Scriptwriting).

Tinderbox
First produced 2013 by Tredwood Productions at Theatre 19, Darlinghurst (dir. Zoe Carides, with Alan Lovell, Nastassja Djalog and Benjamin Ross).

Titania's Boy
First produced 2003 in Wagga Wagga and Griffith by Riverina Theatre Company (dir. Nic Clark, with Georgina Naidu, Alex Papps and Zeke Castelli).

Tricky Girl
Presented 2013 at Bell Shakespeare Rehearsal Space, Sydney.

Unlikely Excursions
Episodes broadcast 2002 (Turkey, the Seychelles) and 2004 (Macau) on 'Radio Eye' (ABC Radio).

Various Angels
Rehearsed reading 1991 at Belvoir St Theatre, Sydney (part of Playworks Showcase).

Walk a Mile in My Shoes
Performed by Barefoot Divas: Ursula Yovich, Ngaiire, Emma Donovan, Whirimako Black, Merenia Gillies and Maisey Rika
First produced 2012 at Sydney Festival and New Zealand International Arts Festival with Vicki Gordon Music Productions. Broadcast 2012 on 'Into the Music' (ABC Radio). Album released 2012. Produced 2013 at the Queensland Music Festival, 2014 in the US and Canada (tour), and 2015 at the Hong Kong Arts Festival. All productions directed by Alana.

Watermark
First produced 2008 by Katherine Regional Arts. Produced 2009 at Katherine Festival and Darwin Festival. All productions directed by Alana. Received a 2009 AWGIE Award (Community and Youth Theatre). Broadcast 2010 on 'Airplay' (ABC Radio).

Wayside Bride
Funded 2016 by the City of Sydney, auspiced by Griffin Theatre Company and supported by the Wayside Chapel.

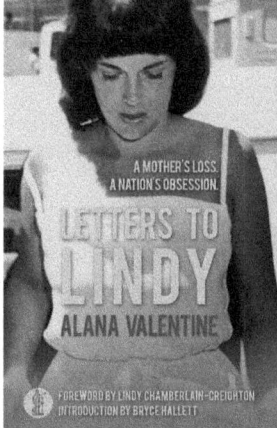

15 Alana Valentine plays
available from Currency Press

Barbara and the Camp Dogs (2017)
Co-written with Ursula Yovich, 978-1-76062-044-8

Cold Light (2017)
978-1-76062-049-3, ebook also available

Cyberbile / Grounded (2013)
978-0-86819-984-9, ebooks also available

Ladies Day (2016)
978-1-92500-564-6, ebook also available

Letters to Lindy (2017)
978-1-76062-024-0, ebook also available

Love Potions / Savage Grace (2006)
978-0-97755-020-3

Parramatta Girls / Eyes to the Floor (2014)
978-1-92500-516-5, ebooks also available

Run Rabbit Run (2004)
978-0-86819-747-0

Shafana and Aunt Sarrinah (2010)
978-0-86819-882-8, ebook also available

Singing the Lonely Heart / Ozone (2008)
978-0-97755-021-0

The Sugar House (2018)
978-1-76062-208-4

www.currency.com.au

Visit Currency Press' website now to:

- Order books
- Browse through our full list of titles including plays, screenplays, theory and reference/criticism, performance handbooks, educational texts and more
- Choose a play for your school or performance group by cast specs
- Seek performance rights
- Find out about performing arts news and sign up for our newsletter
- For students: read our study guides
- For teachers: access free curriculum information and teacher notes

We are also on Facebook and Instagram (@currencypress). Join the conversation!

The performing arts publisher

www.ingramcontent.com/pod-product-compliance
Lightning Source LLC
Chambersburg PA
CBHW040256170426
43192CB00020B/2819